# PENTECOSTAL PERSPECTIVES

# PENTECOSTAL PERSPECTIVES

Editor
**Keith Warrington**

paternoster press

This book is printed using Suffolk New Book paper which is 100% acid free.

Cover design by Mainstream, Lancaster.
Typeset by WestKey Ltd, Falmouth, Cornwall
Printed in Great Britain by Clays Ltd., St Ives PLC.

# Contents

# Preface

Classical Pentecostalism is, by a large, a twentieth century phenomenon. Throughout the world, Pentecostals are seeing massive church growth and mission expansion. This growth has been accompanied by an increased desire to develop Pentecostalism's own theological pedigree and re-examine its fundamental beliefs. To this end, theological conferences for leaders within Classical Pentecostalism have recently debated such issues as the role of women in ministry, healing and exorcism, the infallibility of the Bible, the nature of Hell, eschatology, and church leadership. The Pentecostal and Charismatic Research Fellowship has also been initiated to encourage analysis and interaction on issues of particular pertinence to Pentecostals and charismatics.

Many within Classical Pentecostalism today realise that an emphasis on the Spirit has to be accompanied by a stress on the Bible and the gift of teaching in order to guard from error and lead into truth. The classic statement of Pentecostal beliefs was produced over twenty years ago in 1976 in the book *Pentecostal Doctrine*, edited and produced by P.S. Brewster. However, Classical Pentecostalism has developed its theology in recent years as it has interacted with many other Christians in an attempt to better articulate its own beliefs and practices. As a body, in which there are both distinctive and subtle nuances, it has matured theologically. That is not to say that its forefathers were theologically illiterate or biblically naïve: such an assessment would be inaccurate and based on superficial research. However, Pentecostalism has increasingly reflected on its beliefs and its mission to the world and the Church, as a result of which it can more accurately plan for growth and the achievement of its goal, under God, of leading people into all truth.

Such a process has involved change flowing from study, debate and the ability to learn from one another. Although sometimes painful, the aim has been to follow the leading of the Spirit who sovereignly leads us to truth.

The papers that follow reflect current Classical Pentecostal belief, although it must be recognised that the topics chosen do not represent all the important beliefs and practices of Classical Pentecostalism. Pentecostals would closely align themselves to conservative Evangelicalism and its beliefs. Indeed, although not so long ago Pentecostalism was distinct in many respects, recent years have seen significant changes in the church of Jesus Christ. These have occurred partly as a result of the charismatic renewal, the Restoration Movement, a greater awareness by mainstream traditional churches of the role of the Spirit and a maturation within Pentecostalism itself. As a result, Pentecostalism is not as different as it once was. This should not be interpreted negatively; rather it should be valued as a sign that believers are willing to learn from each other and move on together to new levels of maturity and stability. The early opposition to Pentecostals has largely subsided and has been replaced by cross-denominational fellowship, leading to a honing of beliefs and practices and a greater awareness and appreciation of the value of self-analysis by all concerned.

The first two chapters of this book survey the history, beliefs, practices and development of the two major British Classical Pentecostal denominations. The chapters that follow deal with some of the significant issues that have characterised Pentecostalism. Their analysis of various beliefs and practices is pertinent not only to Pentecostal and Charismatic believers, but also to all who are desirous of combining the study of the Scriptures with a sensitivity to the Spirit. It is the hope of all concerned that these pages will stimulate further discussion and edification that will affect our lives and bring glory to our God.

The writers present general overviews of their topics, often tracing developments in belief and praxis, while at the same time offering some discussion or development of thought and providing suggestions for change. An attempt has been made to eliminate any overlapping or repetition of content in these chapters, except when such repetition is important to the particular point that an author wishes to make.

Classical Pentecostals are found in the Elim Pentecostal Church, the Assemblies of God, the Apostolic Church and rapidly increasing

Black Pentecostal churches. Where any one of these groups has distinctive beliefs or practices, these are mentioned. However, the very nature of Pentecostalism involves a certain fluidity and so it is to be expected that not all nuances will be represented. Nor will all Pentecostals identify with all the views expressed in these pages.

Classical Pentecostalism in Britain sprang from the Welsh Revival, and throughout its history it has sought to follow the leading of the Spirit. In recent years, it has come to realise in a fresh way that the Spirit of revival is also the Spirit of the Word. God has entrusted to us the privilege of interacting with his Word and applying it to our lives. This particular book represents an opportunity to do this, as a result of which we hope to increasingly mature in our faith and in the knowledge of our God.

Keith Warrington

# Contributors

*Richard Bicknell*

Richard was born in Aldershot and is currently working there as a cabinet maker while assisting in the ministry of his local Fellowship. He gained a Cambridge Diploma in Religious Studies and a BA (Hons) in Ministry and Theology while studying at the Elim Bible College. His interest in the historical celebration of the eucharist has led to a number of published and unpublished papers on the issue, particularly in relation to the eucharistic understanding of the Elim Pentecostal Church.

*James Glass*

James has been a minister in the Elim Pentecostal Church since 1993. He grew up in County Armagh, Northern Ireland, and read Classics in Dublin. He then worked in financial services before entering the Elim Bible College where he gained a BD.

*Malcolm Hathaway*

Malcolm was born in India of missionary parents and is the grandson of one of Elim's pioneers. He has been an Elim minister for over twenty years, pastoring three churches. His involvement in Christian education began when he pioneered the UK division of the ICI Bible Study in 1975. Shortly after this, he became a lecturer at the Elim Bible College where he taught Church History and Theology for eighteen years. Since then, he has ministered at the Salisbury Elim church. He is involved in ministerial training, functioning as Training Officer for the Southern Region of Elim.

He has a BD and a particular interest in the life and work of the founder of the Elim Pentecostal Church, George Jeffreys.


## Neil Hudson

After studying at London Bible College, Neil became a minister of the Elim Pentecostal Church in 1985. He went on to serve as the pastor of an inner-city church in Salford (where he is still part of the leadership team) before joining the faculty of Regents Theological College, Nantwich, in 1994, He specialises in Cross-Cultural Communication and Theology, and is the course leader for the MTh in Applied Theology. Currently, he is engaged in doctoral research into the history of the Elim Church, in particular its survival after the loss of George Jeffreys in 1940.


## William Kay

William is Senior Research Fellow at the Centre for Theology and Education at Trinity College, Carmarthen. Prior to this, he was a lecturer at Mattersey Hall. He is a minister in the Assemblies of God. He has a Master's degree and Doctorate in Education (Reading) and a Doctorate in Theology (Nottingham). His publications include *Inside Story*, and he has collaborated in other works including *Drift From the Churches*, *Research in Religious Education* and *Fast Moving Currents in Youth Culture* and *Pastoral Care and Counselling*.


## Richard Massey

Richard is the Principal of Birmingham Bible Institute and lecturer in Doctrine and Church History. Formerly, he was the Director of the Deo Gloria Trust and involved in pastoral ministry. He studied under Donald Gee at Kenley Bible College, and has a BD (London) and an MA (Leicester). He completed his PhD at Birmingham, under the supervision of Walter Hollenweger, studying the history and theology of early British Pentecostalism. He is a founder and chairman of the Management Committee of the Donald Gee Centre for Pentecostal and Charismatic Research. His publications include *Another Springtime: Donald Gee – Pentecostal Pioneer*.

## David Petts

David has been an Assemblies of God minister since 1962 and has been Principal of Mattersey Hall since 1978. He is chairman of the Executive Council of the Assemblies of God, of the Association of Bible College Principals and of the European Pentecostal Theological Association. He is also vice-chairman of the Pentecostal European Fellowship and a member of the Advisory Committee of the World Pentecostal Conference.

A former exhibitioner of Brasenose College, Oxford, his academic qualifications include an MA (Oxon.) and an MTh and PhD from Nottingham University.

## Siegfried Schatzmann

Born and raised in Switzerland, Siegfried first pursued a banking career, followed by initial theological training at the Elim Bible College in London. His ministry has been shaped by pastoral and missionary service in Switzerland, Lesotho (Southern Africa) and the USA. He moved to the USA in 1972 to pursue further theological studies and earned a BS (1974) in Bible and Theology at Bethany Bible College, an MDiv (1976) and a PhD (1981) at Southwestern Baptist Theological Seminary. His publications include *A Pauline Theology of Charismata*.

He was Professor of New Testament at Oral Roberts University before joining Regents Theological College, Nantwich, in 1991 as the Director of Studies and New Testament Lecturer. Currently, he also serves on the team of elders at his church.

*Keith Warrington*

Keith Warrington has been a lecturer in New Testament at Regents Theological College, Nantwich since 1981. He ia also Director of Postgraduate Studies. Prior to this, he worked with Operation Mobilisation in Europe and pastored two Elim churches in the north of England. He has a BA from London Bible College and has completed an MPhil based on an exegesis of James 5:13–18. He is currently engaged in doctoral research on healing and exorcism.

He is the editor of the *Journal of the European and Pentecostal Theological Association (EPTA)* and shares with Neil Hudson the chairmanship of the Pentecostal and Charismatic Research Fellowship. He has served on a number of Elim committees. He also serves on Acute, a theological forum initiated by the Evangelical Alliance. His publications include *The Healings and Exorcisms of Jesus: Paradigm or Phenomenon.*

Chapter One

# The Elim Pentecostal Church: Origins, Development and Distinctives

Malcolm R. Hathaway

Of the three main streams of the early Pentecostal movement in the British Isles, Elim is uniquely the product of pioneer evangelism and church planting by its founder, George Jeffreys (1889–1962). Jeffreys filled many of the largest halls in the country and saw tens of thousands converted to Christ during a career which spanned half a century. His most successful period was from 1926 to 1934. At the height of his success in 1930, he held a six-week-long campaign in Birmingham, which resulted in over 10,000 converts. More than a thousand were baptised and a similar number gave testimony to being healed. Three Elim churches were established, which grew to eleven, six years later. In addition, one of the converts founded the independent Hockley Mission.[1] By 1933, there were 153 Elim churches in Great Britain and Northern Ireland. George Jeffreys is probably, to date, the most successful British evangelist of the twentieth century. The highly respected Pentecostal statesman and contemporary Donald Gee characterised him as 'easily the most gifted preacher that the British Pentecostal Movement has produced. He had a voice like music, with sufficient Welsh intonation to add an inimitable charm. His platform personality at times was magnetic and his face was appealing. Although lacking academic training, he possessed a natural refinement that made him acceptable in all circles. He presented his message with a logical

---

[1] D.W. Cartwright, *The Great Evangelists* (London: Marshall, Morgan & Scott, 1986), 103–106.

appeal and a note of authority that was compelling.'[2] His preaching and singing can still be heard on archive recordings.

George Jeffreys was born in Wales, where religious commitment had reached its zenith after the 1859 Revival. Up to 80% of the Llynfi valley population were regular church-goers. There was room enough for most of the population in the many large chapels. But by the turn of the century, religious zeal had been eroded by theological liberalism and biblical criticism. The new faiths were science and socialism and churches were losing their people to pubs and clubs. The remarkable Welsh Revival broke out in Loughor in early November 1904 and reached the Llynfi valley within weeks. Evan Roberts was to visit the area three times, resulting in 5,414 conversions. The revival transformed the Welsh valleys morally and spiritually.[3] On 20th November, George and his brother Stephen were converted in their home church, Siloh Congregational, under the ministry of the pastor, W. Glasnant Jones. George became active in the revival alongside his pastor who records 'at the open air revival services I always found young Jeffreys at my side. I was privileged to give him his early religious tuition and a splendid scholar he was. Superior to other lads, there was a character in his face: I knew he was a "chosen vessel" '.[4]

## Origins of Pentecostalism

The Welsh Revival was evangelical, with a strong emphasis on the Keswick message of 'deeper life', but it was not Pentecostal. No reliable evidence has been found for the distinctive Pentecostal sign of glossolalia during the year-long revival. When it came two years later, there was strong opposition from the established churches and revival leaders. George and Stephen Jeffreys initially shared this hostility to Pentecostalism. However, the revival was the fire which ignited the flame of the British Pentecostal movement.

Most of its leaders were either converted in the revival, such as the Jeffreys, Daniel P. Williams and Donald Gee, or were deeply influenced

---

[2]   D. Gee, *These Men I Knew* (Nottingham: Assemblies of God, 1980), 49.
[3]   E.J. Orr, *The Flaming Tongue* (Chicago: Moody Press, 1973), chapter 3.
[4]   W.G. Jones as quoted in E.C.W. Boulton *George Jeffreys: A Ministry of the Miraculous* (London: Elim, 1928), 11.

by it, such as Alexander Boddy, Cecil Polhill and William O. Hutchinson. The revival was also the catalyst in the events in Azusa Street, Los Angeles, where the Pentecostal movement began in April 1906. There were, however, other and deeper roots to the Pentecostal movement.

Donald Dayton traces the origins of the Pentecostal Spirit baptism to the Wesleyan doctrine of perfection, developed by Wesley's successor, John Fletcher, and revived in the mid-nineteenth century by Phoebe Palmer.[5] The doctrine was cultivated in Oberlin College by its president, Asa Mahan, and theology professor, Charles Finney. It matured into a belief in a distinct crisis experience of sanctification, a second work of grace by which a Christian may be entirely sanctified. Holiness groups proliferated in the second half of the century, fuelled by the 1858 Revival, the background of the American Civil War and increasing secularism. As the doctrine matured, the language of perfectionism gave way to the more inclusive and biblical terminology of Spirit baptism. This can be seen in the writings of Phoebe Palmer, *The Promise of the Father* written in 1859, and of Asa Mahan, *The Baptism of the Holy Ghost* published in 1870. With the focus on the book of Acts, the emphasis on sanctification broadened to embrace the theme of 'power for service'. As a result, the Holiness movement began to diverge into two camps, destined to be reflected in the twentieth century Pentecostal movements. One emphasised a two-stage process, in which holiness and power were united in the post-conversion crisis experience. The other taught a three-stage process, with the purifying work of the Spirit a prerequisite for the baptism of power. Charles Finney, meanwhile, had moved away from the emphasis on sanctification to focus exclusively on the baptism of the Spirit as the source of power to fulfil the Great Commission.

The Keswick movement played a seminal role in the origins of the Welsh Revival and the Pentecostal movement. It raised the level of spiritual life and commitment in the churches, against the wider background of decline caused by higher criticism, theological liberalism and the religion–science conflict.[6]

---

[5] D. Dayton *Theological Roots of Pentecostalism* (Metuchen: Scarecrow, 1987) L, II.

[6] The causes of religious decline in the period are analysed by Owen Chadwick in *The Victorian Church*, 2nd ed. (London: A & C. Black, 1972), vol. 2, part 1.

The Keswick message prepared the way for the Pentecostal doctrine of a Spirit baptism, evidenced by charismatic gifts, which gave power for Christian service. This was to find fullest expression in the 'power' evangelism of Smith Wigglesworth, the Jeffreys and others, with their emphasis on healing as part of the gospel and a sign to confirm its authenticity. In letters from the campaign trail to his headquarters, George Jeffreys regularly included reports of conversions, healings and Spirit baptisms.

The chief distinguishing feature of twentieth century Pentecostalism is glossolalia (tongues speaking). Although only one of the charismata claimed as normative by Pentecostals, it became the key for two reasons: firstly, the extraordinary and dramatic nature of the gift, which marks it out from other gifts, and secondly because it was seen as a proof of Spirit baptism, in accordance with the doctrine of initial evidence, established from the narratives in the Acts of the Apostles.

Accounts of glossolalia and xenolalia (the supernatural gift of foreign languages, usually understood to be a gift for world missions, as manifested on the day of Pentecost) occur sporadically throughout church history. The most notable precursor to the Pentecostals in Britain was Edward Irving. An outbreak of glossolalia occurred in his church in London in 1831 and led to the setting up of the Catholic Apostolic Church. Edward Irving spoke of glossolalia as the 'standing sign' of the baptism in the Holy Spirit, thus anticipating the Pentecostal doctrine of initial evidence. Although his teaching was known to early Pentecostals, there is no evidence that they received the doctrine from him. It is more likely that they came across his writings subsequently and found them useful as reinforcement of their position in the climate of severe hostility to Pentecostalism in the 1920s and 30s. Like the Pentecostals, Irving encountered hostility and ostracism.

The pioneer of the distinctive Pentecostal doctrine of initial evidence was Charles Parham of Kansas. A radical prophet of the American Methodist–Holiness movement in the late nineteenth century, Parham made the vital connection between the baptism of the Holy Spirit as a source of spiritual zeal and power, and the gift of tongues as its sign and seal. This was to be the bedrock of Pentecostal doctrine. He also emphasised the urgency of world mission and healing, both vital ingredients of the Pentecostal message. In the development of his Pentecostal position, Parham drew on Quaker spirituality, the Holiness doctrine of a baptism of the Holy Spirit for sanctification, the premillenialism of J.N. Darby and his own personal experience of healing. His ideas were matured through the pages of his weekly journal *Apostolic Faith*, a name later adopted by the first American Pentecostal church, in Los Angeles, and the first British Pentecostal church, in Bournemouth. Theory became practice at Parham's Bethel Bible School when, on 1st January 1901, Agnes Ozman, a mature student, spoke in tongues. Two days later, so did Parham and half the remaining students. The Pentecostal distinctive of tongues as the initial evidence of Spirit baptism was forged in the fire of the Bethel experience.[7]

Despite the disintegration of Parham's work at Bethel over the next few years, the message was promoted in his new Bible School in Houston, Texas in 1905, from where graduates spread the doctrine across an America in full flush of the 1905 revival. It was one of these graduates, William J. Seymour, who took the message to a revival hot-spot, the Azusa Street Mission, Los Angeles where, in April 1906, it ignited the Pentecostal movement. Parham's pioneering role in the Pentecostal movement was eclipsed in the explosive growth which followed. He was sidelined because of some unconventional doctrinal views, including British Israelism, annihilationism and the belief that all tongues were actual foreign languages given for the task of world mission to herald the parousia. His 'fall from grace' in 1907 ensured his journey to obscurity for a generation.[8]

The British Israel theory was to be adopted by William Hutchinson's Apostolic Faith Church, Bournemouth, and later by George Jeffreys. Most Pentecostals rejected it. The doctrines of divine healing and premillenialism became major planks of the Pentecostal platform. The scene was set for the adoption of a fourfold Pentecostal mission proclaiming salvation, healing, Spirit baptism and an imminent parousia to usher in an earthly millenial kingdom. It was to prove a powerful combination in America and Britain where religion was being rocked by the implications of biblical criticism, the theory of evolution and the social gospel. Both nations were also grappling with the impact of a devastating World War and a growing financial and

---

[7]   J.R. Goff, 'The Theology of Charles Fox Parham' in Gary McGee (ed.) *Initial Evidence* (Peabody: Hendrickson, 1991), 65–66.
[8]   *ibid.*, 66–67.

social crisis. In this climate, such a radical fundamentalism held a compelling attraction.


## Origins of the Foursquare Gospel

The concept of a fourfold mission was already in place in the Christian and Missionary Alliance founded by Albert Benjamin Simpson (1843–1919). Simpson coined the motto 'Fourfold Gospel' in 1890 to summarise the Alliance's essential message of Christ as saviour, sanctifier, healer and coming king. It was enshrined in his hymn, 'Jesus only is our message', included in many Pentecostal hymnals. James Bradley has demonstrated that the Pentecostal evangelist, Aimee Semple McPherson (1890–1944) 'borrowed' and adapted the motto in 1922 for her International Church of the Foursquare Gospel, despite her claim to have received it by divine revelation.[9]

George Jeffreys changed the name of the Elim movement to Elim Foursquare Gospel Alliance less than two years after his visit to McPherson's Angelus Temple in Los Angeles in 1924, claiming direct, biblical inspiration for the motto.[10] In both movements, sanctification was replaced by baptism in the Holy Spirit. Where this was understood in Pentecostal terms as power for service, rather than a baptism of holiness, there was a danger of losing the emphasis on sanctification, a point raised by Donald Gee.[11]

Simpson was raised in the Scottish Presbyterian church in Canada and nurtured in its staunch Puritanism. This gave him a disciplined, biblical foundation, which kept him from experiential extremism when he became involved in the Holiness movement. Simpson was ordained into his first Presbyterian pastorate in Hamilton, Ontario, in 1865. He came in to the 'second blessing' experience of sanctification in 1874 whilst reading William E. Boardman's, *The Higher Christian Life*, a book which also influenced the Keswick movement. As his own understanding of holiness matured, he took a position distinct

---

[9]　C.W. Nienkirchen, *A.B. Simpson and the Pentecostal Movement* (Peabody: Hendrikson, 1992), 37.

[10]　G. Jeffreys, *The Miraculous Foursquare Gospel – Doctrinal* (London: Elim, 1929), 1:1.

[11]　D. Gee, *The Pentecostal Movement* (London: Victory Press, 1941), 164f.

from the rather sterile debate between 'eradicationists' and 'suppressionists', focusing on the primary result of Spirit baptism as a deeper relationship with the indwelling Christ.[12]

To this, Simpson added the doctrine that healing is included in the saving work of Christ and available by faith for all Christians. His acceptance of this doctrine was influenced by Charles Cullis, an Episcopalian advocate of the position and leader of a number of holiness and healing centres. Simpson's own experience of healing confirmed his belief. He became an international spokesman for the doctrine following his involvement in the 1885 International Convention on Holiness and Divine Healing in London. This alienated him from more conservative holiness teachers.[13] Finally, he exchanged his Puritan eschatology for premillenialism, which aligned him with the growing Adventist movement. It undergirded his missionary emphasis, especially his conviction that the evangelisation of the world would usher in the second advent.[14]

It was not the uniqueness of Simpson's doctrines that marked him out, for each of his four elements was represented by a substantial spiritual movement in the late nineteenth century. Rather, it was his original combination of them, expressed in a forceful motto and an aggressive missionary movement, that distinguished him. The Christocentric interpretation of Spirit baptism reinforced the burden for evangelism and mission. It met a ready echo in the hearts of the new Pentecostals who emerged from the 1905 Revival fired with crusading zeal. His openness to the restoration of the charismata of 1 Corinthians 12, even though he never personally experienced them, meant that he anticipated and embraced all aspects of the Pentecostal movement with the exception of initial evidence.[15] Simpson regarded the insistence on tongues as the first and primary evidence of Spirit baptism as biblically unsound and divisive. However, throughout the turbulent period of 1906–1912, he maintained his openness to tongues, properly controlled, as a valid manifestation of the Spirit,

---

12  Nienkirchen, *A.B. Simpson*, 7.
13  *ibid.*, 13–19.
14  *ibid.*, 20–25.
15  *ibid.*, 13–19; Simpson encouraged Christians to seek all the charismata of 1 Corinthians 12 as early as his first published work, *The King's Business* (New York: Word, Work and World, 1886).

despite many defections from the Alliance to the Pentecostals at home and on the mission field.[16]

His opposition to the doctrine of initial evidence, which was axiomatic to most Pentecostals, was shared by George Jeffreys and the Elim movement. Both were perhaps influenced in this by their preoccupation with the mission of the church rather than the charismata. Significantly, on his 1924 North American tour, Jeffreys was more impressed with the success of the Christian and Missionary Alliance than with the Assemblies of God, who seemed to be disastrously embroiled in internecine conflict. In a letter home, he commented that 'nearly all the noted evangelists that have received the baptism of the Holy Ghost have left the old movement and joined it'. He wanted his movement 'to be in Great Britain what the CMA is in America, with the difference that we retain the whole truth of Pentecost with signs'.[17]

## British Pentecostal Pioneers

The Pentecostal movement spread to Europe through the influence of Thomas Ball Barratt, a Cornish missionary to Norway and leader of the Christiana (Oslo) City Mission, a Methodist Holiness work. Barratt had been an advocate of the doctrine of heart-cleansing and the baptism of the Holy Spirit for twenty years. He was greatly interested in the Welsh Revival and reported its progress in his weekly magazine. He corresponded with Evan Roberts and began prayer meetings for revival in Norway.[18] Whilst on an abortive fund-raising tour of America in the autumn of 1906, he heard of the meetings in Azusa Street through reading a copy of the first issue of *The Apostolic Faith* paper. At the time, he was staying at the Christian and Missionary Alliance home in New York. Here he sought the baptism of the Holy Spirit and on 7th October records, 'I received the baptism of the Holy Ghost, and five weeks later, at a prayer meeting with some friends, I received the Tongues with an increase of power'.[19] In the interval of

---

[16]  *ibid.*, 73–100.
[17]  George Jeffreys, unpublished letter to E.J. Phillips, London (5 August 1924), Elim Archives, Cheltenham.
[18]  E.J. Orr, *The Flaming Tongue*, 180.
[19]  T.B. Barratt, *In the Days of the Latter Rain* rev. ed. (London: Elim, 1928), 144.

five weeks, he corresponded with friends in Los Angeles to receive further news and teaching on the new doctrine.[20] On returning to Norway, the Pentecostal movement rapidly developed there.

Alexander Boddy, vicar of All Saints, Monkwearmouth, near Sunderland, was also in touch with the Welsh Revival and with the events in Azusa Street. Hearing of Barratt's experience, he invited him over. His visit brought the Pentecostal message to Britain. On 1st September, as many people gathered in Sunderland to seek the baptism of the Holy Spirit, the Pentecostal revival came. As ministers and laymen from all over the country came to Sunderland over the next few months, they returned with the Pentecostal experience and doctrine. By April 1908, some 500 British people were believed to have experienced the baptism.[21] In the fertile soil of a church in revival, the movement soon took root and flourished. Notable centres at that time were Westport Hall, Kilsyth (Pastor Andrew Murdoch, Independent), All Saints, Sunderland (Church of England) and Emmanuel Mission, Bournemouth (Pastor William O. Hutchinson, Independent).

A.A. Boddy was the most prominent leader of the British Pentecostal movement from its inception in 1907 to the outbreak of the First World War. In the early days, meetings were held in Sunderland every day, except Fridays. From 1908 to 1914, an annual Whitsun Conference was convened at Sunderland fostering the growth of the movement. Around 120 came from a distance to the first conference in June 1908 and some 500 attended in all. In April 1908, Boddy published the first monthly issue of *Confidence*, the oldest and most influential Pentecostal magazine in Britain. The doctrine of the baptism of the Spirit was expounded by him in the same issue.

Among the leaders and speakers at the first Sunderland Conference was Thomas Jeffreys (no relation to George Jeffreys), a Welsh Congregational pastor from Waunlwyd, Monmouthshire. He was listed in the fourth issue of *Confidence* in July 1908, as the representative of one of only three centres of the Pentecostal movement in Wales, the others being in Victoria and Port Talbot.[22] Jeffreys had heard of the movement at a meeting in November 1907 led by a pastor from England who had received the experience in Sunderland and a visitor

---

20   Nienkirchen, *A.B. Simpson*, 33.
21   A.A. Boddy, *Confidence*, (April 1908), 5.
22   *Confidence* (July 1908), 3.

from Los Angeles, en route to Ceylon. After holding 'tarrying meetings' (times of waiting for the baptism experience) for some time,
Jeffreys and others 'received the baptism' in December and believed
their experience to be the first in Wales. They were able to carry the
majority of their church with them, and begin to spread the message
around the country.

However, other voices were raised against the new movement in
Wales, including those of the leader of the Welsh Revival. Evan
Roberts retired from revival ministry, physically and emotionally
exhausted, early in 1906. He was taken in by Mrs Jessie Penn-Lewis,
who became one of the most vociferous opponents of Pentecostalism.
She had been a key organiser of the Keswick-style convention in
Llandrindod Wells in 1902. Together, they wrote *War on the Saints*
which attacked Pentecostal 'extremism' and characterised it as
demonic.[23]

It is difficult to place the occasion when George Jeffreys entered
the Pentecostal experience. There were Pentecostal meetings in
Maesteg in 1910, organised by a former Baptist minister, William G.
Hill, and the Jeffreys brothers attended these meetings. According to
Jeffreys' reminiscences in the Christmas 1929 edition of the *Elim
Evangel*, he experienced the Spirit baptism in the old Duffryn Congregational chapel.[24] However, this sits uneasily with his earlier
testimony in a letter written to William Hutchinson, Bournemouth,
and published in his magazine *Showers of Blessing* in September 1910.[25]
This indicates that he probably received the experience during his
visit to Bournemouth. Later reluctance to acknowledge this may be
attributed to the need to distance himself and the Elim movement
from the increasingly eccentric doctrinal position of the Apostolic
Faith Church (AFC) after the War and the personality cult which
developed around its leader, William Oliver Hutchinson. This would
have been reinforced by the hostility of the mainstream Pentecostal
movement to the ecclesiology and other doctrines of the Apostolic
Church of Wales, itself an offshoot of the Apostolic Faith Church in
1916.

---

[23]  J. Penn-Lewis, *War on the Saints*, abridged reprint, (Poole: Overcomer
Literature Trust, 1977).
[24]  *Elim Evangel* (25 December 1929), 529.
[25]  *Showers of Blessing*, issue 5.

George Jeffreys' contact with Hutchinson was through James Brooke, a former Baptist minister who had joined Hutchinson and was then the pastor of the work at Belle Vue Chapel, Swansea.[26] It seems likely that George Jeffreys' first ordination was to the pastoral charge of the Independent Apostolic Church (Emmanuel, Christ Church), Maesteg.[27] Jeffreys was at pains to conceal this from wider knowledge in later years.[28]

His link with Hutchinson was broken long before the latter developed his unorthodox doctrines. How was one to know who to associate with in those early days of the Pentecostal movement? Guilt by association could have a serious effect if seized upon by the many enemies of the movement. A number of leading Elim ministers had early connection with Hutchinson which they later regretted and wished to forget.

## Origins of the Elim Foursquare Gospel Alliance

Having become Pentecostals, the brothers Stephen and George Jeffreys came to regard their infant baptism as insufficient. They wrote to Price Davies, a young man under the care of the Pentecostal minister, Thomas Jeffreys, asking him to baptise them by immersion. George was baptised on 11th April 1911, and by this action cut himself off from any ministry ambitions within his own denomination.[29] His Pentecostal experience prevented him from applying to other denominational colleges for training.

At this point, his contact through Sunderland with Cecil Polhill was to prove invaluable. Polhill was one of the Cambridge Seven, a group of Cambridge graduates who went as missionaries to China in 1885. He had inherited wealth in 1903 and, after being invalided home from China and Tibet, had thrown himself into the promotion

---

[26] Later he became a missionary to South Africa and, in 1926, co-founder of the break-away United Apostolic Faith Church.

[27] B. Richards, *History of the Llynfi Valley* (Cowbridge: D. Brown, 1982), 255.

[28] Letters between George Jeffreys and E.J. Phillips, Elim Archives, Cheltenham.

[29] Cartwright, *The Great Evangelists*, 26.

of world missions. He came into the Pentecostal experience in 1908 in Los Angeles. The following year he was one of the founders at Sunderland of the Pentecostal Missionary Union, the first British Pentecostal missionary organisation. It established a number of training centres for missionaries and a Bible school for men in Preston, led by Thomas Myerscough, a former Brethren. Recognising potential in Jeffreys, Polhill offered to finance his studies at Preston. After a commissioning service in Maesteg, he entered the school in November 1912.[30] Fellow students included William F.P. Burton and James Salter, later pioneer missionaries of the Congo Evangelistic Mission, Robert Ernest Darragh, his first and longest-serving team member, Percy N. Corry, later Dean of Elim Bible College, and Ernest John Phillips, another team member and later his chief administrator.[31]

Jeffreys was not to stay long at Preston. His brother Stephen was holding a successful mission in Cwmtwrch, near Swansea in early 1913. So great was the response that he called for his brother George to come and assist him. The mission lasted seven weeks and saw 145 conversions. News of the mission drew Polhill to visit and report the results in his paper *Flames of Fire*. Another report was published in *Confidence*.[32] The mission catapulted the Jeffreys brothers onto the national stage, leading to many requests for them to conduct missions. It was for both the first of many remarkably successful campaigns in Britain and overseas.

At the annual Whitsun Convention in Sunderland that May, George preached for four evenings in succession, with great impact, gaining a widening reputation. Among those impressed was Irishman, William Gillespie, who with his brother George, invited Jeffreys to Belfast, paying his fare. His visit there was to lead to the establishment of the Elim Evangelistic Band (January 1915), the founding of the first Elim Church in Hunter Street, Belfast (June 1915) with Jeffreys as pastor and the first Statement of Faith, 'What we believe.' From the outset, Jeffreys' aim was evangelism and church planting. He was nominally the pastor of the Belfast church, but spent most of his time conducting missions across Northern Ireland. Until 1921, when Irish unrest made mission difficult there, he remained committed to the

---

[30]  *ibid.*, 27–28.

[31]  Boulton, *George Jeffreys*, 13.

[32]  *Confidence* (February 1913), 27.

region, explaining his occasional visits to England as primarily for raising funds for the work in Ireland.[33] By 1922, some twenty-two churches had been established in Northern Ireland.

## The Forming of the Denomination

In common with other early Pentecostals, Jeffreys had no expectation or intention of forming a new denomination. The work in Ireland had resulted in a network of churches, a growing mission team and a missionary arm, but the emphasis was on reaching the country with the Pentecostal message and winning converts to Christ. These were the aims of a forward movement, rather than those of an ecclesiastical body. In retrospect, it is clear that, unless the churches were to be made fully independent and self-governing, the formation of a new denomination was inevitable. Laudably, Jeffreys included in the principles of his first church the ruling 'that no member of any other assembly be asked to join the church'.[34] Of course, transfer growth did take place, but by discouraging proselytising in other churches, Jeffreys eased the high tension a new movement causes. His irenic, if not ecumenical, spirit is evidenced in his long association with Thomas Hackett, a Church of Ireland minister, and with other denominational leaders.

In October 1918 the Belfast diaconate approved Jeffreys' proposal that the growing work be called The Elim Pentecostal Alliance to unite the different ministries. This would be governed by a representative council which would hold property in trust for the Alliance. The council comprised Jeffreys and five other members of the Evangelistic Band, one of them (Rev. Thomas Hackett) a Church of Ireland minister. The decision was influenced by a substantial legacy to George Jeffreys for his work. He was advised to receive the money as a representative of a charitable or missionary cause. The formation of the Alliance constituted the movement as a new denomination. Governing power was no longer in the hands of local church officers, but in the hands of the Council. The diaconate's decision reads, 'And

---

[33]  Minute book of Elim Tabernacle, Belfast (6 June 1922), Elim Archives, Cheltenham.
[34]  *ibid.*, (August 1915).

we therefore acknowledge a representative body of control with plenary powers and known as the Council of the Elim Pentecostal Alliance'. [35] Appointments to the Council were in the hands of Jeffreys. A revision of the constitution in 1923 tightened control of ministers.

Publishing had been crucial to the development of Pentecostalism in America and Britain. In December 1919, Elim added its own magazine, *The Elim Evangel*. This was the official organ of the denomination until its demise in 1989 and its replacement by a glossy monthly, *Direction*. Like many such publications, the former began life modestly and was published quarterly. It comprised a mixture of homily and testimony, but soon became a useful tool for publicity, fund-raising and generating a sense of family among adherents. After two years, the publication became monthly, enabling more reporting of the new pioneer campaigns in England. The need for more frequent reporting was temporarily met by the publication of a weekly news-paper, *The Foursquare Revivalist*, until this was amalgamated into a weekly *Evangel*. In later years, strong editorial control ensured that the *Evangel* conveyed the views of the leadership. Nowhere was this more in evidence than when the founder left Elim.

### Relationships with Other Pentecostals

Throughout the period before the First World War, the Pentecostal movement remained non-denominational. A.A. Boddy remained committed to the end to the principle of a renewal within the existing churches, but the opposition encountered by many Pentecostals led increasingly to the formation of mostly small, independent Pentecostal churches. Not for ever could the question of their relationship be left unanswered. For a time, the unifying effect of the annual conferences at Sunderland and Kingsway Hall and the united missionary work through the Pentecostal Missionary Union proved sufficient. How-ever, a number of factors gave impetus to the formation of other denominations.

Hutchinson's Apostolic Faith Church in Bournemouth was build-ing a network of churches in Wales, England and Scotland, with increasing centralisation of authority under the Chief Apostle. In

---

[35]  *ibid.*, (October 1918).

1916 the Apostolic Church in Wales was formed as a break-away from this body and soon began making approaches to the Assemblies of God in the USA with a view to a formal relationship. Richard Massey has highlighted reasons for the formation of the Assemblies of God in Great Britain and Ireland. These include the positive desire to preserve the Pentecostal testimony and to co-ordinate the work of the movement. There were also concerns about error and discipline, such as the influence of A.E. Saxby, a Pentecostal leader in London, who held to the ultimate reconciliation of all souls to God. His well-articulated views were gaining a following in Pentecostal churches. With the move of Jeffreys from Ireland to England, there was added concern to avoid conflict (and losses) in centres where his missions were held and the possibility of churches being drawn into the centralised Elim movement.[36] A number of churches did join Elim, as they found the successful evangelistic work to be what they were looking for.

Before the move to England, there had been close co-operation between Elim workers and the other churches, with the exception of the Apostolic Church. Many Pentecostal pastors had close links with the Elim Evangelistic Band and some had been members. Leading pastors, such as Donald Gee, contemplated joining Elim and entered into negotiations.[37] At the various conventions, Elim leaders and others shared together. They were jointly supportive of the Pentecostal Missionary Union, founded in Sunderland in January 1909.[38] As Elim gained momentum in the early twenties, the relationship changed. At first, there was a common desire for some basis of unity. Jeffreys was a keen participant in the united conferences in Swanwick in 1920 and 1921 and in the Sheffield unity initiative of 1922. However, fears of Elim's centralised structure and the powers of its leaders over property and ministers made many leaders of independent churches wary of Jeffreys and Elim. The emergence of J. Nelson Parr as a leader in the formation of the Assemblies of God in 1924 probably sealed the outcome.

---

[36] R.D. Massey, 'A Sound and Scriptural Union: An Examination of the Origins of the British Assemblies of God during 1920–25' (unpubl. PhD thesis, University of Birmingham, 1988), section 3.
[37] *ibid.*, 57–64.
[38] *Confidence* (January 1909), 13.

Jeffreys and other Elim leaders were not invited to the initial conference which formed the constitution for the new fellowship, and only came in on the main conference at the last minute. There was an attempt at this late stage to find a role for Elim as the home-mission arm of the new denomination, but it was not to be. Jeffreys visited the USA later that year and was unimpressed with the Assemblies of God there. The ten-year-old denomination was going through a difficult period and seemed to confirm Jeffreys' doubts about the British group. On his return, the Elim Evangelistic Band held their annual meeting in Belfast and decided not to join the new denomination. Relationships remained cool between the two groups for some time. There were several occasions when a new church was opened near to one of the other denomination, although informal agreements sometimes minimised this.

**Expansion into England**

From 1921, Jeffreys' attention switched progressively to England and Wales, with the first Elim church opened that year in Leigh-on-sea, Essex. After a successful campaign in Clapham, London with his brother Stephen, George moved his headquarters (a quasi-military term borrowed from the Salvation Army) to London. From here, the missionary activity developed at a frenetic pace, with Jeffreys rarely at home for long. Much of the planning and organisation of the rapidly expanding denomination was handled on-the-hoof. The administrative load fell increasingly on the shoulders of Jeffreys' 'Secretary-General', Ernest Phillips, in Clapham. Property acquisition went on apace, most of it being redundant buildings of the declining older denominations.

In retrospect, it is easy to see that rapid expansion on this scale could lead to cash-flow problems. In the mid-thirties, congregations facing the financial hardships of the Depression were hard pressed to supply the funds to cover the mortgages on property and the high running and maintenance costs of crumbling architecture. Without the charisma of the founder, many pastors were unable to maintain the number of adherents in the local churches. Times were often hard, especially when, following the decision to make each church self-supporting, the pastors' wages were seen as the last call on church income.

In the development of his evangelistic missions, Jeffreys was influenced by the strategy of Charles Finney and the campaigns of Dwight Moody and William Booth. There was emphasis on sin and its consequences and on the need for repentance and faith to be openly testified. Penitents were invited to respond to the message preached and take their stand for Christ. Emulating the methods of his revivalist mentors, Jeffreys bought a large marquee for his missions. As crowds grew, some of the largest halls were also filled by the evangelist, including Bingley Hall, Birmingham, the Crystal Palace and the Royal Albert Hall, London, as well as city halls, guildhalls and theatres across the country.

Central to the success of his missions was the emphasis on divine healing. Often missions started with limited response until a dramatic healing was reported in the local press, bringing crowds to the meetings. In the days before television and with limited radio entertainment, a healing crusade meeting could draw a crowd as easily as a theatre performance or a music hall. Missions lasted from a few days to six weeks, with the longer campaigns often leaving the strongest churches. Where numbers were strong enough, a church was established and left to the charge of a fresh recruit, often with minimal training.

Press coverage of Jeffreys' campaigns and those of his brother Stephen, who worked under the Elim banner from 1915 to 1925, was mainly positive. Albert Edsor[39] (1910–), who joined Jeffreys in 1928 as pianist, secretary and car driver, holds many such press cuttings from 1927 onwards. A notable exception to this was the magazine *John Bull*, which published a highly critical and unsubstantiated attack on Jeffreys and many other healing evangelists.[40] Hostility came mainly from religious leaders. Donald Gee bemoaned the fact that from earliest days, 'only at the cost of great reproach could believers join themselves to any of the despised little pentecostal meetings'. He had first-hand experience of this as a pastor in Leith, Edinburgh. It was his assessment that 'in Britain the Pentecostal movement probably received the most determined, capable and prejudiced opposition that it encountered anywhere in the whole world'.[41] Stephen Jeffreys encountered such

---

[39] A.W. Edsor, *Set Your House in Order* (London: New Wine Press, 1989), 49–54.

[40] Cartwright, *The Great Evangelists*, 100–102.

[41] D. Gee, *These Men*, 88–89.

hostility when the minister of Horbury Chapel, Kensington, published an attack on him in 1922.[42]

Following the move of the headquarters to London, the decision was taken to establish a printing press and publishing company. A purpose-built press was opened in April 1924. Elim was the first Pentecostal body to move into independent publishing. A steady stream of pamphlets and books undergirded the growing movement. Ernest Boulton promoted the ministry of Jeffreys in the first biographical account, *A Ministry of the Miraculous* (1928). Jeffreys defined Elim beliefs in the multi-volumed *The Miraculous Foursquare Gospel* (1930), *Healing Rays* (1932) and *Pentecostal Rays* (1933). Pentecostal distinctives were developed by William Hathaway, *The Gifts of the Spirit in the Church* (1933) and Charles Kingston, *Fullness of Power* (1939). Other Pentecostal leaders used the publishing house to launch their writing careers. By 1936 over 50 books had been published.

The annual Easter Conventions in the Royal Albert Hall, London, raised the profile of Jeffreys and Elim. At the first one, in 1926, Aimee Semple McPherson was guest speaker. Her flamboyant, Hollywood style was not to London taste, but her high profile and the press coverage certainly helped the launch of these Easter Conventions. The relationship with McPherson undoubtedly emboldened Jeffreys for the more dramatic occasions. However, the media love for her sensational style caused Elim embarrassment when she visited again.

Jeffreys filled the Royal Albert Hall (10,000 people in those days) the following Easter without Aimee. Significantly, Ernest Boulton devoted a whole chapter of his book to the 1927 Convention, yet made no mention at all of the 1926 one.[43] In 1928, 1,000 people were baptised in the Royal Albert Hall on Good Friday, in a specially constructed tank.[44] The Easter meetings became an Elim hallmark until the 1990s when costs became prohibitive and restrictions too limiting.

In the early days, the main body of the denomination was governed directly by Jeffreys by means of rules and regulations which were frequently updated and extended. Control was strict and somewhat paternalistic, but then the pastors were often young with little training

---

[42]   Cartwright, *The Great Evangelists*, 49.
[43]   Boulton *George Jeffreys*, chapter 16.
[44]   *ibid.*, 319.

and could be in charge of large congregations. The style of leadership was reminiscent of the Salvation Army, with Jeffreys in command and the work divided into districts under superintendents from 1929. Ministers had little say in their affairs, a factor which caused increasing unrest as the denomination matured. Churches which had joined Elim were more independent, governed either by their own founder, or by deacons. These were included in an umbrella organisation, the Elim Church Incorporated, started in 1926. This dual-track situation made it difficult to weld the work into a unified structure, a problem which remains today.

In 1929 some ministers were called to the Bible College to discuss revised regulations. Then in 1932, Robert Tweed, Northern District Superintendent, called a conference of ministers in Glossop. The first national conference of ministers was held in 1933; laymen were not included. The conference discussed Elim's organisation at length, but had no powers to make any changes for executive power lay with Jeffreys and Phillips. In 1934, a deed poll transferred government to an executive council of nine members, three of whom were nominated by Jeffreys and four by the conference, the others being Phillips and Jeffreys. This left Jeffreys without overall control.

## Elim Bible College

Jeffreys and Phillips had both received training under Thomas Myers-cough at the Preston College of the Pentecostal Missionary Union. The PMU was a participant in the formation of the British Assemblies of God in 1924. Elim, meanwhile, was beginning to expand in England, with Jeffreys opening new churches. Some pastors were recruits from other denominations, but many had received no formal training. A training centre was required to serve the growing movement and supply pastors for the new churches.

The *Elim Evangel* of 1st May 1925 reported, 'Elim Bible College: Our readers will rejoice to hear that studies in connection with the above have already commenced in the minor hall of the Elim Tabernacle, Park Crescent, Clapham. Like many other Elim undertakings, the school has begun in an unostentatious manner, with five students. The overseers of the Alliance are looking to the Lord to supply the need of a suitable home in London where the students can live and study under the same roof.' The prayers were soon answered and in January 1926, the Elim Bible College was established in a former Redemptorist convent building in Clapham Park, which was soon named 'The Woodlands'. It was to be home for the college for thirty-nine years.

In the early days, the study programme was very basic, majoring on Pentecostal doctrines and practice, and evangelism. There were no qualified tutors, no theologians or biblical scholars. No minister held a theology degree. The course of training could be very short, many students staying only a few months, before the demand for pastors placed them in charge of new churches with perhaps hundreds of new converts. Even as late as the mid-1950s, students could be taken from college after only a few months and appointed to churches.

The first principal of the college was Jeffreys himself, although he was rarely there to teach. There could only be one principal in Elim and very quickly the title stuck to him as a kind of honorary rank, quite apart from its link with the college. E.J. Phillips soon took to calling him 'Prince' in his correspondence. The daily oversight of the college was in the hands of the dean, the first dean being Phillips, though his heavy administrative load left him little time to give to the college, so the first tutor was the minister of the Clapham church, Robert Mercer. Even prior to the schism in 1939, the pace of church planting had slowed dramatically. Few churches were opened after 1935 as the growing crisis of leadership and direction diverted activity. Jeffreys' time was partly spent in successful campaigning in Switzerland, partly in touring the established churches, partly in working for reform in Elim's constitution. With the decline in demand for new pastors, the college's activity contracted. In the early 40s, the combined effect of the schism and the war led to the temporary closure of the college. After the war, as Elim made new efforts in church planting the college's work expanded. In the early 1950s, J.T. Bradley, then principal, established a more structured curriculum and a one-year course. English Language tuition was offered for overseas students, an activity which continues successfully today. Over the years, many language students have continued on to the Theology course and some into the Elim Ministry or Missions. A number have married Elim pastors.

## British Israelism (BI)

A strong emphasis on eschatology was a distinctive feature of early Pentecostalism. For the most part, this meant the premillenial, dispensationalist teaching inherited from J.N. Darby through the Holiness movement. There was no place for postmillenialism or amillenialism in the apocalyptic vision of the Pentecostal evangelist. Variations of interpretation within the premillenial framework were hotly debated, especially between historicists, who saw most biblical apocalyptic as already fulfilled in history, and futurists, who believed most remained to be fulfilled in imminent climactic events. The futurists had the edge in generating a sense of urgent expectation of Christ's return in the hard times of the twenties and thirties.

British Israelism offered a quite different prophetic interpretation. The theory is based on a distinction between the Jews and Israelites. The Jews were believed to be only the descendants of those people who formed the southern kingdom of Judah – those from the tribes of Judah and Benjamin. It was held that in the return from exile, only the Jews returned to Palestine. The Israelites were the descendants of the ten tribes who formed the northern kingdom of Israel which was exiled by Assyria. They were scattered and had not been part of the return to Palestine. Instead, they had migrated across Europe by land and sea to Britain and parts of continental Europe. During and since the Reformation, 'Israel' had re-emerged. The Anglo-Saxon race was believed to be in direct descent from Israel. This included those who had migrated to the New World and now formed the USA. Britain was identified with Tarshish. It was the Jews alone who had rejected their Messiah. Israel had received him and was enjoying his blessing in Britain, the USA and Northern Europe. The prosperity and worldwide power of Britain and the USA were directly attributable to God's providence. Salvation still required faith in Christ and still included Jews and Gentiles, but it was Israel who enjoyed the special favour of God.[45]

Charles Parham held the BI view at the turn of the century. However, the liberation of Palestine in 1918 and the prospect of a

---

[45] The Pentecostal version of this theory is developed at length in *Showers of Blessing* from issue 27 (May 1922) on; for a Pentecostal refutation see C. Palmer, *British-Israelism* (London: Victory Press, 1942).

revived state of Israel intensified interest in the place of Israel in God's
purposes. It also gave a stimulus to the growth of British Israelism in
Britain and the USA. Many arguments for the theory were advanced,
from studies of human migration in European history to etymology
of British names. It was a mixture of legend and pseudo-science. It
was also believable as an explanation for the largest empire the world
had yet seen. In the twenties and thirties, the theory prospered and
under the banner of the British-Israel World Federation, meetings
were held across the country. After the Second World War and the
withdrawal of European nations from imperialism, it was less tenable
and by the 1960s, the movement was a lost cause, though it still has
its adherents today.

In Britain, as in the USA, some of the earliest Pentecostal leaders
were attracted to the BI view. William O. Hutchinson adopted the
position in December 1919 after reading an article in the *Daily Express*.
His Apostolic Faith Church was transformed into a BI movement very
rapidly and the doctrine was taken to extremes. George Jeffreys held
the view from around 1920, possibly influenced towards it by John
Leech KC, one of his closest advisors and a strong advocate of the
view. There is little mention of BI in Elim until the early thirties. After
what was to be his last major church-planting crusade, Jeffreys wrote
'My main supporters believe God is fulfilling prophecy in the British
Empire'.[46] Later, Jeffreys attended and shared the platform at BI World
Federation meetings.

The BI view was discussed at the Glossop conference in 1932,
where Jeffreys urged Elim's alignment with it though he received little
support. At the first national conference in 1933, the issue was debated
at length and the final vote showed only 16 men in sympathy with
BI. Agreement was struck neither to preach it nor oppose it in any
Elim Church. The agreement did not last long and in 1934 a full-scale
debate was proposed. In favour of BI was John Leech, a skilled lawyer
and debater, whilst against him was the college dean, Percy Corry.
Corry withdrew at the last minute and it was left to Ernest Phillips to
oppose the view. Phillips was of Jewish descent on his mother's side.
He stayed up all night to prepare. The debate and discussion lasted a
day and half, and in the final vote only 13 out of 78 ministers present
supported the BI view. The outcome was a ban on the preaching of

46   Cartwright, *The Great Evangelists*, 120.

BI in centrally governed Elim churches.[47] The conference could not bind locally governed churches. One of the main causes of the schism between Jeffreys and Elim in 1939 was thus established. Relationships between Jeffreys and Phillips, formerly inseparable partners in Elim's expansion, were strained and dissension hit a number of churches whose pastors held the view.

Not content with the decision of the 1934 conference, Jeffreys sought executive council authority to preach BI in the centrally governed churches. Despite his allies on the council, he failed to gain the freedom he wanted. Increasingly he spent his time in visiting locally governed churches. Pressed on this, he agreed in 1935, not to raise BI again in the conference and not to spend all his time in the locally governed churches. In fact, he persisted in raising the issue in correspondence and at the executive meetings. In 1937, one of his appointees to the executive and head of Elim's Youth work, James McWhirter broke the moritorium by publishing his book *Britain and Palestine in Prophecy*. Opinion is divided to this day over the part played by the BI issue in the schism of 1939. Whilst it may not have been the single cause of the break, it was a major contributory factor. It certainly galvanised Jeffreys' determination to introduce local government to all Elim churches. Significantly, those churches he founded after this were brought in under local government.

## Jeffreys' Schism with Elim

The primary cause of the schism, according to Jeffreys and leaders of the Bible Pattern Fellowship, which he founded afterwards, was the issue of Elim's government. In 1924, Jeffreys had written from the USA declaring his opposition to democratic forms of government. Ten years later, he was of a different persuasion and became the champion of local government, with churches controlling their buildings through local trustees and free from central control. He was persuaded to this view in part by his visits to Sweden where the Baptist-originated Pentecostal churches had no central control and were flourishing. He had a similar impression in Switzerland. At home, the financial burdens of the central administration worried

---

[47] Elim Conference Minutes (1934), Elim Archives, Cheltenham.

him. During a period of illness, he came to believe he had a call
from God to 'set your house in order'.[48] Various schemes were put
forward by Jeffreys and discussed, but there were difficulties in
changing the constitutional structure, established in the denomination's Deed Poll of 1934. There were also financial and practical
obstacles to the various schemes. In any case, the executive council
was not in favour of major changes. Jeffreys stood to gain from a
devolution of power. He had lost personal control of the movement
in the Deed Poll of 1934, had no freedom to express his BI views
in centrally governed churches, and thus had no direct access to the
people. How far such considerations influenced his desire for reform
is a matter of debate.

The story of the schism itself is outside the scope of this study. It
was a sad episode lasting a number of years.[49] The outcome was that
Jeffreys resigned from Elim at the 1939 Conference, leaving with a
few ministers and their churches and launched the Bible Pattern
Church Fellowship. The schism demoralised Elim and it was re-
enacted in some local churches which also divided. In churches which
followed Jeffreys, there were battles over buildings. All this came only
months after the outbreak of a war which halted expansion, left a
number of church buildings destroyed or damaged, and further
eroded church attendance. It took many years of post-war effort to
regain the lost ground. Elim revised its constitution in 1942, trans-
ferring overall control from the executive council to the conference.
This was now in two sections. The Ministerial Session had responsibility for the admission and discipline of ministers. The Representative Session, comprising all ministers and one lay representative
from each church, had final authority in all other matters. The
executive council had various delegated powers and responsibility to
implement conference decisions. This Presbyterian-style structure
remains today. It went some way to meeting Jeffreys' aims for lay
participation, but came too late for a reconciliation. Happily, a
reunion of many Bible Pattern churches with Elim has been effected
recently, largely ending the schism.

---

[48]  Letter to E.J. Phillips (28 January 1937), Elim Archives, Cheltenham.
[49]  For a fuller discussion, see Cartwright, *The Great Evangelists*, chapters
16–17.

## Elim Ministers

Elim's earliest leaders were members of the Elim Evangelistic Band.
The Band continued to operate until the late twenties. Its members
were evangelists first and pastors second. They looked for inspiration
and leadership to Jeffreys, their role model and director. By the early
thirties, there was a growing body of pastors whose role was to care
for the local church. Their relationship with Jeffreys was different. In
his sociological study of Elim in 1961, Wilson characterised the pastors
as 'the trained, controlled agents of headquarters', indoctrinated at the
College and then controlled by the centralised administration.[50] He
was building a case for his thesis that Jeffreys' schism with Elim was a
classic break between the simple, charismatic leader and his bureaucratic, centralised organisation. It is certainly the case that ministers
depended increasingly on the headquarters machinery and relied for
an opportunity to have a voice in decision-making on the annual
conferences from 1932. There was a growing demand for a say in the
movement's affairs and to help shape its future. However, that demand
was as much targeted against the executive and headquarters as it was
on Jeffreys. The Deed Poll of 1934 gave the ministers in conference
the power to appoint four of the nine members of the executive. If
the ministers were unhappy with their appointees to the executive,
they would have to vote them out at the conference. Until the Deed
Poll revision in 1942, after the schism, this was the only power the
ministers held.

In the early days, strict and detailed regulations covered the function
of the minister. All appointments were made by the Stationing Committee at headquarters, with neither minister nor churches having a say
in the matter. Later, churches were permitted to refuse a proffered
minister, and in this case another name would be offered. Similarly, the
minister was allowed to refuse an appointment and would be offered
another. Not until the 1970s did the policy change to allow minister
and church leadership to meet and interview each other to assist the
decision. Until the 1970s, ministers required headquarters approval to
marry and even to begin or end a relationship. A minister (in theory)
could not preach in churches outside Elim without permission from

---

[50] B.R. Wilson, *Sects and Society*, (London: Heinemann, 1961), 61ff.

headquarters. Such regulations in part reflect the different attitude to authority in the pre-war and immediate post-war periods. They also reflect the youth and inexperience of many ministers in those early days. The changed attitude today owes more to the relaxed individualism of the prevailing culture than to any review of principle.


## The Impact of the Charismatic Renewal and House Church Movement

For the few short years from its beginning to the outbreak of the Great War, the Pentecostal movement in Britain was mainly a renewal movement within the established churches. In this, it followed the Keswick and other Forward movements of the late nineteenth century. Boddy hoped that the movement would accomplish wholesale renewal of the church. He remained opposed to the formation of Pentecostal denominations to the end.[51] It was not to be, and from the outset the Pentecostal message was divisive in its effect. The Pentecostals were rejected by the established churches because of their teaching and practice, reinforced by the problems of excesses and disorder. In their turn, the Pentecostals rejected the older churches as 'dead' and resistant to God's Spirit. They saw no way that the new Pentecostal believers could be grafted into these churches.

Hocken regards the charismatic renewal, which began in the 1950s, as the second wave of the Pentecostal movement, as it owed a great deal to the influence of leading Pentecostals. These included David Du Plessis (1905–1987), General Secretary of the Apostolic Faith Mission in South Africa, and Donald Gee, Principal of the British Assemblies of God Bible College and editor of *Pentecost*, the magazine of the World Pentecostal fellowship.[52] Both were widely travelled and held broad perspectives on the world Pentecostal movement. Smith Wigglesworth (1860–1947), the Pentecostal evangelist, had prophesied in 1936 that Du Plessis would be used by God to bring the message to the older

---

[51]   M. Robinson, 'The Charismatic Anglican' (unpubl. MLitt thesis, University of Birmingham, 1976), 82, 102.

[52]   P. Hocken, *Streams of Renewal* (Exeter: Paternoster, 1986), 21; see also chapter 8.

churches.[53] The role was not an easy one, as many Pentecostals remained suspicious of the renewal, especially of the Roman Catholic phase. Du Plessis and Gee broke boundaries when they attended and spoke at the World Council of Churches' meeting on Faith and Order in 1960. Du Plessis said at the meeting 'I am privileged to share in two Pentecostal revivals: one still outside the WCC and the other more recent one, inside the historic churches within the ecumenical movement.'[54] There is still strong feeling about the WCC among many Pentecostals, which shows the radical nature of these leaders' involvement at that time. Gee regarded Pentecostalism as a revival rather than a movement, sharing Boddy's disappointment at the formation of the denominations. He encouraged openness to the renewal in Pentecostal editorials and published news of its spread. This served to inform Pentecostals and encourage a favourable response. Both men looked on the renewal as a second phase of one divine work.

In the early 1960s, there was increasing contact between Pentecostals and the older churches. This reflects a re-assessment of Pentecostalism, with many of the churches now less hostile. Negative reaction to them narrowed to evangelicals in the Puritan tradition, notably in the FIEC and Brethren churches. Pentecostals share the broader, catholic roots of the Anglican and Methodist tradition. The renewal spread to the Church of England in the early 1960s. Michael Harper, whose influence may be compared with that of Boddy, came into the Pentecostal experience in September 1962. Other early leaders were David Watson and David McInnes, who came into the experience in 1964. Harper organised renewal meetings from his base at All Souls Church, Langham Place, London, and hosted a visit of Du Plessis in 1964. That year he left All Souls Church to work full-time in the renewal, and in September he launched the Fountain Trust to promote it, *Renewal* magazine providing the modern equivalent of *Confidence* to spread information about Renewal.

By the early 1970s, the movement was widely spread in the established churches and conventions, such as the international one hosted by Harper at Guildford Cathedral in 1971, attracted leaders from many different churches. The Fountain Trust brought together the many streams of the renewal, including many Pentecostals. It was

---

[53] *ibid.*, 19.
[54] *ibid.*, 64.

terminated in 1980, believing its task to be completed, though the
*Renewal* magazine continues its monthly publication.

The renewal began in the Roman Catholic Church at meetings in
Notre Dame University, Indiana, USA, in the spring of 1967,[55]
American Assemblies of God pastors playing a key role. The Church
proved to be very responsive, helped by the fact that Catholic theology
had always allowed for the supernatural, in contrast to the Protestant
theology of the Reformation. The second Vatican Council (1962–65)
encouraged openness to the Holy Spirit and greater lay activity. This
undoubtedly contributed to the spread of the renewal in the Church
two years later. The Catholic charismatic renewal was to become a
substantial movement and receive recognition in the Vatican.

Pentecostal reaction to the renewal was muted. Some were hostile,
others openly supportive, most indifferent. Few could see how far it
was to spread or its consequences. However, the reaction to the
house-church or Restoration movement was very different. From its
outset, this phase of the renewal was divisive in Pentecostal circles,
as it was in the older churches. A number of renewal groups in the
older churches broke away to form home-based churches. As in the
early Pentecostal movement, some jumped while others were pushed.
The earliest groups were formed in the mid-60s, but the period of
rapid expansion was in the 1970s. Walker regards the conference of
leaders in 1965 as the effective beginning of the Restoration movement.[56] Seen from this distance, the movement may be interpreted as
the denomination-forming phase of the renewal. This made it preda-
tory on less 'charismatic' or 'renewed' churches, including Pentecostal ones. Many of the latter were going through a second-generation
identity crisis. The subculture of pre-war Pentecostalism had in many
cases resulted in a traditionalism which lacked the vitality to change.
These churches were vulnerable to the youthful dynamic of the new
movement.

There were also deeper issues at stake in the new movement, which
were not immediately apparent to those attracted from the renewal
or Pentecostalism. The formation of house churches was not merely

---

[55]    E. O'Connor, *The Pentecostal Movement in the Catholic Church* (Notre
Dame: Ave Maria Press, 1971), 38.
[56]    A. Walker, *Restoring the Kingdom* (London: Hodder & Stoughton, 1985),
40.

to escape from hostile churches. There was a strong Brethren element to the new movement, which influenced the anti-clerical, anti-denominational stance it developed. It also encouraged the emphasis on eldership. Key early leaders with a Brethren background included Arthur Wallis, acknowledged 'father' of the movement, Campbell McAlpine, David Lillie, Sidney Purse and Graham Perrins. Purse remained independent of the main Restoration movement, as did some other house-churches. The Restoration movement had another attraction – its eschatology, which undergirded its message. This was not the premillenialism of the older Pentecostals, with their apocalyptic vision of the imminent end. That doctrine met a ready response in the dark days of the 1920s and 30s when the prospect of an imminent parousia was appealing. The new message was postmillenial, although it was dressed in the language of 'restoration'. This was not an appeal to defeatism, but a promise of a powerful, flourishing church influencing and changing society so that it would be fit for Christ to return as king.[57] It was an optimistic doctrine, similar to that of the early and medieval church and more recently of the Latter Rain movement and it caught the popular mood of the 1970s and 1980s.

Among the things to be 'restored' were strong leadership and discipline, locally through elders and nationally through the apostles and prophets of the movement. A new, relaxed and exuberant style of worship arose, interpreted through contemporary music and song-writing. The Pentecostals were still largely singing the hymns and songs of the pre-war revival. The few new songs they had lacked depth while the restoration songs reflected the new, triumphalist doctrines of the movement and began to influence many Pentecostals.

Many, including Pentecostals, were drawn to the annual camp meetings established by leaders of the restoration movement, the first occurring in 1970 in South Wales. By the late 1970s, attendance at the annual week in the Yorkshire Dales was reaching 8,000 and other events were added in the South of England and Wales. In these conventions, the ideology of the movement was cultivated and propagated.

In Britain, as elsewhere, the Restoration movement had a dual effect. Some churches embraced the new themes while others resisted and many lost members as a result. Some leaders and whole churches

---

[57] *ibid.*, 125.

were lost to the movement and the impact was felt keenly in Elim. In the late 1970s, national leaders feared that a schism was imminent. In the end, only a few churches left Elim, along with a few pastors and members. The pressure of the restoration influence reached crisis point in 1981 when there was much discussion at the annual conference about the movement's response. The outcome was a re-convening of the ministers' section of the conference in that autumn in Southport. The Southport meetings were a watershed, and during them Elim came to terms with the issues of the Restoration movement. This can be seen in the keynote address by J.C. Smyth and in the papers and reports of the discussion groups and plenary sessions.[58] The conference averted a schism, although a few were impatient with the speed and extent of change and left. However, a number of changes were agreed over the next few years.

Elim in Ireland had established elders in the local churches from the start. Elsewhere, churches were governed by deacons elected every two years. Some had elders, but this was more an honorary recognition of long-serving deacons. The difference was highlighted by the restoration teaching on eldership. Many in Elim wished to have elders for spiritual oversight, being convinced that this was the biblical ideal. There was distaste for the democratic process. There was also, perhaps, the hope that by following the restoration teaching greater spiritual renewal would ensue. The matter was discussed at the 1981 Southport Conference and a steering committee was established to prepare for changes at the 1982 Conference. In the event, further consideration proved necessary and it was only in 1983 that arrangements for local church oversight were loosened. Each church was permitted, within certain guidelines, to determine its own local leadership structure.[59] A number of churches implemented changes and three main styles emerged. Those keeping the original structure elected deacons; some chose to have elders, nominated by the church session and confirmed by a vote of the members; while others chose to have elders appointed without a vote of the members. Those with elders have various administrative arrangements, either in the form of deacons appointed by the eldership or elected, or management committees.

---

58    Southport Conference papers, published internally by the Elim Church, Cheltenham.
59    Elim Conference Minutes (1983).

The house church movement had developed effective care for leaders and this highlighted the limited nature of this in Elim. Much discussion and consultation took place between the first Southport Conference in 1981 and that in 1984 over the desirability of appointing men to the care of pastors. The outcome was the regionalisation of the movement in 1985, with regional superintendents responsible for pastoral supervision.[60] The result was a rather bureaucratic structure which inhibited the original objective. Regional superintendents require administrative skills to handle their regional duties, and those best suited to the pastoral care of pastors do not necessarily have these. In addition, the financial burden of supporting regional superintendents has been difficult to sustain, especially as the original seven regions have been extended. Attempts to regionalise many central functions proved abortive and the system has not worked as well as had been hoped and is currently under review.

The Restoration movement began to fragment in 1975 and by the early 1980s had lost much of its early drawing power. By the same time, Elim and other Pentecostal groups had changed considerably, absorbing many features of the movement and the wider renewal. There is now a fair measure of mutual trust and respect between the movements and other issues exercise the minds of leaders. The overall impact can be fairly judged as beneficial to the Pentecostal movement, shaking it out of the traditionalism and insecurities of the post-war period and giving it much greater self-confidence.

## Changing Distinctives – Social

### *Identity*

The primary distinctive of Elim in its early days was not doctrinal, Wilson noting that in those days; 'Elim was more characterised by its revivalism than by its Pentecostalism'.[61] Whilst Jeffreys and his team were all products of the Pentecostal movement of the pre-First World War period, their motive for working together was always mission and church-planting. The founding meeting on 7th January 1915 in

---

[60] Elim Conference Minutes (1985).
[61] *Sects and Society*, 61.

Monaghan, Ireland, was arranged in order to discuss 'the best means of reaching Ireland with the Full Gospel on Pentecostal Lines'.[62] They were more concerned to offer an alternative to modernism than to promote Pentecostalism. The hallmarks were thus evangelism, adventism and healing, and in the pioneering days of the 20s and 30s, Elim was more akin to Wesley and Booth than to Boddy. Wilson thus comments, 'George Jeffreys did not preach pentecostal teaching in his revivals, nor claim authority by asserting his own possession of the gifts of the Spirit'.[63]

Elim has always considered itself a movement rather than a denomination. This is more than just a desire to avoid institutionalism; it represents the consciousness of the leadership that they are united in a mission organisation, not a settled church. The tension between the two is reflected in the schism of 1939, but the mission-consciousness did not leave with Jeffreys. It was continued by P.S. Brewster, who pioneered some forty churches, and other evangelists in the post-war period. It was seen in the Challenge '94 Mission, a Pentecostal evangelistic campaign in 1994, and the strategies of the denomination for church planting in the 1990s. This sense of being a movement reinforces the value of central government, which can initiate programmes of mission and call for local response.

The impact of the charismatic renewal in the 1960s and the house church movement in the 1970s and 80s has changed the local self-consciousness dramatically. No longer do local pastors need to travel to Elim district rallies to get fellowship and support. Such events have all but vanished. The same is true of district youth functions or ministers' fraternals. Now the Elim pastor can enjoy acceptance with local clergy, many of whom will be charismatic. He even enjoys the status of being a Classical Pentecostal. He is more likely to build relationships with local evangelical and charismatic pastors than to build them with other Elim pastors, other than those nearby, or those who are close personal friends, perhaps from college days. If the sense of a movement is no longer strongly felt by ministers, it is almost absent in local churches, except among the older members of Elim. Many churches have little contact with the wider denomination,

---

[62] Minutes of Elim Evangelistic Band (January 1915), Elim Archives, Cheltenham.
[63] *Sects and Society*, 61.

except through reading the *Direction* magazine or through an occasional preaching visit by the regional superintendent. Many members have little or no awareness of what the movement means to them. An exception to this is Northern Ireland, where the number and size of the churches and specific local factors foster a stronger Elim identity.

## Anti-intellectualism

Few early Pentecostal leaders had received a university education and many, such as Smith Wigglesworth, were barely literate. University degrees were even considered a hindrance to Pentecostal ministry and anti-intellectualism was a common early feature. The movement has struggled for most of its life with the mind – Spirit tension. There was a deep suspicion of contemporary theology, with its higher criticism and modernism. Pentecostals were not equipped to engage the academics and were thus content to condemn. They needed no further evidence of the 'evils' of such doctrines and of the influence of Darwin, than the decline in the older churches. The answer was not viewed as being located in theological debate, but in a practical demonstration of spiritual power.

The earliest leaders and teachers at Elim's Bible College had no formal higher education though the appointment in 1958 of G. Wesley Gilpin as principal led to a change. Wesley Gilpin had undertaken some formal theological training, and under his 21-year leadership the college established a two-year course from 1958 and a three-year course from 1975. The college relocated to larger premises in Capel, Surrey, in 1965. Here the Theology School reached a new level of 125 students with the addition of the third-year course in 1975. The college relocated again in 1987, to Nantwich, Cheshire. In 1992, the college was validated by the Open University Validation Service, successor to the Council for National Academic Awards, for the award of a Diploma in Theology and Christian Ministry, and in 1993 for a Bachelor of Arts degree currently with three different tracks specialising in various aspects of biblical studies and Christian ministry. In 1994, the degree was validated by Manchester University. Enrolment reached a new peak of 140 students in 1994. Today, alongside the principal, there are six full-time faculty with theology degrees and a panel of qualified external lecturers. The college

changed its name in 1996 to Regents Theological College to reflect
its wider enrolment and appeal, and also commenced an MA and M
Theol. in Pentecostal and Charismatic Studies, the latter being
dedicated to those in Christian (pastoral) leadership. Elim currently
expects two years of training of its pastors, although many now
complete the three-year course.

The charge of anti-intellectualism against Pentecostalism is no
longer justified. There remains a higher proportion of less-educated
people in Pentecostal ministry than in other denominations, but
increasingly the trend is for ministers to be college trained, now with
validated qualifications. Pentecostals generally align themselves with
the broader conservative evangelical theology. Whilst still rejecting
liberal theology, they base their defence on the evangelical doctrine
of Scripture, rather than solely on charismatic experience. The higher
level of training enables Pentecostals to embrace a wider social band,
but it must also endanger their ability to effectively serve the less-
educated and socially-deprived sections of the community. Like
Methodism, the Salvation Army and other movements which had
their roots in these communities, the Pentecostal movement has
experienced upward mobility.

**Changing Distinctives – Doctrinal**

Elim's first Statement of Fundamental Truths was published in 1923,
as Elim expanded into England.[64] It was based on a statement drawn
up at the founding of the first church in Belfast in 1915. In common
with statements of faith by other new religious movements, it was
more a statement of distinctives than a statement of faith. It served
to define the movement's boundaries against evangelical, as well as
modernist churches. Thus there were incomplete statements on
matters over which there was no dispute with traditional creeds.

For example, the only statement on the person and work of Christ,
and on salvation was: 'We believe that through the death and risen
power of Christ all who believe are saved from the penalty and power
of sin'. There was no statement on the person and work of the Holy
Spirit, other than on the Pentecostal enduement. On the distinctives,

---

[64]    *Elim Evangel* (August 1923).

there was more detail. For example, on the charismatic gifts, it was declared: 'We believe that God is restoring all the gifts of the Holy Ghost to the Church, which is a living organism, a living body composed of all true believers'. It was important for Elim to define who they were in the religious milieu of the early twentieth century.

A revised and fuller statement was prepared for the 1934 Deed Poll which established a constitution for the denomination.[65] Some statements were unchanged, some were revised and some added. There were now statements on the nature of the church, the fruit of the Spirit, a list of the gifts of the Spirit (1 Cor. 12:7–10) and a statement on the ordinances recognised by Elim – communion, baptism in water, and the laying on of hands and anointing of the sick with oil. There was no improvement on the statement concerning Christ and salvation and there was still no statement on the person of the Holy Spirit.

Revisions in the Fundamentals were contemplated at times in the post-war period and in the 1960s, a doctrine of the Church committee spent much time preparing a report and a revised Statement, but no action was taken to implement it. The 1970s and 1980s turned attention to the more pressing matter of response to the growing charismatic and house church movements and any doctrinal revisions were suspended. The issues of the day were worship, leadership, discipline and the need to respond to the challenges of the new movements. Creative thinking was focused on organisational restructuring. Not until a theological conference was called to address current doctrinal issues did the thought of revising the Fundamentals arise again. This conference was held in October 1991 at the Swanwick Centre, and a committee was established to revise the Statement of Faith. It represented a preliminary report to the 1992 General Conference and a full revised Statement the following year.[66] The revisions were vigorously debated, but finally received overwhelming support. The 1993 Fundamentals represent a significant shift in key aspects of Pentecostal doctrine.

---

[65] The text of this statement can be found in Elim Pentecostal Church yearbooks published prior to 1993 by Elim Church Headquarters, Cheltenham.

[66] The text of the revised statement can be found in the Elim Pentecostal Church yearbooks from 1994 on.

*Initial Evidence*

In the early days, Elim held to the usual Pentecostal position on initial evidence. The 1923 Fundamentals stated: 'We believe that the present latter day outpouring of the Holy Ghost, which is the promise of God to all believers, is accompanied by speaking in other tongues as the Spirit gives utterance.' However, Jeffreys held lightly to the view that tongues are the initial evidence of Spirit baptism. A more eclectic view appeared in the 1934 Fundamentals: 'We believe that our Lord Jesus Christ is the baptiser in the Holy Ghost and that this baptism with signs following is promised to every believer.' The Assemblies of God regarded the Elim position as fudging the basic Pentecostal distinctive. The 1993 Fundamentals maintain the same position, with emphasis on the enduement of power that the Pentecostal experience brings to equip the believer for the ministry of the church. This maintains the focus derived from Keswick and from A.B. Simpson.

*Healing*

In common with most early Pentecostals, Jeffreys held the view that healing was provided for in the atonement of Christ and thus available by faith for all believers.[67] Early articles in the *Elim Evangel* suggested that Christians had no need of medical aid, but this position was soon dropped. The doctrine of healing in the atonement is enshrined in the 1923 Fundamentals: 'We believe that deliverance from sickness is provided for in the atonement, and is the privilege of all who believe.'

In 1934 it changed to: 'We believe that our Lord Jesus Christ is the healer of the body and that all who will walk in obedience to His will can claim Divine Healing for their bodies.' Here, obedience is added to the prerequisite of faith, while there is no mention of the atonement, though this is assumed. The believer does not have to depend on God's discretion, but can claim healing. Over the years, many have been uncomfortable with this emphasis, and in the revision of Elim's Fundamentals in 1993 it was dropped. However, in its place is the concept of deliverance, also controversial as it may reflect the view of some that all sickness is the work of the devil, which can be overcome

---

67    G. Jeffreys, *Healing Rays* (London: Elim, 1932), 154.

through exorcism. The wording, however, is broad enough to embrace a variety of positions and reads: 'We believe that the gospel embraces the needs of the whole man and that the Church is therefore commissioned to preach the gospel to the world and to fulfil a ministry of healing and deliverance to the spiritual and physical needs of mankind.'

### Eschatology

On other issues as well, the 1993 Statement of Faith carefully steers its way through the doctrinal minefield to accommodate varying opinions. Eschatology had always been an area of debate, but the original two Statements had included premillenialism as a fundamental belief. In the early days this caused little difficulty, but as the movement matured, a wider range of opinions developed. Men holding an amillenial or postmillenial position were excluded from the ministry as they could not subscribe to this tenet of faith, supporters of the premillenial position regarding it as non-negotiable. When the revised Fundamental was put to the 1992 Conference, it was hotly debated, but eventually passed and now reads: 'We believe in the personal, physical and visible return of the Lord Jesus Christ to reign in power and glory.' By leaving out any reference to the millenium, the drafters of the statement sidestepped the issue – successfully. The statement would now be acceptable to any evangelical Christian.

### The Spirit of Christ

Apart from his adherence to the BI position, Jeffreys also held to another minority view. He believed that there is a distinction between the Spirit of Jesus and the Holy Spirit. This distinction was held by some other Pentecostals, but was never a mainstream view for it clashed with orthodox evangelical theology, though it did offer a theology to interpret Pentecostal experience. It provided a convenient distinction between the Spirit of Christ, received at regeneration, and the subsequent reception of the Holy Spirit at the Pentecostal baptism. It finds its biblical support in Romans 8:1–17 where the Apostle Paul uses the terms Spirit of Christ and Spirit of God alternatively. Most exegetes, however, regard these uses as interchangeable, but Jeffreys saw in them a real distinction and expounded the view in *Pentecostal*

*Rays*.[68] His position was not widely supported in Elim, but is accommodated in the wording of the 1934 Fundamentals, which refer to the fruit of Christ's Spirit (8) and the gifts of the Holy Spirit (9). For those not holding Jeffreys' view, there was no difficulty in subscribing to the statement, but it allowed for his minority view. The revised Fundamentals of 1993 incorporate the phrase 'fruits of the Spirit' in a more complete statement about salvation, and include the phrase 'gifts of the Spirit' in the statement on the ministries of the church. There is no accommodation to Jeffreys' view.

### Other Doctrinal Issues

The 1934 Fundamentals served the movement indifferently for almost 60 years. On the major evangelical themes they were orthodox, but incomplete. On Pentecostal distinctives they were unnecessarily pedantic and sometimes excluded worthy men from the Elim ministry. They stood the test of time partly because, until legal opinion was obtained, the prevailing belief was that they could not be altered, since they were enshrined for ever in the 1934 Deed Poll. The 1993 Fundamentals are altogether a more complete and more sophisticated statement of faith. They represent the maturing thought and theological reflection of a denomination in its third generation, with competent theological advisers. They also reflect the burning issues of the day.

The revisers faced strong representations on the wording of the statement on biblical inerrancy, a contentious issue in evangelicalism generally in recent times. They were reluctant to be tied in a way which might later appear as pedantic on this issue as the early Statement was on the issues of the formative years.

Another minority view today – annihilationism – was not accommodated at all, despite its support by a few leading evangelicals and charismatics and the Statement reads: 'We believe in the resurrection of the dead and in the final judgement of the world, the eternal conscious bliss of the righteous and the eternal conscious punishment of the wicked.'

The 1993 Fundamentals provide Elim with the framework for a Pentecostal theology which is more thoroughly integrated into the

---

[68]   G. Jeffreys, *Pentecostal Rays* (London: Elim, 1933), 39ff.

received evangelical theology. The consensus in Elim in that it is unlikely that there will be further revisions for a considerable time.

## Conclusion

Eighty years after its foundation, Elim is full of vitality and determination to fulfil its mission. It has survived the tragic schism of 1939 and the ravages of war and materialism. It has allowed the fresh winds of charismatic renewal to reinvigorate its life and mission and it has been innovative in mission and social involvement. Today, it is growing strongly in many areas, though stagnant in others.

In February 1996, the author attended the London Alpha Conference at Holy Trinity, Brompton, along with some eight hundred church leaders from Britain and across the world. A more thoroughly Pentecostal event and programme could hardly be imagined. It would have gladdened the heart of A.A. Boddy to see the realisation of his dream – an Anglican church fully embracing Pentecostal doctrine and practice. Donald Gee and, the author suspects, George Jeffreys also, would have shared the delight. However, here lies the rub for classical Pentecostal denominations, such as Elim. They have become victims of their own success. It could be said that they have lost their distinctiveness but not yet found a role. Adjustment to the new realities has been the struggle of Pentecostals throughout the last quarter of the twentieth century. The struggle is not yet over. The flirtation of some Pentecostals with the so-called 'Toronto blessing' is symptomatic of the desire to maintain a radical edge and be distinctive.

It is the author's conviction that the true role of Pentecostals in the future lies in wholehearted alignment and co-operation with Christians of all denominations who share their evangelical and charismatic convictions and mission. The challenge for British Pentecostals in the new century will not be to maintain minor doctrinal or charismatic distinctives, but to join a concerted attack on the humanist roots of the secular culture that dominates Britain today and proclaim the powerful message of the gospel to every person in the land. It is a challenge to restore to Britain, in the new millenium, the moral, social and spiritual values that the twentieth century has seen destroyed.

Chapter Two

# Assemblies of God: Distinctive Continuity and Distinctive Change

## William Kay

A two-part thumbnail sketch of the formation of the British Assemblies of God and the changes which have taken place over the past seventy years is given here. The first part deals with the period before 1939 and the second with the post-war period. Each part consists of a brief account of the major events in the period, and is followed by a historical, theological and sociological analysis of the events.

The reason for adopting this approach is that there are various schools of historiography, none of which is suitable for modern church history. The general process of historiography has been influenced by developments within the field of science. For this reason, history has, since the rise of science, attempted to present itself as a scientific enterprise, claiming to make use of 'historical facts'. The problem with this is that there is considerable disagreement about the 'facts'; consequently, the attempt to build history on undisputed facts is bound to fail. Moreover, even when there is agreement concerning facts, these facts must be interpreted by placing them into a sequence and selecting between the significant and the insignificant. Thus, there is bound to be an element of subjectivity within the presentation of any historical narrative. Moreover, even when there is agreement about which facts are significant, they must be placed in a framework against which their significance is measured. The Marxist historian is concerned to support the case for dialectical materialism. The Christian historian will, in most cases, wish to see the hand of Providence.[1]

---

[1] For a fuller discussion see W.K. Kay, 'Three Generations On: The Methodology of Pentecostal History', *EPTA Bulletin* 10. 1 and 2 (1992), 58–70.

The approach used in this chapter pays particular attention to the interpretation of events as they were understood by participants. For this reason, Parr's and Boddy's own understanding of the baptism of the Spirit is mentioned. Participants are in a uniquely privileged position in relation to events through which they live and, though there may be later rationalisations or judgements made with the benefit of hindsight, it would be absurd to pretend that such factors are automatically absent from a historian's mind.

If, indeed, it is the job of the historian to try to trace a causal sequence through a mass of events, then it makes sense to invest the decision-makers in any situation with a special importance. Such a view is not without critics, especially among those who have a deterministic understanding of the historical process.[2] The account presented here, however, attempts, in the historical and theological analyses, to do justice to the personalities in the story. In the socio-logical analysis, on the other hand, a more deterministic tale is told and the reader must judge which account is the more persuasive.

## The History of the British Assemblies of God before 1939

The Welsh Revival of 1904, the outpouring of the Holy Spirit in Azusa Street from 1906 to 1913 and the visit by T.B. Barratt to A.A. Boddy in Sunderland in 1907, which were directly or indirectly crucial to the arrival of Pentecostalism in Britain, have been described and analysed in greater detail elsewhere.[3] The events which stabilised and dissemi-nated Pentecostalism in Britain included the Sunderland Conventions from 1908 to 1914, the publication of *Confidence* magazine (1908–26),

---

[2] E.H. Carr, *What is History?* (Harmondsworth: Penguin, 1964); see also Leo Tolstoy's appendix to *War and Peace*, first published in Russian (1869), now available in many translations.

[3] W.K. Kay, 'A History of British Assemblies of God' (unpubl. PhD thesis, University of Nottingham, 1989), published with minor amendments as *Inside Story* (Mattersey Hall: Mattersey Hall Publ., 1990); D. Allen, 'Signs and Wonders: The Origins, Growth, Development and Significance of Assemblies of God in Great Britain and Ireland, 1900–1980' (unpubl. PhD thesis, University of London, 1990); R.D. Massey, 'A Sound and Scriptural Union: An Examination of the Origins of the British Assemblies of God during 1920–25' (unpubl. PhD thesis, University of Birmingham, 1988).

the meetings held at Sion College, London, from March 1909 onwards, the formation of the Pentecostal Missionary Union in the same year and the founding of the Elim Evangelistic Band in 1915.

These events resulted in an indeterminate number of people in the first two decades of the twentieth century who believed that the gift of tongues did not die out with the early church but was available to contemporary believers. The exact number of people who believed this, and the number who not only believed it but experienced it, must be a matter of speculation, though there is evidence that the number of tongues-speakers in Britain in 1908 amounted to about 500.[4] We must also speculate on the number of congregations which accepted the experience and functioned in a Pentecostal dimension. By 1920, if we estimate the number of people who subscribed to *Confidence*[5] (and after 1925 the number who subscribed to *Redemption Tidings*[6]), and the numbers who attended specifically Pentecostal conventions at the Kingsway Hall, London, from July 1925,[7] we arrive at a figure of between 4,000 and 8,000 people. If each congregation numbered 50 people (an admittedly arbitrary figure) we arrive at between 80 and 160 congregations. Certainly the British Assemblies of God counted 200 congregations by 1929[8] and Elim 70 congregations[9] in 1928, though

---

[4]  M.J. Taylor suggests that when he launched the first issue of *Confidence* in 1908, Boddy knew 500 tongues-speakers (*Confidence*, April 1908, 3); in the January 1910 issue (page 12), Boddy thought he had 20,000 readers – a figure which looks rather high. ('Publish and Be Blessed: A Case Study in Early Pentecostal Publishing History, 1906–1926', [unpubl. PhD thesis, University of Birmingham, 1990], 343).

[5]  Printing costs are given for the 1913 issue. From the cover price and the printing costs, it is possible to calculate roughly what the print-run must have been. See Kay, 'A History', 32.

[6]  From comments made in the April 1925 issue of *Redemption Tidings* we deduce that the circulation was less than 5000, but that 5000 was a target within reach.

[7]  In July 1925, *Redemption Tidings* estimated the attendance at the Kingsway Hall as 'approaching 2000', though Gee thought 1500–1600 would be a more accurate estimate.

[8]  Kay, 'A History'. 88 f.

[9]  D.W. Cartwright, 'Elim Pentecostal Church' in S.M. Burgess, G.B. McGee, P.H. Alexander (eds.), *Dictionary of Pentecostal and Charismatic Movements* (Grand Rapids: Regency, 1988), 260.

some of the latter were in Ireland. What we may suppose is that the number of tongues-speakers rose from about 500 in 1908 to approximately ten times that figure twenty years later.

In their autobiographies, both John Carter[10] and Nelson Parr[11] give insights into the growth of individual Pentecostal assemblies during and after the First World War. In some instances, existing assemblies were 'pentecostalised' and in others they were started more or less from scratch. These assemblies were not connected by any constitutional mechanism. They were scattered and diverse but, judging from Carter's autobiography, they were joined by the view that speaking in tongues indicated the fullness or baptism of the Holy Spirit, a view which in Carter's case was strengthened by the ministry he and his brother received at the Sunderland Conventions.

Parr's autobiography devotes a chapter to his search for the power of the Holy Spirit. He began by attending prayer meetings in 1908. He heard preachers speak of the 'Second Blessing', 'the Cleansing Baptism', 'Entire Sanctification' and the 'Baptism of Fire'. At the interdenominational evangelical conventions at Keswick, he went forward to receive the 'Gift of the Holy Spirit'.[12] The fluidity of terminology reveals the unsettled nature of the doctrine surrounding the experience. In about 1909, Parr heard a missionary who had passed through North America and had witnessed scenes where speaking in tongues had taken place. This intensified Parr's interest, but it was as a result of contact with the Sunderland Conventions that his quest for the baptism in the Spirit accompanied by speaking in tongues became 'very desperate'. On Christmas Day 1910, Parr found what he was looking for during the morning service and he spoke in tongues for several hours. Not long afterwards, a mini-revival took place in his congregation, though many local ministers condemned from their pulpits what was happening.

---

[10] J. Carter, *A Full Life* (London: Evangel Press, 1979).

[11] J.N. Parr, *Incredible: The Autobiography of John Nelson Parr* (Fleetwood: private publication, 1972).

[12] T.A.C. Bush points out that the Keswick teaching on the baptism in the Spirit is to be contrasted with the 'eradication of sin' concept which came from the Wesleyan holiness tradition ('The Development of the Perception of the Baptism in the Holy Spirit within the Pentecostal Movement in Great Britain', *EPTA Bulletin*, 10. 1 and 2 [1992], 24–41).

It was, however, not until 1924 that the British Assemblies of God was formed. Two years previously, W.P.F. Burton, on furlough from the mission field, had attempted to call the various Pentecostal assemblies together into some kind of collaborative unity.[13] Boddy, who was by now in his seventieth year, had no desire to form a new denominational group. It was Nelson Parr, who belonged to the next generation of Pentecostals, who called the 1924 meeting, partly prompted by news that the Welsh assemblies were considering applying for special membership of the American Assemblies of God, which had been formed in 1914. His letter of invitation[14] gave five reasons for the gathering: to preserve the testimony of the full gospel, to strengthen fellowship, to present a united witness, to exercise discipline over immoral believers and to save assemblies from falling into unscriptural practices. In 1924, 74 assemblies pledged themselves to join the newly formed group.

The organisational structure adopted by the new group had two levels: a local level and a national level. Each assembly welcomed at the local level was required to endorse certain 'fundamental truths' drawn from the Bible. These truths were very similar to the usual

---

[13]  Burton's name heads a broadsheet listing those who called a two-day conference in Sheffield on May 23–24, 1922; George Jeffreys' name was also prominently displayed. The conference resulted in a resolution to set up a provisional council 'for the advice and assistance of Assemblies in the United Kingdom and Ireland'. John Carter in his autobiography (*A Full Life,* 57) makes the point that in 1923 Archie Cooper of South Africa put the idea of a further meeting to Nelson Parr and Thomas Myerscough. Allen ('Signs and Wonders', 102) points out that there had been Pentecostal conferences at Swanwick in 1920 and 1921 where informal discussions about organisation probably took place.

[14]  The invitation was issued to R.C. Bell of Hampstead, Charles Buckley of Chesterfield, Howard and John Carter of London, Mrs Margaret Cantel, also from London, J. Douglas of Stratford, Donald Gee from Edinburgh, Tom Hicks from Cross Keys as a representative from Wales, Arthur Inman of Mansfield Woodhouse, B.W. Moser from Southsea, Fred Watson of Blackburn and Arthur Watkinson of York. Thomas Myerscough, who was invited, was ill and unable to attend the meeting, which took place in Aston, Birmingham, 1 February 1924. According to D.W. Cartwright ('Elim', 29) Lewi Pethrus, who was visiting the country at the time, was also invited.

evangelical statements of faith, but included premillenialism[15] and an emphasis on the experience of the baptism with the Holy Spirit evidenced by speaking in other tongues.

From 1925 onwards, the Pentecostal Missionary Union was incorporated with the Home Missionary Reference Council of the British Assemblies of God. In other words, there was grafted into the young British Assemblies of God a complete missionary arm which was fully formed and active, though short of financial muscle. The next ten to fifteen years saw steady growth in Britain, stimulated by sporadic but large-scale evangelistic healing crusades directed at unbelievers and holiday-time conventions directed at believers. Sometimes, the two directions were combined in missionary conventions, while, at other times, missionary conventions helped recruit new overseas workers or financial support.

Local presbyteries (later called District Councils and then Regional Councils) were formed. Each local assembly was allowed to send someone (usually the pastor) to local meetings and those endorsed at these local meetings were allowed to attend the Annual General Conference where decisions affecting the fellowship as a whole could be made. Those who attended the Annual General Conference were able to vote for nominees to national committees or councils, the chief of which was the Executive Presbytery (later called the Executive Council). For many years this council included at least three men who had attended the inaugural meeting called by Parr in 1924.

### Historical Analysis of the Period Before 1939

Boddy and Parr were natural leaders – adventurous, persuasive, organised, decisive and communicative. Boddy, an Anglican vicar, wished to see the Pentecostal experience used for a renewal of the established church and all other churches. He understood the experience as enabling the creation of unity among all kinds of evangelical Christians. At the same time, he saw the outpouring of the Spirit as being related to an end-time calendar involving both the Jews, the re-establishment of the kingdom of God (we are at the 'toes' of history

---

[15]   The Scofield Reference Bible which taught the premillenial return of Christ was first printed in 1909.

in Daniel's vision[16]) and the return of Christ, for he believed he might live to see the return of Christ, assuming that the First World War was a preparation for the upheaval which Christ's return would entail.

Parr had no vision of a renewed national church. He was confirmed in the Church of England at the age of twelve but was expelled from the Sunday school for misconduct. He attended a Bible class later, in what seems to have been an independent Protestant mission, and learnt there to beware of the snares of biblical criticism. After 1910, he was rejected by those who thought that speaking in tongues was devilish at worst and divisive at best. His pacifism and reliance on divine healing placed him apart from the majority of his compatriots and, after the war had finished and life had begun to return to normal, he thought it wise to call like-minded Christians together so that resources could be pooled and evangelism intensified. Parr also saw the outpouring of the Holy Spirit in eschatological terms but he seems to have been more open about exactly what shape the future would take. His belief in the premillenial return of Christ made room for the possibility of a persecution of the church *or* a revival. Had he opted for a postmillenial position, he would have had to accept the gradual improvement of the world situation as a prelude to Christ's millenial reign.

Another indication of Parr's realistic view of the future is his inclusion of a pacifistic statement about war within the constitution of the British Assemblies of God. He knew that such a statement would greatly aid conscientious objection in the event of future military conscription.[17] He had observed the less-than-sympathetic hearings given at tribunals to young ministers of unattached congregations who claimed exemption from military service on conscientious grounds.

### Theological Analysis of the Period Before 1939

Theology is a discipline which is defined neither by its method nor its content. Its methods are diverse and its content has reflected the changing historical circumstances of the church. In its systematic and dogmatic forms, it attempts a coherent presentation of Christian doctrine. The theological analysis presented here explores the balance

---

[16]  A. Boddy, *Confidence* (December 1910), 283.
[17]  Parr, *Incredible*, 26f.

and relationship between the twelve points in the first Statement of Fundamental Truths adopted by the Assemblies of God in 1924. The preamble is considered separately.[18]

The first statement asserted the divine inspiration of the Bible. This was the starting point, and the other truths followed in a more or less logical order. The trinity of God was stated next, followed by the fall of man, the means of salvation through faith in Christ's death, the place of baptism by immersion in water and, after this, baptism in the Spirit evidenced by speaking in other tongues.

Baptism in the Spirit is, in this context, seen as following water baptism; all the biblical references relating to the baptism in the Spirit are taken from the book of Acts. The implications of this are well known: the church of today is directly linked with the early church; the nature of speaking in tongues in the early church is the same as the nature of speaking in tongues today; and the baptism in the Spirit is an experience distinct both from salvation and from water baptism.

What this suggests is that Parr had come to a clear-cut decision on the terminology to describe the experience of the Holy Spirit and on the evidential nature of tongues. His autobiography shows that the terminology before 1910 was not standardised and was drawn from Holiness traditions (the 'cleansing baptism', for example). Between 1910 and 1924, the terminology becomes biblical, almost certainly as a result of the formation of the American Assemblies of God and its adoption of a Statement of Fundamental Truths in 1916.[19] Boddy, however, apparently softened his stress on the evidential nature of tongues after contact with Europeans from about 1912 onwards and after experience of unholy fanaticism by tongues-speakers at various times. Both Van der Laan[20] and Taylor[21] argue that Boddy came to the

---

[18] The text of this Statement can be found in the Minutes of the Assemblies of God in Great Britain and Ireland (January to May 1924), Donald Gee Centre for Pentecostal and Charismatic Research, Mattersey Hall, Mattersey.

[19] The linkage between the British and American Statements of Fundamental Truths can be seen in the similarities of phraseology and in the fact that both omitted reference to the virgin birth.

[20] C. van der Laan, 'Proceedings of the Leaders' Meetings (1908–1911) and the International Pentecostal Council (1912–1914)', *EPTA Bulletin* 6.3 (1987), 76–96.

[21] 'Publish', 220.

view that the baptism in the Spirit was evidenced by tongues *and* divine love, and both interpret this as a diminution by Boddy of the value of tongues as the sign of the baptism in the Spirit. This is supported by the prominence given to the teaching position of Boddy's wife in the pages of *Confidence*. She was not prepared to accept that speaking in tongues is 'necessarily a convincing sign'.[22] However, it is also true that the article quoted by Van der Laan is entitled by Boddy 'Tongues: the Pentecostal Sign; Love: the evidence of continuance' which suggests a more nuanced position.[23] Tongues were, for Boddy, still an *initial* evidence or seal, but love was the continuing evidence.[24]

The seventh point in the statement of belief asserts that holiness of life and conduct are enjoined upon Christians. Following on from the discussion above, its inclusion at this point may be explained: holiness is the true continuing outcome of the baptism of the Spirit.

The eighth point states that divine healing is provided for 'in the Atonement'. The issue here is not only that healing is available to contemporary Christians, but also that healing is directly connected with Christ and the cross. It is directly offered as a result of faith in Christ and 'artificial' means of healing are therefore not necessary.[25] Yet the healing spoken of here, because of its link with Christ, should not be confused with 'faith healing' or spiritualism.

The ninth point states that breaking of bread, or communion, is expected of believers. Breaking of bread is presumably mentioned partly to distinguish Pentecostal churches from the Salvation Army.

The final three points are more miscellaneous. The tenth asserts the premillenial second coming of Christ as the blessed hope set before all believers; the eleventh, the everlasting punishment of those 'who

---

[22] M. Boddy, 'The Real Baptism of the Holy Ghost', *Confidence*, (November 1909), 260.

[23] *Confidence* (November 1910), 260.

[24] In fact, the insistence on tongues *and* divine love, that is, two criteria to be applied jointly instead of one criterion on its own, actually consolidates Boddy's characterisation of the baptism in the Spirit.

[25] Parr took the view that 'it is unscriptural to seek help from drugs or physicians in order to escape the chastisement or discipline of the Lord'; see D. Petts, *Healing and the Atonement*, Unpubl. PhD, University of Nottingham, 1993), 39.

are not written in the Book of Life'; and the last affirms belief in the gifts of the Spirit and the offices (apostles, prophets, evangelists, pastors and teachers) as recorded in the New Testament.

The premillenial second coming of Christ was connected in the minds of early Pentecostals with the outpouring of the Spirit on the twentieth–century church. The Spirit was given to prepare the church for Christ; in other words, the giving of the Spirit has eschatological significance. It was the 'latter rain', given to facilitate the final harvest. The reality of divine punishment was presumably inserted to combat universalism which had troubled sections of Pentecostalism since A.E. Saxby's espousal of it.[26] Belief in the gifts of the Spirit and the New Testament offices come at an odd place in the list. They present an ecclesiology which allows for the full expression of Pentecostalism within congregational life, and for this reason would have been better placed after reference to holiness or the breaking of bread.

The preamble to these statements explains that they are not to be taken as a 'creed for the Church' but rather as 'a basis for unity for full Gospel ministry'. The statements were not intended to rule out dissidents or to define heretics but to allow practical collaboration. They provided the minimum platform on which individual preachers and congregations could stand together.

### Sociological Analysis of the Period Before 1939

Sociological analysis inspects social institutions and the forms of relationship they generate.[27] The organisation formed in 1924 was marked as voluntary, task-orientated, disciplinary, doctrinally powered and, in a measure, non-sectarian.

---

[26] A.E. Saxby had been one of the few older and more established preachers who had accepted the baptism in the Spirit and speaking in tongues. After beginning to play a leading role in the young Pentecostal movement, Saxby wrote *God's Ultimate* (London: Stockwell, n. d.) and other texts to advance his universalistic views. Such views, which were implicitly propagated by Spiritualism, found a ready acceptance in the Europe of the 1920s after the death of so many young men in the First World War but were fiercely opposed by Pentecostals.

[27] M. Ginsberg, *On the Diversity of Morals* (London: Heinemann, 1956), 164.

It was clearly voluntary and individuals and churches could join without financial cost or compulsion. Donald Gee's hesitation at the inaugural meeting was produced by his need to consult the congregation of which he was pastor,[28] and we must assume that similar consultations took place elsewhere. It was also task-orientated in the sense that the preamble to the Statement of Fundamental Truths speaks of 'a basis of unity for full Gospel ministry'. Ministry was at the forefront of Parr's mind, and in his case, ministry usually meant evangelism. The disciplinary function of the new organisation is spelled out in Parr's letter of invitation and in the insistence on holiness of life and conduct in the twelve statements. The doctrinal element is found both in the letter of invitation ('to preserve the testimony of the full Gospel') and throughout the twelve statements. The non-sectarian nature of the organisation is to be seen in its voluntariness and in its unwillingness to define itself as standing against other groups. Yet it was sectarian in the sense that it was exclusive to those who took a certain doctrinal position.

The relationships brought into existence by the formation of the new organisation only became clear later. The disciplinary function required procedures for dealing with errant ministers or congregations. The New Testament offices referred to in the biblical texts supporting the last of the twelve statements presumed that people could be recognised as pastors or evangelists, for instance, though what needed to be worked out was how such people might be related to the structures or functions presumed by the twelve statements.

Any social group which is to survive over a period of time with its identity intact must have a method both of agreed change and of removing destructive or self-seeking individuals. The attention to 'immoral believers' and the need to 'save assemblies from falling into unscriptural practices' in Parr's inaugural letter, and the reference to holiness in the twelve statements allow for this. Difficult individuals or congregations could be dismissed from fellowship.

### Distinctives in the Period Before 1939

When we consider the distinctives of the early British Assemblies of God, there are four factors to bear in mind. First, distinctives are only

---

[28]   R.D. Massey, 'A Flirtation with Elim: Donald Gee's negotiations to join the Elim Pentecostal Alliance in 1923', *EPTA Bulletin* 8. 1 (1989), 4–13.

distinctives if they differentiate one group from another. If the climate changes, those things which distinguished one group from two others may make all three more similar to each other than to a fourth. The distinctives of the early British Assemblies of God, therefore, must be set against the prevalent norms in church life in the 1920s and early 1930s. Secondly, distinctives are not chosen for their social function, though they may have a social or, indeed, a historical function. Distinctives are given, and in theological terms they are given by God. The distinctives of circumcision or dietary laws with regard to Jewish, Islamic or Hindu groups are unavoidable and deeply embedded in a theological worldview. Thirdly, distinctives are not chosen for their perpetuative function; they are not chosen because they are easy to hand on to the next generation. They may or may not be easy to hand on, but that is not the reason they are distinctives. In this sense, distinctives are separable from initiatory rites, although they may operate in that way when new people join groups of certain kinds. Fourthly, distinctives are of different kinds: some may be core distinctives and others may be auxiliary distinctives. In essence, this chapter argues that the core distinctives of the British Assemblies of God have remained unchanged, but that auxiliary distinctives have altered.

The core distinctive was the belief that the baptism in the Holy Spirit is accompanied by evidential tongues. All the other distinctives were auxiliary.

## The History of the British Assemblies of God After 1939

Evangelistic campaigns were almost impossible in the 1939–45 war years. Yet missionaries who had been forced to return to Britain by fighting elsewhere in the world often made good pastors and revitalised stagnant churches. The sense of unity at annual conferences, too, was remembered with affection. Removal of ministerial status would have immediately forced non-combatant pastors to face conscription or investigative tribunals, and therefore all behaved themselves and built up the fellowship as a whole.

After the war, the same leadership remained in place, but they were largely men who had been born in the previous century and were coming to the end of their normal working lives. Discussions arose about methods of leadership and about the need to evangelise. Though the national leadership (in the form of the Executive Council) tried to recapture the glory of the great crusades of the 1920s and 30s, they failed to do so for times had changed. Church-going, as a whole, had fallen off, partly or largely as a result of the displacement of the population in the war. The National Health Service, provided by the new 1945 government at the taxpayer's expense, reduced the attractiveness of divine healing campaigns. In the years between 1951 and 1964, ownership of television sets rose from one million to three million.[29] Inflation drove up the wages of factory workers while those of pastors often remained at pre-war levels.[30] In addition, the appearance of the family car, which permitted outings on Sundays or holidays, made trips organised by churches less of an exceptional event. In the same way, mothers who earned money outside the home reduced the pool of people on whom the local congregation could call.[31] Conventions where locally known preachers could teach became less appealing and, quite soon, the invention of the portable tape recorder enabled people to hear famous preachers at little or no cost in the comfort of their own homes.

Nevertheless, there was steady growth and consolidation. The Bible College at Kenley was presided over by Donald Gee, and in some areas hard-working pastors, like W.T.H. Richards, managed to build up new assemblies from nothing. There were relief programmes for impoverished Europeans and Unity Conferences among the total Pentecostal constituency.[32] The arrival of commercial air travel made the mission field closer and broadened the horizons of those able to afford the tickets. Against this moderately encouraging background, warning voices were raised. John Wallace, in 1950, wondered where the Pentecostal movement was going. There was a period when it was

---

[29]  A. Hastings, *A History of English Christianity: 1920–1985* (London: Collins, 1986), 413.
[30]  Kay, 'A History', 238.
[31]  Prior to 1920, 10% of married women were employed outside the home. In 1951, this figure rose to 21%. By 1966, the figure had risen to 38% and by 1976, it had increased to 49%. (A.H. Halsey, *Change in British Society*, 2nd ed. [Oxford: Oxford University Press, 1981]).
[32]  Meetings were held in 1948 between leaders of the Elim Foursquare Alliance, the Full Gospel Testimony, the Apostolic Church, the Bible Pattern Church and the Assemblies of God.

thought that by tinkering with a constitution, bigger problems could be solved.

Part of this constitutional change involved the setting up of new bodies recognised by the General Conference. Excellent work was done by the National Youth and Broadcasting Councils. It would be inaccurate and unfair to characterise this period as bedevilled with failure. There certainly were notable successes but, just as certainly, there were in the 1960s and 70s attempts to refresh the Pentecostal movement as a whole.[33] Donald Gee delivered his famous 'Another Springtime' sermon as Conference chairman in 1960 and, on other occasions, Howard Carter did his best to spur the younger generation into zealous and sacrificial activity. Gee's prescription was an overall increase in spirituality rather than constitutional reform. Carter, though he inspired faith, was occasionally in danger of alienating those to whom he was appealing.[34]

Such was the strength of feeling at the General Conferences in the early 1970s that an impasse was reached. Those who wanted change were opposed equally strongly by those who only wanted change within the mechanisms provided by the constitution. Those who wanted change were often the most successful pastors with the largest congregations, who were most attracted to the new wave of Spirit-filled activity which began to occur outside the bounds of Classical Pentecostalism. Some of these pastors left, and took their congregations with them. Nevertheless, the figures show that in the decade from 1970 to 80, there was a 5% growth in the number of assemblies, though only a 3.5% growth in the number of full-time ministers, which suggests that many of the new assemblies were unable to support a full-time pastor. The general picture is of a smaller number of large, established congregations and a larger number of small and struggling ones.

In the 1980s, the subject of the constitution was raised yet again, this time successfully. By the mid-1990s, the constitution of the Assemblies of God had been altered extensively. Voting was almost entirely removed from the Conference floor and leadership was more

---

[33]   In 1963 a meeting between the two groups suggested amalgamating the Assemblies of God and Elim but it foundered on the issue of the evidential nature of tongues.

[34]   Kay, 'A History', 263.

clearly vested in local superintendents who had a proven pastoral ministry to other pastors.[35] The Conference itself was seen more as an opportunity to receive ministry, and church planting was put on a different basis by pastors who had had successful experience with housegroups rather than large crusades. Housegroups could become the nuclei for new growth and, when there were enough of them, could be combined into congregations.

## Historical Analysis of the Period After 1939

The story of the period after 1939 can be seen as one of generational change. The early pioneers were beginning to die while the next group of men were, in many instances, less pioneering and less able to cope with changing circumstances. They had inherited a system rather than built it. When they became the most senior men in the movement, they were, in most cases, middle-aged. It was therefore from the third generation that many of the most radical ideas came, and so the struggle over the constitution was often conducted along age-related lines, though there were notable radicals among some of the more maverick older men.

It must also be recognised that an important background to these generational changes was created by the huge alterations to the quality and texture of life in Britain. The social changes of the twentieth century, the loss of Britain's empire, the devaluation of sterling (which had an impact on missionary work), the rapidity of transport and communication, the breaking down of class barriers, the growing emancipation of women and the rising standards in state-maintained education[36] made many alterations to the working practices of ministers inevitable. To take two examples, the motorway network allowed ministers to travel much further to preach or to attend regional meetings and the old district council groupings became less important and less meaningful. Secondly, in the life of the congregation, the use of the telephone made pastoral visits less haphazard and less necessary.

Pentecostalism, which was strongest in the industrial north of England, felt itself to be failing to make an impact on the post-war

---

[35]    Though it is important to note that local superintendents were *voted* into office; democracy operated at this point.
[36]    The compulsory school-leaving age was raised by one year in the 1970s.

world, particularly in the south of the country. There were three reactions to this sense of failure. Firstly, there was a call for greater holiness and dedication and more crusading. Secondly, there was a desire to modernise, and this often meant modernisation in the style of music, clothing and services: Beatle haircuts, flared trousers and electric guitars began to appear in church meetings. Thirdly, there was a desire to explore new methods of evangelism or church structure and housegroups were an obvious outcome of this latter emphasis.

The outpouring of the Spirit on non-Pentecostal denominations posed a problem for Pentecostals. When there was no mass exodus of these people into the promised land of Pentecostal assemblies, the Pentecostals began to question the validity of the experience enjoyed by the new charismatics. When the genuineness of the experience was beyond doubt, they began to question the doctrine which new charismatics came to propound as a way of harmonising traditional doctrine with a new experience. Thus Roman Catholic tongues-speakers came to talk more of a 'release' of the Spirit than a baptism in the Spirit because they argued that they had already received the Spirit in infancy at baptism.[37]

### Theological Analysis of the Period After 1939

The theological basis of the Assemblies of God has not changed since its beginning. A comparison between the Statement of Fundamental Truths approved in 1924 and that adopted in 1994 shows very little variation. References to the new birth, the virgin birth and the bodily resurrection of the redeemed have been added, and the statement relating to the gifts of the Spirit and New Testament offices has been moved nearer to the group dealing with church life. None of these changes does more than make explicit what was previously implicit.

Five matters claimed attention, however. There was a muted and ill-considered attempt by ministers who had been in touch with other denominations who had been baptised in the Spirit to soften the Assemblies of God stance on evidential tongues. This was met by teaching seminars at the General Conference at which the traditional position was reasserted. Once the premise is granted that the Book of

---

[37]  S. Tugwell, *Did You Receive the Spirit?* (London: Darton, Longman and Todd, 1971), 47f.

Acts provides a suitable template for Christian doctrine, and once it is further granted that there is direct continuity between the church of today and the early church, the case for evidential tongues can be made strongly.

The second matter concerned the premillenial return of Christ. Similar forces were at work to cause some Pentecostals to reconsider their fundamental truths. Forceful Christians who had been baptised in the Spirit argued for the postmillenial return of Christ and the gradual dominance of the church as a prelude to the millenium.[38] Psychologically, such a view facilitated triumphalism and optimism and was attractive to ministers who had suffered too long from a siege mentality. Again, but without reference to the psychological correlates of doctrine, the premillenial position was reasserted at teaching sessions in the General Conference and the issue faded away.[39]

Thirdly, there was discussion about the possibility of Christians who had been baptised in the Holy Spirit being inhabited by demons. This point of view had never been entertained by the early Pentecostals; indeed they had argued strongly against it when Penn-Lewis and others stated that speaking in tongues was itself demonic. The source of the idea was again from Christians who had been baptised in the Spirit who operated in a nonconformist context. The appeal of the doctrine was that it explained hitherto insoluble pastoral problems, but it was met with articles in *Redemption Tidings* and private discussions. There was a general wish not to become involved in confrontations and, though some ministers wanted the publication of 'position papers' like those produced by the American Assemblies of God which would clearly state that Spirit-filled Christians could not, by definition, be troubled by internal demons, the issue subsided without official resolution.

---

[38]   A. Walker, *Restoring the Kingdom* (London: Hodder & Stoughton, 1985), 117–136.

[39]   In a paper on 'The Premillenial Return of Christ', delivered at the Assemblies of God General Conference at Minehead in 1987, D. Allen had no difficulty in showing that a belief in the millenium was held as early as Justin Martyr and maintained as a shibboleth of orthodoxy as much as the resurrection of the body. Similarly, a year later, David Petts argued for evidential tongues.

Fourthly, the emergence of the housegroup as a way of organising large congregations produced a set of active lay people whose role was undefined by the Assemblies of God constitution and whose theological position was unclear from the New Testament. Were housegroup leaders small-scale pastors, trainee pastors, undefined associates, or should they not be fitted into a scheme which had no obvious place for them? The issue remained ambiguous. The preferred term came to be 'leaders' and, on Regional Training Days, for example, pastors could bring along their 'leaders' without having to specify an exact title or function for those attending.

Fifthly, though the actual wording of the statement about healing said, with almost no variation, what it had always said, its interpretation began to be modified. As early as 1952, Donald Gee's book *Trophimus Have I Left Sick*[40] made room for the use of medical means in the combating of illness. A more thorough theological discussion of the atonement by L.F.W. Woodford[41] emphasised that Christ atoned specifically for sin, though the ultimate removal of sickness in the world, like the ultimate removal of sin, lay in the future. Woodford believed that healing was available to the believer through the charismata and the laying on of hands as a way of mediating Christ's victorious authority.

### Sociological Analysis of the Period After 1939

The work of Weber is a sociological starting point for much analysis of historical events concerning religious groups. Weber made a distinction between charismatic and bureaucratic leadership and between charismatic and bureaucratic authority.[42] He saw an inevitable conflict between these two types of authority and two types of leadership, and he also saw the creation of a bureaucracy as almost an inevitable consequence of the success of charismatic leadership. In the stage following the success of the charismatic leader, the bureaucratic organisers begin to control the charismatic leader's circle of action. This leads to various forms of division and, if such a bureaucratic

---

[40]  D. Gee, *Trophimus Have I Left Sick* (London: Elim, 1952).
[41]  L.F.W. Woodford, *Divine Healing and the Atonement: a Restatement* (London: Victoria Institute, 1956).
[42]  D.G. MacRae, *Weber* (London: Fontana, 1974).

ascendancy occurs after the death of the charismatic leader, then the movement which has been founded in a lively and innovative way becomes stereotyped and fossilised.

It is, therefore, sensible to look at the history of the Assemblies of God to see whether the theoretical expectations of Weber are fulfilled. As is evident from the pages proceeding, it *does* appear that the period, particularly the 1970s and 1980s, saw some elements of a struggle between the bureaucrats, who in this instance are the constitutional-ists, and the charismatics, who in this instance are those who embraced new theological ideas.

The constitution became far more obtrusive than it had been in the early days. Skilled debaters could raise constitutional objections to any proposed initiative, and when the number of ministers present at the annual Conference grew, the machinery governing debate began to stand in the way of collective decisions. Time prevented everyone who wanted to from taking part, and many ministers returned from these gatherings dispirited and exhausted.[43] At their worst, these gatherings resulted in disagreements between one constitutionally appointed body and another, as happened when a Select Committee disagrees with the Executive Council.[44] In addition, the issue of ministerial status was invested with an importance beyond the original conception.[45] There were occasions when ministerial gatherings were treated like an exclusive club and jealously guarded.[46] Those who wished to join the Assemblies of God were hardly welcomed and inevitably the growth of the fellowship as a whole slowed almost to a halt.[47]

Some people wanted to abolish democratic procedures at local and national level ('there is no voting in the Bible'), while others main-tained that it was their birthright and fundamental to the kind of fellowship they had joined. In a sense, too, there was a bottleneck at

---

[43]  Kay, 'A History', 296.
[44]  *ibid.*, 242.
[45]  *ibid.*, 293.
[46]  I have in mind a District Council meeting I attended in the 1980s. A black minister who wished to bring his congregation into the Assemblies of God was treated with great insensitivity.
[47]  The number of assemblies on the list dropped from 535 in 1966 to 531 in 1970 (Kay, 'A History', 272).

the top of the movement when men in middle age found it impossible to be 'promoted' onto the Executive Council because the now venerable pioneers were still in place.

The constitutional changes which eventually took place may be interpreted as an attempt to place charismatic leaders within a constitutionally-defined zone of activity. Constitutional authority and charismatic authority were thereby reconciled. The new system allowed appointments to office to be made by a small National Leadership Team and confirmed, in key instances, by the whole General Council.[48] The lengthy voting procedures of the old system were largely dropped, though in some cases, postal ballots were held.

As part of the shake-up produced by the introduction of superintendency at national and regional level, and of the National Leadership Team's role in promoting the 'vision' of the fellowship, a Leadership Review Committee was commissioned by the 1996 General Conference to report on the future leadership structure and resolve questions such as: how should the Executive Council relate to the National Leadership Team and the levels of superintendency? and how should the departmental heads relate to each other?

### Distinctives in the Period After 1939

Throughout the changes of the twentieth century, the core distinctive of the Assemblies of God has remained intact: the belief in evidential tongues remains. The other issues (which were less distinctive than they had been) namely holiness of life, healing, premillenialism and belief in the gifts and offices of the New Testament have also remained, whilst the issue of holiness of life has been redefined. The possession of a television is no longer sinful and the watching of a film or video is not condemned. Fashionable clothes are acceptable and those who minister to young people show that trendiness and Christian commitment can be combined. Christian rock concerts have been accepted, and in some assemblies teetotalism has been relaxed.[49] If holiness to the early Pentecostals was separation, to the generation of the 1990s it is expressed by attendance at Christian events, by financial giving and by sexual abstinence before marriage. Missionary work continues,

---

[48]  That is, those eligible to attend the Annual General Conference.
[49]  Personal observation.

though an examination of the changes in this area would require a separate study.

Divine healing is retained, but there is an equal willingness to see the provision of drugs and doctors as God-given, very much in line with Gee's position outlined earlier. Divine healing was frequently seen by the early Pentecostals as being available through the ministry of the famous visiting evangelist; the modern Pentecostal is happy to be prayed for by his or her housegroup leader. It is not that divine healing has been relegated by routine, but rather that less hangs on it; it is seen less as a sign of the truth of the full gospel and more as bread for the ordinary believer (Mark 7:28). In this respect, Woodford's view has effectively been accepted.

Organisationally and constitutionally there have been changes. The constitution has certainly grown in complexity and length, and it requires a quasi-legal mind to master its intricacies. The aims expressed by the constitution, however, have not changed. It still exists to enable collaboration at local, national and international levels. It defines the relationship between the various parts of the Assemblies of God. The mode of church government is still congregational in the sense that no ecclesiastical rank has been called into being. Superintendents may be voted out of office and pastors, whose relationship with their congregations is on a church-by-church basis, cannot be interfered with by denominational officers.[50] The Assemblies of God has become more permeable to outside influences while retaining much of its original identity.

## An Empirical Postscript and Conclusion

In the spring of 1995, the author supervised a project designed to elicit information from all the full-time Assemblies of God ministers in Britain, numbering 635. A survey was conducted using the 1994–1995 Year Book as the basis for a mailing to all full-time ministers,

---

[50]   This is the theory, though in practice it is not entirely clear where the authority of the local superintendent begins and that of the local pastor ends. Generally speaking, local superintendents cannot be called into local churches against the wishes of the pastor without an invitation from a substantial proportion of the congregation.

excluding probationers, those on the mission field and those retired. The questionnaire was completed anonymously and returns were facilitated by a freepost system. Background information about ministers was elicited in the first section and beliefs were investigated in the second section. Neither section made use of open-ended questions. Beliefs were assessed by presenting ministers with statements to which they were required to respond on a five-point scale ranging from *agree strongly*, through *agree*, to *not certain, disagree* and *disagree strongly*.[51]

At the stage at which it was analysed, the sample comprised 105 full-time Assemblies of God ministers (of whom two were female). Slightly more than half (54%) of the respondents were under 49 years of age, but 20% were aged over 60.

Nearly a third (30%) of ministers had been baptised within the Assemblies of God, 10% had come from Baptist backgrounds, 35% from a Church of England background, 7% from a Methodist background, 3% from a Roman Catholic background, 3% from a Presbyterian/URC background and 1% from an Elim background. More than half (58%) reported that their religious commitments had begun in childhood.

All the respondents spoke in tongues at least occasionally, and 89% nearly every day. Only 23% of ministers claimed never to have been healed as a result of prayer; 56% had been healed physically, 2% had been healed mentally and 13% had been healed mentally and physically. Altogether, 43% had undertaken formal, full-time training for ministry and 13% had undertaken part-time training.

These background variables, taken together, show several consistent features. For example, all respondents spoke in tongues and a large proportion had been healed in answer to prayer. The early religious commitment shown by many of these ministers indicates an exposure to Christianity at a young age, though the various backgrounds from which they came showed that many had made a spiritual pilgrimage of some distance. It is unlikely that those from Church of England, Methodist, Roman Catholic or Presbyterian backgrounds would have experienced speaking in tongues in childhood.

---

[51]   A preliminary report on the findings of the questionnaire was presented at the Society for Pentecostal Studies (SPS) and the European Pentecostal Charismatic Research Association Conference (EPCRA) at Mattersey Hall, England, in July 1995.

Turning to the beliefs of ministers, there were various surprises. For example, 8% did not believe that 'speaking in tongues is necessary as initial evidence of the baptism in the Holy Spirit' and 28% accepted that 'baptism in the Holy Spirit can occur without speaking in tongues'. Further, while 98% believe that 'God heals the sick today', 2% disagreed strongly with this statement. Similarly, 4% disagreed that 'healing is provided by Christ's atonement'.

Turning to eschatology, 3% disbelieved in a literal millenium and 15% were uncertain while 8% did not believe that the church would be taken from the earth before the millenium.

The distinctive beliefs in tongues as the initial evidence of baptism in the Spirit, in healing (particularly healing in the atonement) and in the millenium (particularly the millenium after the rapture of the Church) are not accepted by a proportion of the Assemblies of God ministers. The most widely unacceptable belief concerns the role of speaking in tongues. Nevertheless, the number of ministers who do not adhere to Pentecostal theological distinctives is small, and does not threaten the unity of the churches.

On moral matters, the survey shows that standards appear to have altered greatly, though no empirical benchmark from any previous survey of the Assemblies of God ministers exists against which the current findings can be compared. Nevertheless, the impression given by the findings on cinema-going (71% disagree with a prohibition), drinking alcohol (51% disagree with a prohibition), social dancing (46% disagree with a prohibition) and sporting activities on Sundays (44% disagree with a prohibition) suggests that a radical change has taken place in social attitudes. Correspondence and articles within early Pentecostal literature make it highly unlikely that such a large percentage of a previous generation of ministers would have supported such 'worldly' activities.

In a series of stages since the late 1980s, the Assemblies of God has altered its constitution to introduce a General Superintendency (with a team of three) and Regional Superintendents. Consequently, some ministers have expressed concern about a threat to their traditional autonomy and about 'creeping centralisation'. The statistics gathered here show that 14% of ministers think that the Assemblies of God is now too centralised, but exactly half expressed a concern about the future of their denomination. The problems, as they are perceived by the sample of ministers reported on here, include centralisation, but are not confined to this issue. If this had been the case, then the same number of ministers who are worried about centralisation would also have been worried about the future.

Undoubtedly, the British Assemblies of God is influenced by the social and theological context in which it operates. Its distinctives have remained largely intact, though the empirical information presented here, together with the historical and theological analysis which informs it, show that change and continuity continue to exist in tension.

Chapter Three

# The Word of God: 'Thus Saith the Lord'

Richard D. Massey

This chapter surveys Pentecostal attitudes to the Bible in terms of its inspiration and authority as well as its use in the churches, particularly for preaching. Attention is given to the relationship between Scripture and contemporary prophecy as this represents one of the main debates within Pentecostalism at this time.

## The Inspiration and Authority of the Bible

As regards the inspiration and authority of the Bible, the Pentecostal churches are still firmly within the conservative evangelical tradition. The Statements of Faith of the main groups describe Scripture variously as 'the inspired Word of God, the infallible, all-sufficient rule for faith and practice', and warnings are given, 'that none may add thereto or take away therefrom except at their peril'.[1] The line from B.B. Warfield through to J.I. Packer is firmly held, concluding with the affirmation that 'what Scripture says, God says'.[2]

---

[1]  See W.J. Hollenweger, *The Pentecostals* (London: SCM 1972) appendix 1.
[2]  See the wide use of these authors by G.W. Gilpin, 'The Inspiration of the Bible', in P.S. Brewster, *Pentecostal Doctrine* (Cheltenham: Elim, 1976), 127 ff. and in the unpublished papers on the 'Sufficiency of Scripture' given at a theological colloquium of Elim leaders at Swanwick in 1992.

Similarly, the Chicago Statement on Biblical Inerrancy drawn up by some 300 theological scholars and church leaders in 1978, in which Packer took a leading role, represents the kind of stance on Scripture approved by modern Pentecostals.[3] Some of the issues which gave rise to that statement will be discussed below, but if an overview is required of current Pentecostal thinking – not necessarily charismatic thinking – on the status of the Bible, then no better description could be given than the 'Short Statement' or summary, given at Chicago:

1. God, who is Himself Truth and speaks truth only, has inspired Holy Scripture in order thereby to reveal Himself to lost mankind through Jesus Christ as Creator and Lord, Redeemer and Judge. Holy Scripture is God's witness to Himself.
2. Holy Scripture, being God's own Word, written by men prepared and superintended by His Spirit, is of infallible divine authority in all matters upon which it touches: it is to be believed, as God's instruction, in all that it affirms; obeyed, as God's command, in all that it requires; embraced, as God's pledge, in all that it promises.
3. The Holy Spirit, its divine Author, both authenticates it to us by His inward witness and opens our minds to understand its meaning.
4. Being wholly and verbally God-given, Scripture is without error or fault in all its teaching, no less in what it states about God's acts in creation, about the events of world history, and about its own literary origins under God, than in its witness to God's saving grace in individual lives.
5. The authority of Scripture is inescapably impaired if this total divine inerrancy is in any way limited or disregarded or made relative to a view of truth contrary to the Bible's own; and such lapses bring serious loss to both the individual and the Church.[4]

This kind of view is held by Pentecostals to come out of Scripture's own teaching about itself. Overall, the general theory of inspiration is based on such passages as 2 Timothy 3:16 and 2 Peter 1:21 where the Scripture is seen as a creative act of God, more 'breathed out' than 'breathed into', under the guidance of the Holy Spirit. Jesus himself is seen to give the general imprimatur to the concept of the 'word of

---

[3] See J.I. Packer, *God Has Spoken* (London: Hodder & Stoughton, 1979), 139 ff. for the full statement and its exposition.
[4] Packer, *God has Spoken*, 143.

God written', when he frequently uses Scripture in an authoritative manner.[5]

Inspiration and authority are recognised in regard to both the Old and New Testaments. The passages given above refer primarily to the Old Testament and yet in many ways they anticipate the New Testament. Scholars have drawn attention to the inclusive scope of 2 Timothy 3:15f., which makes it clear that the salvation-history of the Old Testament finds its fulfilment in Christ. Hence, the story of the New Testament, namely how Christ is the fulfilment of the Old Testament, becomes the ongoing Scripture that is being breathed out by God, the message of 2 Timothy.[6] Stott suggests that in this passage Paul may well have been close to seeing his own writings as Scripture already, in the sense that his exposition of the gospel is the ongoing Word of God.[7]

However, for Pentecostals in particular, and for many others as well, a significant factor in the New Testament's inspiration and authority is the Holy Spirit. The Spirit of truth and the testifier to Christ was given at Pentecost to reveal Jesus as the fulfilment of the Old Testament purposes of God and enable the emerging church to understand and interpret the work of Christ.[8] Whatever the exegesis of 2 Peter 1:19ff., it must surely imply something about the New Testament's inspiration by the Holy Spirit through the apostles and prophets.[9]

The human involvement in inspiration leads on to questions about 'theories' and 'models' of inspiration. This in turn leads to wider questions about the inspiration of prophecy in today's Pentecostal churches, to be examined in the final part of this chapter.

The modern Pentecostal sits easily with conservative evangelical colleagues about how inspiration works and what it effects. Certainly they reject the idea that the Holy Spirit simply illuminated the biblical writers so that their writings were merely perceptive and uplifting. On the other hand, the much-maligned and often attributed 'dictation

---

[5]   See Matt. 4:1–11; 5:18; John 10:35.
[6]   See Luke 24:27; for an exegesis of 2 Timothy 3:15f., see, J.R.W. Stott, *Guard the Gospel: The Message of 2 Timothy*, (London: IVP, 1973).
[7]   See I Thess. 2:13.
[8]   See John 14:26; 15:26; 16:13–15.
[9]   See 2 Peter 3:15, 16.

theory' is also rejected; the pages of Scripture did not appear on the screens of the minds of biblical writers like teletext or an auto-cue apparatus. Rather, the 'supervisory' or 'concursive' theory is mainly held, which implies God working in and through the human faculties and personalities of the writers. One recent Pentecostal minister expressed inspiration in the familiar image of light shining through the stained glass windows of the human personality and taking on some of the colours as it passes through the glass. Interestingly, he went on to develop the model by commenting 'But what if God Himself is the creator of the glass and that He produced the glass to His own precise specifications with the purpose of producing the exact colours that He desired. This is in fact what has happened. God carefully prepared the men that He wished to use in the production of Scripture. Their upbringing, character and training being exactly that which He required to produce the Scripture. When God wants to create the Epistles of the Apostle Paul, He produces an Apostle Paul to write them.'[10]

This, of course, raises the question of whether the imperfections of human personality reflect on the truthfulness or infallibility of Scripture. Here again, the decisive truth-revealing role of the Holy Spirit has to be affirmed, if not fully understood in its operation. Moreover, issues about the culturally relative nature of Scripture cannot be avoided. Possibly this is best approached by taking a more dynamic view of progressive revelation, namely, that the Holy Spirit, as well as unfolding aspects of truth progressively within Scripture, can also continue to make truth plainer in successive generations of the church. Thus, questions about the cultural limitations of the Bible are more a question of hermeneutics than of dogmatics. Pentecostals would say what most other evangelicals say, that the truth of Scripture lies in it being rightly interpreted and understood through the Holy Spirit.

Such a position would want to avoid the twin rocks of either knowing the truth only through the teaching magisterium of church authority or subjective Barthianism, which seems to imply that the Bible only becomes scriptural truth when it is so revealed to us by the Holy Spirit. Most Pentecostals would prefer something of both

---

[10] J. Burgan, 'The Sufficiency of Scripture' (paper presented at a theological colloquium of Elim Pentecostal ministers at Swanwick, 1992) 16f.

emphases, recognising the importance of the corporate views of church teachers together with the confirmation or 'inner testimony' of the Holy Spirit. However, as we will see later, both of these extremes have emerged in their own way within Pentecostalism and need to be addressed.

One of the major debates within evangelicalism itself has concerned the infallibility and inerrancy of Scripture. This debate has been popularised as the 'battle for the Bible', a slogan taken from the title of a book by Harold Lindsell.[11] Lindsell, a former vice-president of Fuller Theological College, challenged some of the faculty there, together with other scholars, to define more clearly what was meant by the infallibility of scripture. He claimed that some leading evan-gelical scholars were happy to recognise that the Bible was authorita-tive in what it taught about salvation and faith, but not necessarily in peripheral details of history and geography. That is, the Bible is infallible in its revelation, but not inerrant in all its details. This debate has spread to Britain and has threatened aspects of the long-established unity within evangelism concerning biblical authority. Pentecostals have come out strongly on the side of inerrancy, pointing out that this applies to the text as originally given and to the text rightly interpreted. In other words, as already noted, they would align themselves with the Chicago Statement on Biblical Inerrancy.

However, despite this firm stance, or indeed as a result of this kind of thinking, Pentecostal churches and scholars have had to accept elements of change and development in their approach to Scripture. A prominent area of change has been in the growing use of modern versions of the Bible as against the once universal, virtually dogmatic, use of the King James or Authorised Version. Inevitably, this has resulted in the assimilation of the results of textual criticism, involving the change of vocabulary in some familiar passages and also the omission of some verses, including most importantly, the longer ending of Mark's Gospel with its 'Pentecostal' elements.

Some of these issues are being addressed by the wider theological training that the Pentecostal denominations are offering in their Bible colleges. Both Regents Theological College, previously known as the Elim Bible College, at Nantwich and the AOG College at Mattersey have recently had their courses validated by external universities. At

---

[11]   H. Lindsell, *The Battle for the Bible* (Grand Rapids: Zondervan, 1976).

least a greater understanding of critical methods of theological study is now part of ministerial training, even though the more negative forms of such criticism are not encouraged or accepted.

This means that the problems relating to Scripture raised by modern scholarship can be intelligently explained to church members. As part of this change, a growing number of members of the faculties of the Pentecostal Bible colleges are well qualified and engaged in research for higher degrees with British universities. Most of these changes have occurred in the last ten years and are quite remarkable when one considers that Classical Pentecostals have been somewhat hostile to the idea of theological qualifications and discouraged the use of degrees after the names of their pastors.

However, this was a bubble waiting to burst, and the change had been anticipated by more forward-looking leaders. The later stages of this debate, as it affected the AOG in the 1970s and 1980s, has been chronicled by William Kay.[12] It was Donald Gee who, as principal of the AOG Bible College from 1951–1964, did much to encourage a more positive approach to theological education. In one of his many articles, he perceptively draws on his early experience among Pentecostal leaders and notes both the strengths and weaknesses of a non-theologically trained leadership, writing:

> More solid ground for saying that Bible Schools were unnecessary was the fact that among my colleagues in those pioneering days of the Pentecostal Movement were several rugged old pioneers who, like myself, had never been to any Bible School, but were doing solid work for God. They were however, men of strong natural intelligence and ability. Moreover the baptism in the Spirit had given them such a passionate love for the Bible that it would hardly be too much to affirm that in certain aspects of scriptural knowledge in which they specialised they became true scholars. If they were self-taught, they were certainly not ill-taught. But they were exceptional men, doing exceptional work. Truth requires us to admit that alongside them there were scores of other men who accomplished little through sheer lack of ability.[13]

---

[12] *Inside Story* (Mattersey Hall: Mattersey Hall Publishing, 1990), 317ff.
[13] *Redemption Tidings* (February 1958); for a fuller description of Gee's role see R. Massey, *Another Springtime: Donald Gee, Pentecostal Pioneer* (Guildford: Highland, 1992), 152ff.

So far, we have been looking at Scripture from the standpoint of the doctrine of its authority and the more technical and academic issues arising from this. Yet by far the most frequent and significant use of the Bible for Pentecostal churches lies in preaching.

## The Use of the Bible in Preaching

Sermons are still a major part of the public services on Sundays and often at mid-week Bible studies. Pentecostal preaching tends to be enthusiastic and challenging, frequently occupying some thirty minutes of the service time. Above all, it is usually biblically centred with a traditional text or short passage as its base. Many members of the congregation still bring their own Bibles to church and follow the sermon from it. In this tradition, the Pentecostals set a high and enviable standard.

The quality of the content and structure varies, especially where lay or untrained ministry is involved. In the context of preaching and Scripture, one area that needs to be examined by Pentecostals is the focus on the allegorical or spiritualised use of a text rather than its plain or original sense. As we shall see below, true Pentecostal preaching is inspirational or prophetic, and more dynamic than the colourful imagination or typological ingenuity found in much sermon material. There is a need for a genuine critique of preaching within Pentecostalism, leading to better expository ministry and less of the 'promise-box' sermons still found today.

Nevertheless, some of the finest modern preachers are still found within the Pentecostal churches and this explains some of the growth and vibrancy of these groups. However, the centrality of the sermon has been under threat in recent years from the increasing place that congregational worship now occupies in Pentecostal meetings. The strength of Pentecostalism lies in the liveliness and devotion of its corporate worship.

However, in recent years, the growth of gifted song writers and the use of worship groups and musicians in local churches, has placed pressure on sermon space within the framework of the service or liturgy.

A similar, but subtle, extension of this challenge to the biblical sermon has come from the growing practice of having several short 'sound-bite' sermonettes interspersed throughout the service, coupled usually with personal, prayer ministry to those who respond, and frequently followed by testimonies from the beneficiaries. Here the problem lies not merely in the reduction of sermon time but in the very nature of sermon exposition itself, which when reduced to brief homilies does not allow for either depth or development of the text in a meaningful way. Likewise, the extension of this into personal testimony means that a strongly subjective and even triumphalist element dominates the preaching time within the service. Creating balance in all these demands is one of the key issues facing Pentecostals today as they seek to maintain their strong biblical witness through preaching.

## Prophecy and Scripture

Perhaps some of the most interesting and challenging recent discussion deals with the nature and status of Pentecostal prophecy. This has both a theological dimension in relation to how prophecy relates to Scripture in terms of authority, and a pastoral dimension in connection with how such prophecies are judged and received in the local church. Much is being written on this topic and my purpose here is to give a survey of some of the views in relation to Scripture and to draw some conclusions.

Walter Hollenweger, in his seminal study on Pentecostalism, suggests that with few exceptions, biblical prophecy is absent from the modern Pentecostal movement. This is because once Pentecostal groups settle down into institutional organisations, prophecy of a challenging kind, especially that which does not 'evade the problems for which the world and the church cannot find answers', is rarely found and only prophecy of the 'edificatory and exhortation' type is encouraged.[14]

This is not too far removed from the traditional Protestant and evangelical position that sees prophecy as inspired preaching. Packer, whilst sympathetic to the positive aspects of the charismatic movement, would nevertheless regard prophecy as derivative from scripture

---

[14] *The Pentecostals*, 345ff.

rather than directly revelatory; that is, prophecy is an extension of preaching and application.[15]

Hollenweger was mainly concerned with the Classical Pentecostal groups. With the emergence of neo-Pentecostalism or the charismatic movement, new directions and emphases in prophecy have begun to occur, not the least of which is that revelatory insights are presented in prophecy today. Michael Harper, one of the earliest exponents of the charismatic movement, points out that 'there are surely many times when natural reasoning and intuition is not enough – when the finest education and training is insufficient; then the Holy Spirit will give, if we only believe, the utterance of wisdom and knowledge'.[16]

Harper has continued to encourage the recognition and use of prophetic gifts. He has written suggesting that conferences and local churches should make provision for 'word gift groups', with the proviso that they are in good standing in the church and know when to speak and when to be silent. The leaders of conferences and churches 'can fix an appropriate time when the group can make their contribution'.[17]

The house church movement and the so-called 'Third Wave' movement, the latter of which included personalities such as John Wimber,[18] have carried the prophetic ministry into new areas. They have revived the idea of prophetic offices in the modern church alongside those of apostles, and in the dramatic episode of the 'Kansas City prophets' have brought to the fore the idea of very individualised and personalised prophetic revelations.[19]

This latest development has raised positive and negative responses at various levels of heat and light. Nigel Wright has given a very perceptive critique of the value of such personal prophecy and prefers the prophetic model of such characters as Martyn Lloyd-Jones and Martin Luther King. He concludes, 'a prophetic ministry which

---

[15]   J.I. Packer, *Keep in Step with the Spirit* (Leicester: IVP 1984), 214ff.

[16]   M. Harper, *As at the Beginning* (London: Hodder & Stoughton, 1965), 104ff.

[17]   M. Harper, *These Wonderful Gifts* (London: Hodder & Stoughton, 1989), 77ff.

[18]   K. Springer (ed.), *Riding the Third Wave: What Comes after Renewal?* (London: Marshall Pickering, 1987).

[19]   D. Pytches, *Some Said it Thundered: A personal Encounter with the Kansas City Prophets* (London: Hodder & Stoughton, 1990).

springs out of the exposition of the Scriptures is less likely to become volatile and ensnared in mystical subjectivism. A prophetic ministry which addresses the issues of an unjust world is less likely to become in-house entertainment for the saints.'[20]

Interestingly, this same kind of critique has been raised concerning the Catholic charismatic renewal movement by one of its leading participants and theologians, Peter Hocken. In a recent assessment, he comments on the Catholic charismatics that 'instead of their renewal experience opening them to the saving work of Jesus on the cross and the power of the Holy Spirit to transform, they have majored on revelations and messages'.[21]

On the other hand, some valuable reassessment of prophetic offices and revelations have come from within the new movement itself – not the least from David Pytches. He suggests that prophecy is a 'two-tier' phenomenon.[22] There is the authoritative type of prophecy in which God speaks directly through a person (I Cor. 14:36–38) and there is the 'low-level' prophecy which is commonly found today, in which the revealed truth of Scripture is applied in particular and personal ways to modern situations and people. He quotes with approval David Pawson's observation that 'Scripture only gives general guidance – how to live but not where, how to marry but not who to marry, how to do our job but not what job to do. We need the help of the Spirit to apply the general to the particular.'[23]

Pytches comes to some radical conclusions. First, he accepts the place of the prophet and prophecy today in speaking to individuals, to the church, to the community and to the nation. Secondly, he clearly defines the leadership status of prophets, believing that they rank second only to apostles. From this, Pytches deduces that they are significant but not necessarily the main leaders of a church. Thirdly, he suggests that emerging prophets should be encouraged to begin

---

[20] T. Smail, A. Walker, N. Wright, *Charismatic Renewal: The Search for a Theology* (London: SPCK, 1993), 117ff.

[21] P. Hocken, *The Glory and the Shame: Reflections on the 20th Century Outpouring of the Holy Spirit* (Guildford: Eagle, 1994), 188ff.

[22] D. Pytches, *Prophecy in the Local Church* (London: Hodder & Stoughton, 1993), 14ff.

[23] *ibid.*, 25.

sharing their revelations in their home groups or bringing their prophecies to the leadership.[24]

Despite this somewhat avant-garde approach to revelatory prophecy, Pytches still retains the traditional Pentecostal and charismatic emphasis on judging or assessing the messages given. He suggests that prophecy should be evaluated by its relation to Scripture inasmuch as it will never contradict Scripture, although there may be times when long-held interpretations of Scripture are challenged; by the character of the prophets, in particular, their maturity and status, by the fulfilment of the prophecy, and by the edification and 'resonance' that determines whether there is a sense among the recipients that it is bringing freedom, not bondage.[25]

It is worth noting that in his attempt to re-evaluate the authority of prophecy, Pawson puts the onus on judging the source of inspiration. He concludes: 'Once its divine inspiration has been fully established, prophecy carries the same authority as Scripture, since both carry the authority of the same Lord who has spoken and is speaking. Both are to be obeyed. Yet it is vital to keep a clear distinction between them. In all matters of faith and practice scripture is both final and universal.'[26]

Alongside this discussion about the practice of prophecy, there has been debate concerning the office and role of a prophet. Both Classical Pentecostal and charismatic groups have tended to see the prophetic office as akin to that of the Old Testament prophet and rarely found in the modern church; those exercising the New Testament gift of prophecy are regularly described as having a ministry but not an office. However, the house church movement gave greater prominence to the office of prophet, and saw it as a foundational ministry alongside that of an apostle (Eph. 4:11). Such a prophet would have important revelatory insights which would challenge and give vision to the church.[27]

However, while all this 'in house' discussion has been happening, perhaps the most interesting debate has been taking place in the academic world of New Testament scholarship. There questions are

[24] *ibid.*, 125f.
[25] *ibid.*, 95ff.
[26] D. Pawson, 'Prophetic Foundations: What is the Relationship between Written Scripture and Prophecy Today?' *Today*, (October 1990), 11.
[27] T. Virgo, *Restoration in the Church* (Eastbourne: Kingsway, 1985).

being raised about the precise nature of New Testament prophecy and how it compares or contrasts with Pentecostal practices today.[28]

David Hill[29] broke important new ground in scholarly study by examining the nature of New Testament prophecy and making some general reference to contemporary prophecy. He put a greater emphasis on the revelatory element in prophecy and less on the interpretative element of the inspired preacher. He felt that the current charismatic emphasis on prophecy as 'edificatory exhortation' was nearer to the New Testament than interpretative preaching.

This was followed up by Wayne Grudem's doctoral research into prophecy in 1 Corinthians, published in a more popular form in 1988.[30] The major contribution that Grudem made was to insist that a divine revelation lies behind prophecy but that the words used to announce or declare it are basically human words. It is these human words, as well as the revelation itself, which need to be evaluated by the listening church. Hence, when Agabus the prophet received the revelation of Paul's personal danger and arrest, the words he used to present that message were not entirely precise when judged by the events which took place later; thus, the Jews did not apparently hand Paul over to the Romans; he was arrested directly by them (Acts 21:10 ff. cf. v.33). On the basis of this interpretation, Grudem distinguishes between the Old Testament prophets and their New Testament counterparts, the apostles, who had the authority of actual words which became Scripture, and the New Testament prophets who had authority only in general terms regarding the content of their words, words which are not necessarily equivalent to Scripture. Whatever

---

[28] A valuable summary of aspects of this debate is found in 'Charismatic Prophecy and New Testament Prophecy' by M.J. Cartledge, *Themelios* 17.1 (1991), 11–19; see also M.J. Cartledge, 'Charismatic Prophecy: a Definition and Description', *Journal of Pentecostal Theology* 5 (1994), 79–120; C.M. Robeck Jr., 'Prophecy, Gift of' in S.M. Burgess, G.B. McGee, P.H. Alexander (eds.), *Dictionary of Pentecostal and Charismatic Movements* (Grand Rapids: Regency, 1993), 728–740; G.F. Hawthorne and R.P. Martin (eds.), 'Prophecy, Prophesying', *Dictionary of Paul and His Letters* (Leicester: IVP, 1993), 775–762.
[29] D. Hill, *New Testament Prophecy* (Basingstoke: Marshall, Morgan & Scott, 1979).
[30] W. Grudem, *The Gift of Prophecy in the New Testament and Today* (Eastbourne: Kingsway, 1988).

the criticisms of Grudem, and we shall see that there are some, he does at least give an interesting definition of prophecy with an insistence upon divine revelation couched in general terms. This enables modern prophecies to be treated seriously, while preventing them from having a parallel authority to Scripture and excluding them from being identified as 'the Word of the Lord'.

Grudem has been criticised and modified in two further studies. Max Turner suggests that Grudem's description does not allow for the range and variety of prophetic ministry presented in the New Testament. At one end of the scale there does appear to have been the prophetic impartation of doctrinal 'mysteries' (1 Cor. 13:2), while at the other end there appear to have been 'vague and barely profitable attempts at oracular speech' (1 Thess. 5:19f.).[31] Where Turner is close to Grudem is in his insistence that prophecy is based on a revelatory impulse rather than an interpretative insight into Scripture. This certainly widens the gap between the traditional view of prophecy as preaching and the Pentecostal and charismatic recognition of a revelatory element. However, it may also narrow the gap between contemporary prophecy and Scripture.

Don Carson has also sought to appraise Grudem's position.[32] Like Turner, he feels that Grudem has too easily distinguished between the Old Testament and New Testament prophets. He raises the question of 'training schools' for the Old Testament prophets and whether they all felt confident that their words were God's words. With this in mind, Carson puts considerable emphasis on the judging of prophetic messages in all eras to evaluate their divine origin, rather than focusing on the office the prophets held or the period in which they lived.

Mark Cartledge has examined much of this recent research and arrived at the following conclusions. New Testament prophecy was based on revelatory impulses such as dreams, visions and words. The congregational setting is the main context for speaking out prophecies, thus allowing evaluation to take place, especially if it is true that prophecy has 'only an authority of general content'.[33] Theoretically,

---

[31] M.M.B. Turner, 'Spiritual Gifts Then and Now', *Vox Evangelica*, 15 (1985), 7–64.

[32] D.A. Carson, *Showing the Spirit* (Grand Rapids: Baker 1987).

[33] 'Charismatic Prophecy', 19.

anyone can prophesy, but the end result should always be the building up of the hearers as indicated in 1 Corinthians 14:3.

Thus far we have been looking at the issue of modern prophecy in terms of its definition and practice, and especially in connection with its relation to the authority of Scripture. But where do the Classical Pentecostals fit into all of this? What are their attitudes and distinctives? It is to this we finally turn.

## Classical Pentecostals and Prophecy

The Apostolic Church in Britain has always maintained a greater emphasis on the use of prophecy and the prophetic office than other Pentecostal denominations.[34] They have tended to stress the foundational role of the prophet in church government and personal direction, not dissimilar to some of the recent house church practices. It was partly extremes in this area that led to many of the independent Pentecostal assemblies forming themselves into the Assemblies of God in Britain in 1924.[35] In recent years, those divisions have become less significant, not least in the light of the wider use and practice of prophecy in the charismatic movement. A current study manual used in the Apostolic Church Training School stresses that they do not believe in the infallibility of prophets, but the writer goes on to quote with approval a comment from an Apostolic leader that 'prophets are not infallible but rarely do true prophets make a mistake'.[36] Similarly, they believe that through the office of prophet today, Christ 'reveals His will for the administration of the church', not the least in the appointments for ministerial functions.[37]

The Assemblies of God in Britain have made their contribution to understanding prophecy by an excellent book on this topic from one

---

[34] J.E. Worsfold, *The Origins of the Apostolic Church in Great Britain* (Wellington: Julian Literature Trust, 1991), chapter 4.
[35] R.D. Massey, 'A Sound and Scriptural Union: an Examination of the Origins of the British Assemblies of God during 1920–25' (unpubl. PhD University of Birmingham, 1988), chapter 10.
[36] I. Howells, *Prophecy in Doctrine and Practice* (unpublished study manual, Penygroes: Apostolic Church Training School, 1991), lesson 8.
[37] *ibid.*, lesson 6.

of their leading scholars, William Kay.[38] Kay makes it quite clear that he believes prophecy to be an 'exciting gift today and should be widespread in the church. There ought to be more prophecy in the church today than there is.'[39] He sees prophecy as both for inspirational instruction and general encouragement. However, he takes issue with the Apostolic Church, the Latter Rain Movement and the Kansas City Prophets for their practice of personal and directive prophecy.[40]

Kay is quite clear on the lesser role of prophecy in comparison with the Scriptures, stating 'prophecy must be complemented and balanced by a serious attention to Scripture'.[41] Interestingly, he advises against the writing down and circulating of prophecies because it can wrongly give the impression of canonical status. There is a very real distinction between what he helpfully calls 'pre- and post- Pentecost' prophecy. The latter was to be judged, not by fellow prophets, but by the local church. No penalties were laid down for incorrect prophecies, in contrast to the Old Testament (Deut. 18:20). This Kay suggests, implies the different level of authority between pre- and post-Pentecost prophecy.

Kay includes some helpful, practical sections on receiving and using the gift of prophecy.[42] The one area which he does not address in any detail is Grudem's thesis about the full revelatory nature of prophecy and the form in which that revelation comes and is then announced.

The Elim Pentecostal Church held a leadership conference in 1992 at which they discussed a number of theological issues. One of the topics was 'The Sufficiency of Scripture'. The contributors tended to agree with Grudem's view that prophecy is partly a human account of a divine revelation and such words need to be assessed. Prophecy was mainly to be addressed to the churches and judged by them, rather than to individuals or the nation. It was concluded that prophecy does not have the same authority as Scripture, but even so it should be valued and seen as 'a word of God' even if not 'the Word of God'. Moreover, if there were more exegetical and 'prophetic preaching', speaking directly to individual needs and situations, then the clamour

---

[38]   W.K. Kay, *Prophecy* (Nottingham: Life Stream, 1991).
[39]   *ibid.*, 113.
[40]   *ibid.*, chapter 7.
[41]   *ibid.*, chapter 7.
[42]   *ibid.*, chapter 6.

for 'personal words' of prophecy might decrease. Generally, it was felt that better guidelines should be given to local churches about how to judge prophetic messages.

In seeking to draw some overall conclusions concerning attitudes towards prophecy today, our survey has shown there are a variety of views and practices. Many still see prophecy as derivative from Scripture and exhortatory or applicatory in style. Others are increasingly stressing the revelatory nature of prophecy, albeit presented in fallible words. All seem to agree that Scripture should be the final arbiter in any assessment of prophecy and that the end product should always be the upbuilding of the church. The Classical Pentecostal groups in the main are still fairly conservative in their approach, although they are showing a renewed interest in both the nature and practice of prophecy brought about by pressures from the wider charismatic and house church movements.

The evidence of this chapter points to the central position of the Bible in all aspects of Pentecostal belief and practice. A high status is given to its authority. Its contents and interpretation are given lively exposition in preaching and personal devotion. Despite the tensions created by some newer emphases and practices surrounding the prophetic ministry and gifts, there has been an unswerving endeavour not to surrender the judgement of Scripture either in determining the true nature of prophecy or its evaluation within the Church.

Few Pentecostals would disagree that 'all Scripture is God-breathed and is useful for teaching, rebuking, correcting and training in righteousness, so that the man of God may be thoroughly equipped for every good work' (2 Tim. 3:16, 17).

Chapter Four

# The Gifts of the Spirit: Pentecostal Interpretation of Pauline Pneumatology

Siegfried S. Schatzmann

In keeping with the emphases of the twentieth century Pentecostal revival in general, British Pentecostalism has from its inception placed considerable weight on the practice of the gifts of the Spirit. This is hardly surprising, given the close proximity of glossolalia to the baptism of the Holy Spirit in Pentecostal theology and practice. The experience of the latter opened up the endowment and practice of giftedness in ways that have come to be associated mostly with the Pentecostal – and more recently with the charismatic – churches. Pentecostal dynamism is no doubt fostered by deep, personal devotion to God in gratitude for salvation received through Jesus Christ, by evangelistic and missionary zeal, and, not least, by the fervour with which local congregations desire to practise the gifts within the church context.

Much of the Pentecostal literature addressing itself to aspects of giftedness is, understandably, of the popular type and therefore inten-sively experiential in orientation. The sincerity of early and more recent Pentecostal writers is not in question here at all; though many of their premises and arguments call for theological and hermeneutical re-examination and correction, they do provide us with insights into Pentecostal practice of charismata. In fairness to them, it also needs to be pointed out that they have directly or indirectly contributed to the more recent spawning of significant contributions on the subject, both within newer Pentecostal scholarship and outside the Pentecostal tradition.

Here we are concerned with examining (essentially British) Pen-tecostal views of giftedness in relation to Pauline pneumatology. The focus will be upon the following issues: the problem of terminology, the relationship of the gifts of the Spirit to Spirit baptism and of the gifts to the fruit of the Spirit, the preferential status of some gifts and the purpose and function of gifts.

## The Problem of Terminology

The standard label for the gifts that have come to mean so much to Pentecostals is 'gifts of the Spirit'. This identification is drawn from the term used so prominently in 1 Corinthians 12:1 (and 14:1), 'pneumatikos' (lit. 'spiritual men' or, more likely, 'spiritual things', hence 'spiritual gifts') and in the context reflects more Paul's attempt to pick up one of the preferred identifiers of the Corinthians than his own term.[1] Paul's own preferred identifier, both in the narrow framework of his instruction concerning giftedness in this letter and in his writings as a whole, is the term 'charisma[ta]' (lit. 'gracious bestowment', 'grace enablement'). This concept does not on its own connote any association with the Spirit but more directly points to the various ways in which the grace of God is being manifested in the believers individually (1 Cor. 7:7) and corporately (Rom. 5:16; 6:23). In several instances, however, Paul explicitly links charismata with the powerful work of the Spirit, especially in 1 Corinthians 12:4 ('There are diversities of charismata, but the same Spirit') and 12:9 (to another, charismata of healings by the one Spirit), so it is safe to argue that Paul likely had this association in mind throughout the discussion in chapters 12–14.

On the surface, it may be argued that the Pentecostal label is not far removed from the Pauline intent. What is missing from much Pentecostal literature, however, is an adequate recognition of the *gift* character of these manifestations of the Spirit and, more importantly, of their unmistakable association with God's gracious activity. Perhaps this is partly the case because Paul himself makes the charisma – Spirit link in 1 Corinthians 12:4–10 but does not do so in Romans 12:6–8, the other primary listing of charismata. Thus Canty can assert: 'while all gifts from

---

[1]  This is the most plausible option, especially given the standard Pauline introductory phrase, 'now concerning', signalling a new point that the apostle picks up from the Corinthians' letter to him (cf. 7:1, 25; 8:1; 12:1; 16:1, 10).

God are grace-gifts (charismata), only a few are Spirit-empowered[2] (presumably those listed in 1 Corinthians 12:8–10, given his lengthy treatment of them). Canty's argument is not consistent with the broader witness of the Pauline corpus, however. The relative ease with which the apostle can move from Spirit to grace and vice versa, or link the two, as in the designation 'charisma pneumatikon' ('spiritual gift', Rom. 1:11), indicates that he does not see them in conflict or competition with one another. Indeed, for Paul what is of grace is given by the Spirit and what is of the Spirit is by grace. It does not follow that simply because the recurring reference to 'the one same Spirit' in 12:8–10 is not repeated in such lists as 12:27 ff. and Romans 12:6–8, that Paul viewed the gifts in the latter contexts as less Spirit-charged.

A more likely reason may be found in the fact that some Pentecostal writers prefer to use the adjective 'miraculous' or 'supernatural'[3] when describing the gifts of 12:8–10, thereby disavowing any association with what could be construed as a heightening of natural talents. Countless Pentecostal testimonies echo the observation that because their own experience is often crisis-related and hence resulting in radical turnabouts, Pentecostals are apt to read radical discontinuity also into God's ways of working out his purposes. For them, the Holy Spirit's power and natural talents are mutually exclusive.

Not all Pentecostals dismiss any possible relationship between spiritual gifts and natural talents. Though never equating the two, Donald Gee, without doubt Britain's internationally best-known Pentecostal pioneer, suggested that 'spiritual gifts call for a high level of sanctification if they are to be used for the glory of God, and consecrated natural talents can find their crown in added supernatural gifts'.[4] Gee recognised

---

[2] G. Canty, *The Practice of Pentecost* (Basingstoke: Marshall Pickering, 1987), 97; similarly J.R. Williams refers to Paul's use of pneumatika in 1 Corinthians 12:1 as 'those charismatic expressions that are pneumatic, thus of the Spirit' (*Renewal Theology*, [Grand Rapids: Zondervan, 1990] II. 325).
[3] G. Jeffreys, *Pentecostal Rays* (Cheltenham: Elim, 1933).
[4] D. Gee, *Spiritual Gifts in the Work of the Ministry Today* (Springfield: Gospel Publishing House, 1963), 10. In fairness, the debate of how gifts and talents relate to one another has never been a major Pentecostal concern. Perhaps the best discussion is found in contributions by charismatic writers, such as the Lutheran pastor A. Bittlinger, who, amongst other publications, has written 'The Charismatic Worship Service in the NT and Today', *Studia Liturgica* 9 (1973), 215–229.

the Holy Spirit as the source and giver of all expressions of grace in the life of the believer.[5] This may come close to what Paul intended to convey in 1 Corinthians 12:4; charismata are spiritual gifts because they are graciously bestowed by the Spirit and as such are energised by God. There is therefore no mileage to be gained from rating 'spiritual gifts' as higher than and distinct from 'charismatic gifts'. But there may be another reason, perhaps experientially more important, for associating gifts with the work of the Spirit in the Pentecostal tradition than those we have considered thus far.

## The Relationship of the Gifts of the Spirit to Spirit Baptism

It is well known that Pentecostal pneumatology is based almost exclusively on Acts. The outpouring of the Holy Spirit on the Day of Pentecost (2:4 ff.) became paradigmatic, underscored by the parallel events involving the Samaritans (8:4–25), Cornelius and his household (10:23b–48) and the Ephesian disciples (19:1–6). Despite the fact that what these accounts actually have in common is that all four of them differ at significant points, many Pentecostals have developed a seemingly tight theological construct, based less on convincing hermeneutics and exegesis than on experiential perspectives projected back on Acts and turned into dogma.[6] The point here is not to question the sincerity or validity of the Pentecostal experience of Spirit baptism, whether this be construed as subsequent to salvation (the majority view) or as initiation into the new life in Christ (the minority view). The simple fact is that Pentecostals testify to and take seriously the baptism of the Holy Spirit. By implication (for most) this Spirit baptism becomes the threshold over which the believer must step to

---

[5]   Gee, *Spiritual Gifts*, 18f.

[6]   The best available hermeneutical and exegetical advice by Pentecostal NT scholars to date is 'Acts: the Problem of Historical Precedent' in G.D. Fee and D. Stuart, *How to Read the Bible for All Its Worth* (Grand Rapids: Zondervan, 1982). For a recent scholarly attempt by an American Pentecostal scholar to defend the classical Pentecostal hermeneutic of Spirit baptism based on Acts, see R. Menzies, *The Development of Early Christian Pneumatology with Special Reference to Luke–Acts*, JSNT Supplement 54, (Sheffield: JSOT Press, 1991).

receive the gifts of the Spirit. How closely these categories are intertwined in Pentecostal thought can already be seen in the subtitle to George Jeffreys' 1933 publication of *Pentecostal Rays*, which reads, 'The Baptism and Gifts of the Holy Spirit.'

Problems arise when the Lucan perspective found in Acts is superimposed upon the Pauline perspective found in the letters.[7] Pentecostal experience generally draws its theological underpinning for Spirit baptism from Acts and then turns that into the prerequisite for the Spirit's bestowal of gifts in terms of 1 Corinthians 12:4–10, the latter being a piece of Pauline teaching.

This procedure becomes even more problematic in the majority view which holds Spirit baptism to be subsequent to salvation. In this view, giftedness is contingent upon an experience of the Spirit some time after conversion, a notion foreign to the apostle Paul. What the apostle argues consistently and categorically in his letters is that the (Holy) Spirit indwells every believer (1 Cor. 12:6, 7, 11). This, for instance, is the clear meaning of 1 Corinthians 12:13 where the metaphorical (rather than literal) reference to baptism is set in parallel with the declaration 'we were all given the one Spirit to drink'. It is correct, therefore, to state that to be Christian is to have the Spirit who sovereignly and graciously bestows upon each believer such gift(s) as he sees fit to give (1 Cor. 12:11).

The Pauline perspective, then, of the relationship between Spirit baptism and the gifts of the Spirit is a very natural one in which the former is part and parcel of the believer's initiation into the new life of Christ, of salvation. Pentecostals have at times gone to desperate lengths to find a biblical rationale for an initial experience of the Spirit and a subsequent one. Though perhaps extreme, the example of George Jeffreys illustrates this very painfully. He introduces his chapter on 'The Spirit of Christ and the Holy Spirit', with the following statement:

> Seldom are our minds directed to the difference between the Spirit of
> Christ and the Holy Spirit, yet it is impossible to have an intelligent

---

7   Non-Pentecostal scholarship has consistently faulted this praxis as theologically and literarily suspect (and correctly so). The converse needs to be signalled as well, however. Some non–Pentecostal scholarship has been guilty of the same procedure in reverse; they have tended to superimpose a Pauline grid upon Acts. Neither practice is justified.

understanding of the New Testament Scriptures without recognising such a difference. The way to a right conclusion of the matter is by comparing scripture with scripture, and thus allowing the inspired commentary to explain itself . . . Some Christian teachers maintain that the scripture in Romans 8:9, 'Now if any man have not the Spirit of Christ, he is none of His', emphatically declares that it is impossible to be a believer without having the Holy Spirit. The gift of the Holy Spirit, they say, is identical with regeneration. We maintain that there is a difference, and that the scripture in Romans 8:9 refers to the Spirit of Christ, and not to the Holy Spirit. We teach that the former takes up his abode in the believer at regeneration, and that the latter can only be received by those already regenerated.[8]

Clearly, this position is neither theologically nor exegetically tenable. Most Pentecostals today would distance themselves from extreme and plainly wrong assertions such as this.

With regards to the broader question of the relationship between the baptism of the Holy Spirit and the gifts of the Spirit, the tension in the traditional Pentecostal interpretation remains. For many, the experiential presupposition dictates their theological conclusion. However, when personal experience is submitted to the priority of the text, and its content is evaluated on hermeneutical and exegetical grounds, those given to such exploration generally find their pilgrimage taking them to a position reflecting the one outlined as Pauline above. Suffice it to say here that the Pauline pneumatology does not, a priori, rule out the Lucan emphasis on being filled with the Spirit, though it is important to note that Luke's purpose for writing Acts is substantially different from Paul's purpose for his letters. It is worth noting, however, that Luke's understanding of the work of the Spirit may not be as devoid of a soteriological dimension as some recent Pentecostal writers tend to argue. More likely what is explicit in Paul may be found, somewhat more obliquely, in Luke – Acts as well.[9]

---

[8] Jeffreys, *Pentecostal Rays*, 39f.
[9] See, for instance, Menzies, *Early Christian Pneumatology*, R. Stronstad, *The Charismatic Theology of St. Luke* (Peabody: Hendrickson, 1984); a more balanced view is presented by M. Wenk, 'John's Pneumatic Ministry: Redefinition of the Community "within" Israel – to make ready a people prepared for the Lord (Luke 3:1–18)', unpublished paper presented at the EPTA Conference, Lunteren, April 1995.

## Relationship of the Gifts to the Fruit of the Spirit

For Paul, as for the New Testament in general, salvation is transfor-
mational. Those in Christ have not only been set free from sin, they
have also become slaves to righteousness (Rom. 6:18) and to God
(Rom. 6:22). This new life is described in terms of 'putting off' the
characteristics of the old nature and 'putting on' the new self (Col.
3:5–14). The classic description, of course, is found in Galatians
5:16–25 where the practices of the sinful nature are contrasted with
the characteristics of the new life in Christ, graphically portrayed as
'fruit' (singular). The growing of this fruit is the work of the Spirit,
according to Paul, just as is the gracious bestowal of charismata for
service. Nowhere does the apostle even suggest a qualitative differen-
tiation; neither is optional and both are essential expressions of Christ's
transforming work through the agency of the Holy Spirit.

Generally speaking, Pentecostals have no problems with acknowledging the importance of the fruit of the Spirit, either individually
or corporately. Perhaps the best British Pentecostal contribution is
John Lancaster's lucid essay on 'The Nine-Fold Fruit of the Spirit',
though the title seems rather unfortunate, given that Paul's listing in
Galatians 5:22, 23, like the listing of charismata in 1 Corinthians 12,
is almost certainly not intended to be exhaustive, as Lancaster himself
recognises.[10]

On the whole, however, the Pentecostal emphasis is not on the
fruit of the Spirit as much as on the gifts of the Spirit. To some degree,
this may be in reaction to one of the popular sentiments voiced
polemically by many non-Pentecostal evangelicals, namely that the
fruit of the Spirit is to be regarded as more significant to spiritual life
and growth than the gifts. But this can hardly be seen to reflect what
Paul intended in his pneumatology. More likely, the Pentecostal focus
on gifts over fruit, rather than being deliberately dichotomous, may
be the result of associating the work of the Spirit with the more
spectacular manifestations of his power in signs and wonders. The
growth of fruit, after all, is not conspicuous but a slow internal process
with gradual outward evidence.

---

[10]   In P.S. Brewster (ed.), *Pentecostal Doctrine* (Cheltenham: Elim, 1976),
63–77 esp. 74.

The inadequate recognition of both fruit and gifts as the work of the same Spirit can be seen in such Pentecostal works as J.R. Williams' recent *Renewal Theology*. The dominant emphasis in his second volume is on the work of the Holy Spirit. In it, he (correctly) observes the distinction between gifts that are *given* and fruit that is *grown* and tacitly acknowledges the value of both, though for different reasons.[11] Williams' treatment of the fruit of the Spirit, especially in relation to his gifts, is inferential at best and hence inadequate, as demonstrated by the absence of the topic from his table of contents. This may in fact be a realistic reflection of the situation in Pentecostal churches. Yet we cannot allow this generalisation, true as it may be, to stand without also pointing out that British Pentecostals especially have sought to bring a certain corrective to bear in this regard. Gee, for instance, argued that the issue lies not as much in the 'balanced proportion' of the nine gifts and the nine fruit[s], itself an untenable view, but in how fruit and gifts are interrelated. He is emphatic that neither makes the other superfluous, especially since the Holy Spirit is 'alike the source of fruit and gift'. Pentecostals may well insist on the gifts as a present and necessary reality, though these are frequently dichotomised from the fruit. There may be closer links between the two than even Gee suggests, especially through the Christological confession of 1 Corinthians 12:3 and love as the context within which charismata are to be used in the community (1 Cor. 13).[12]

Canty correctly observes that neither the fruit nor the gifts of the Spirit are the way to, or the guarantee of, the other. Since the Spirit is the source of both, it would be strange indeed if Paul had construed the use of the Spirit's gifts as tenable without the evidence of his fruit and vice versa.[13] More recently, Brewster concluded his study of 'The Seven-Fold Work of the Holy Spirit' with the pertinent observation, 'any manifestation of the gifts of the Holy Spirit without the accom-

---

[11]  J.R. Williams, *Renewal Theology*, II. 330f; see also the critique by T.L. Cross 'Toward a Theology of the Word and the Spirit: A Review of J. Rodman Williams' *Renewal Theology*, *Journal of Pentecostal Theology*, 3 (October 1993), esp. 126.

[12]  D. Gee, *Concerning Spiritual Gifts*, revised and enlarged edition (Springfield: Gospel Publishing House, 1937, 1st ed. 1918), 70f.

[13]  G. Canty, *In My Father's House: Pentecostal Exposition of Major Christian Truths* (Basingstoke: Marshall, Morgan & Scott, 1969), 104ff.

panying fruit of the Spirit becomes unacceptable to God and to the Church'.[14] Pentecostal dynamic and praxis are not compromised by embracing both as vital expressions of the work of the same Holy Spirit.

Indeed, in order to redress the tendency to overemphasise the gifts, pastors and teachers may have to put more weight on the Spirit's work of bringing about in us the conformity with the character of Jesus Christ that is the fruit of the Spirit. Even a cursory reading of the Pauline letters shows how much more the apostle stressed the fruit-aspect of the Spirit's work than the gift-aspect. Yet neither is neglected at the expense of the other: for Paul, Christlike character and behaviour are indispensable to effective charismatic ministry. Should it be any different today?

## Preferential Status of Some Gifts

We have already pointed out above that in many Pentecostal circles the preferred identification of the gifts is the one whereby Paul introduces the subject in 1 Corinthians 12:1: 'Now concerning spiritual gifts', perceiving the gifts listed in 12:8–10 as somehow more descriptive or powerful (or spiritual?) than those listed elsewhere. Paul's likely deliberate shift from 'pneumatika' (12:1) to 'charismata' (12:4) generally has little effect upon Pentecostal exposition and practice of giftedness. Pentecostal literature commonly identifies these gifts as 'gifts of the Spirit' or, more specifically, 'the nine gifts of the Spirit'. Thus for Turnbull, for instance, it is a foregone conclusion that 'when the Holy Spirit came on the day of Pentecost He brought nine gifts with Him which are enumerated in 1 Corinthians 12'.[15] Further, to no one's surprise and in line with the Statement of Beliefs of the Elim Pentecostal Church[16] in use at the time (1976), W.R. Jones'

---

14    Brewster, *Pentecostal Doctrine*, 24.
15    T.N. Turnbull, *What God Hath Wrought* (London: Puritan Press, 1959), 107.
16    Until 1994 it was formulated as follows: 'We believe that the church should claim and manifest the nine gifts of the Holy Spirit: wisdom, knowledge, faith, healing, miracles, prophecy, discernment, tongues, interpretation.'

contribution on the subject in *Pentecostal Doctrine* is entitled, 'The Nine Gifts of the Holy Spirit'. Whether purposely or unwittingly, such identification points to preferential status given to some gifts, if it does not render them exclusive. If 1 Corinthians 12 is thought of as setting the intended parameters of gifts, one wonders why at least the two further gifts cited in 12:28, namely 'helpful deeds' or 'those able to help others' (NIV) and 'gifts of administration' (NIV) or 'acts of guidance'[17] are not deserving inclusion. More appropriately, the gift ministry of the apostle and of the teacher should be included as well, though neither occurs in the preferred list of 12:8–10. Equally strange is the omission of the list in Romans 12:6–8 which the apostle explicitly introduces with the term 'charismata', his own preferred identifier. Gee recognised the inadequacy of the view held by many of his fellow Pentecostals, namely that there were only 'the nine gifts' in 1 Corinthians 12:8–10 which pertained to the church's function, and pleaded for a more inclusive understanding in light of such passages as 1 Corinthians 12:28f. and Romans 12:6–8.[18]

Elim's current Statement of Beliefs, the revisions of which were ratified by the Conference of 1994, reflects its leadership's awareness that the previous statement relative to the (nine) gifts of the Spirit misrepresented the clear Pauline teaching on the subject. The revised statement reads as follows: 'The Ministry: We believe in the ministries that Christ has set in his church, namely, apostles, prophets, evangelists, pastors and teachers, and in the present operation of the manifold Gifts of the Holy Spirit according to the New Testament.' It would be wrong to assume that this correction was the work of a theologically more progressive minority and that this new understanding now needs to filter down to the grass roots. On the contrary, the exegetical and theological maturing in the Elim Pentecostal Church (and likely in the other British Pentecostal bodies as well) in this regard is evident both among a broad representation of pastors and, perhaps even more significantly, in the respective denominational theological colleges.

If the focus is turned on the list of gifts in 1 Corinthians 12:8–10, it quickly becomes apparent that preferential status is also accorded to some gifts over others within the same list. Though six of the nine

[17] G.D. Fee, *The First Epistle to the Corinthians* (Grand Rapids: Eerdmans 1987), 621f.
[18] Gee, *Spiritual Gifts*, 5f.

gifts are actually speech-related and may therefore legitimately be termed 'gifts of inspired speech', much of Pentecostal practice emphasises only the last three of the speech-gifts (prophecy, tongues and interpretation of tongues) plus gifts of healing (both terms are plural) and miraculous powers. While the emphasis may have shifted (and may continue to shift) from one area to another from time to time, overall the three speech-gifts mentioned have dominated. While it would be plainly wrong and illegitimate to denigrate the value of the latter, the net result of their over-emphasis is the dwarfing, if not the total absence, of the other equally important gifts cited in that list in particular and in other lists in the wider frame. If Paul did not intend a hierarchical prioritisation of the gifts, a point which Pentecostals are quick to affirm when non-Pentecostals argue (equally incorrectly, to be sure) that tongues must be least important since this gift (including the interpretation of tongues) is listed last, then the argument must also be applicable to the various Pentecostal ways of according preferential status to one or more of the gifts. While virtually all writers in the popular literature objectively or by their silence recognise that Paul did not intend a hierarchical structure of gifts, what the churches practise all too frequently is another story altogether. The preference for spectacular gifts over non-spectacular ones, or of the popular speech gifts over less attractive service gifts, may have more in common with the proclivity to being entertained, endemic to the western culture, or with a certain 'feel-good' factor resulting from a release of emotions. For Paul, the only legitimate preference or priority is for the gifts that clearly and intelligibly communicate what God desires to say over those that do not, particularly in the community setting (1 Cor. 14).

## The Purpose and Function of Gifts

In the Pauline writings, foremost in 1 Corinthians and Romans, the apostle sets out the purpose of the gifts of the Spirit in several different ways. Fundamentally, Paul calls for gifts to serve a twofold purpose.

Firstly, they are to bring glory to Jesus Christ through the agency of the Spirit who makes possible and meaningful the very confession that Jesus is Lord (1 Cor. 12:3). The lordship of Jesus Christ, then, must be the ultimate touchstone of whether or not the practice of giftedness, however spiritual or legitimate it might be, fulfils its primary purpose. Fee's assessment of this criterion needs to be heard: 'Whatever takes away from that, even if they be legitimate expressions of the Spirit, begins to move away from Christ to a more pagan fascination with spiritual activity as an end in itself.'[19]

Secondly, on the horizontal level, gifts serve to build up the church. Nothing in Paul's instructions in 1 Corinthians 12–14 leads us to the conclusion that gifts are for any form of self-aggrandisement. Nor are they ends in themselves; instead, as Gee observed, they are gateways.[20] The Spirit's gracious gifts are always directed away from the one so endowed to those whom God intends to build up through the sharing of the gift(s). This is precisely why the apostle places such emphasis upon the diversity of gifts, given in order to meet the diversity of needs in the church. God's own character is expressed, Paul tells us, in the framework of unity within diversity; the same is true of the gifts given to the church. There is one Spirit but diversities of gifts, one Lord but diversities of ministries (which one would expect, given that gifts are diverse), and one God but diversities of workings (12:4–6).[21]

This diversity is then illustrated by means of the listing of nine gifts (v. 8–10) that were especially relevant to the Corinthian church and probably intended as a corrective to their tendency to uniformity. By means of the body analogy (v. 14–26), Paul vividly brings home his basic point that unity is best expressed in diversity: the human body is made up of many members; anything less is a monstrosity. The same is true in the community, therefore, where the lordship of Jesus Christ is exalted in the diversity of gifts used for the church's upbuilding. What would seem to make for simple and straightforward exegesis for Pentecostals, however, turns out to be inadequately practised in reality. The objective recognition of the need for diversity often extends only to the more popular gifts of inspired speech, with tongues

---

[19] Fee, *1 Corinthians*, 582.

[20] Gee, *Spiritual Gifts*, 5.

[21] The Greek term 'energémata' may be understood as the effect of what is worked, as in 12:10, but since this expression of diversity is specifically attributed to God, rather than to the Spirit or the Son, the idea may be God's sovereign empowering or energising commensurate with the respective gifts and ministries. However, since the term occurs only in 12:6 and 12:10 in the New Testament, certainty eludes us.

still holding the pole position. The result, all too often, is that those who consider themselves not gifted with glossolalia (or other popular gifts, depending upon the circumstances) are made to feel inferior, which in turn tends to breed a sense of elitism among those who have the 'right' gift. How much of this is actually going on can perhaps be tested by asking the following question: When has a church member graciously gifted by the Spirit with showing mercy or with leadership skills last been shown the same public recognition as one who prophesies or speaks in tongues?

This leads us to make a few observations about the function of gifts. While many non-Pentecostal scholars and church leaders readily acknowledge objectively that the purpose of the gifts is to glorify Christ and to build up his body, the church, they find it more difficult to translate this into viable practice on the local church level. Conversely, Pentecostal communities generally embrace the dynamic exercise of gifts with singular enthusiasm and church members are encouraged to function with the gift(s) they have received. The modus operandi is usually learnt from others, often conforming to patterns provided by the ministers in charge.

Nowhere else is this perhaps more the case than in the practice of glossolalia, which is usually labelled 'messages in tongues'. The implied understanding is that the one speaking in tongues gives a message directed to the congregation in an unknown tongue and that the latter is made intelligible by the interpretation of tongues. In Pentecostal practice and literature, the equation is clear: tongues plus interpretation equal prophecy. Turnbull, for instance, asserts unequivocally, without the slightest support, that 'these two gifts, the Scriptures state, are equal to prophecy'.[22] Gee admits the scant biblical support for rendering tongues and interpretation as broadly equivalent to prophecy. He cautiously points out that the fundamental purpose and direction of tongues is to God; yet he acquiesces to the fact that the popular equation has become habitual and has hardened into a tradition.[23] In his earlier work, however, Gee's position is rather more doctrinaire, asserting that 'it is distinctly affirmed that when these twin gifts of tongues and interpretation were exercised in proper order in the church, they equalled the gift of prophecy (1 Cor. 14:5); and it is

---

22    Turnbull, What God, 167.
23    Gee, Spiritual Gifts, 53.

generally conceded that since such is the case, they provide an equivalent method by which the Holy Spirit can cause his voice to be heard in the church'.[24]

Nothing illustrates Pentecostal pragmatism better than this: we do what we do because it seems to work. It has to be noted, however, that there are some encouraging signs of changes here and there. In the very recent past, for instance, a number of interpretations of tongues given in chapel services at the Elim Bible College have observed their Godward direction; instead of simply turning them into hortatory prophecy, they have reflected the praise and worship of God expressed in the tongue. This surely is what Paul intended in 1 Corinthians 14:2–3 and 14:16–17, 28.[25] The community is thus built up through prayer, praise and adoration, made intelligible by means of the interpretation of a tongue. No doubt some participants sensed a certain unease because this represented a new approach, the unease underscoring just how hard old habits die.

Throughout chapter 14, Paul further emphasises that inspired speech in the community is legitimate only when it is intelligible; otherwise its purpose of building up the body is jeopardised. In 14:22–25 he makes the point that the purpose of prophecy is to convict unbelievers, hence its function is manward, precisely because it communicates intelligibly what God is saying. On the other hand, to unbelievers, tongues are a 'sign' of judgement, confirming them, as it were, in their unbelief.[26] In this context again, Pentecostal pragmatism finds vivid expression in Canty's *The Practice of Pentecost*, for instance. He typically sees tongues and interpretation as equal to prophecy in the sense of the overall purpose of upbuilding. But then in an almost apologetic manner, likely to vindicate Pentecostal practice, he poses the question, 'Why should not the message in tongues (as we call it today) bring an exhortation which exposes to man his own sin?'. But 14:25 simply cannot be stretched to this extent. The convicting work of the Spirit in a meeting where outsiders are present is said to be made manifest through prophecy, not through 'the

---

[24] Gee, *Concerning Spiritual Gifts*, 58f.

[25] For some, Acts 2:11 belongs to this category as well, though the focus there is not on glossolalia but on intelligible languages.

[26] See C.K. Barrett, *A Commentary on the First Epistle to the Corinthians* (London: A. & C. Black, 1968), 323; and Fee, *1 Corinthians*, 680–688.

atmosphere where the gifts of the Spirit are operating' per se.[27] Canty does, in fairness, also acknowledge the essential focus of tongues as Godward, but his vacillation indicates the weakness in much of popular Pentecostal exegesis where recognition of what the text meant and means is sometimes inadvertently, sometimes deliberately, widened to include practices sanctioned by experience and tradition, rather than by the text.

We have already pointed out the Pentecostal tendency to prefer, if not to render exclusive, the gifts identified as 'spiritual' (1 Cor. 12:8–10) and to associate them with the primary purpose of being manifestations of supernatural power. Pentecostals are also ready to agree with Paul's apparent prioritising of Spirit-empowered ministries in 12:28, at least to the extent that these 'ministries' coincide with the listing in 12:8–10. The curious omission of some of the gifts or ministries cited in 12:28 is illustrated by Harold Horton, for instance, who tacitly acknowledges the presence of apostles, prophets and teachers (though for him even these seem to function only if 'the *Gifts*' [emphasis his] render them 'miraculously effective') and then summarises the remainder of the list as 'Miracles, healings, tongues'.[28] Although he cites the text of 12:27–31, Horton, followed by the majority of Pentecostal writers, chooses to ignore both 'those able to help others and those with gifts of administration' (NIV). In all likelihood, at least part of the reason for this omission is the apparent inability or reluctance to come to terms with giftings that in their perception may not qualify as 'miraculous' or 'spiritual'.

A brief examination of 'gifts of administration' indicates that what Paul may have had in mind here, in the first instance, is not administration as a twentieth century business-related skill but something akin to the use of the same Greek term 'kybernéseis' in the LXX version of, for example, Proverbs 1:5 where it is translated as 'guidance'. This is also echoed by the cognate noun 'kybernétés' (Acts 27:11; Rev. 18:17), describing one who is at the helm of, or pilots, a ship and hence 'guides' it. Even the contemporary term 'cybernetics' at least hints at the fact that a form of guidance is still contained in computer-related control systems. In the context of the church, then, the apostle Paul seemed to

---

[27]   Canty, *Practice of Pentecost*, 15f.
[28]   H. Horton, *The Gifts of the Spirit*, (Springfield: Assemblies of God Publishing House, 1934), 35.

use 'kybernéseis' to mean the ability to give direction or guidance in leadership. Paul's listing of this function within the broad range from apostleship to glossolalia can only mean that he understood the exercise of such guidance as no less Spirit-empowered and no less a gracious endowment than any other gift. Here the conflict between what is spiritual and what is natural in much of the Pentecostal tradition is brought out in bold relief. Rather than dichotomising the two realms, Paul seems to integrate them. Outside of Christ, natural talents and skills acquired through learning remain just what they are. But when these are yielded to Christ in salvation, they may well become the Spirit's gracious endowment for the upbuilding of the church. While it is not our intention here to denigrate the supernatural aspect of giftedness or to elevate every talent and skill to the level of giftedness, it is surely more likely that God will equip some to function with gifts of administration who already have such skills or talents than those in whose life leadership and guidance are negligible at best. When God in this way equips a person and redirects such function from selfish use to the use for the common good, it is no less a powerful demonstration of his sovereignty in apportioning gifts to individuals than in the case of miraculous powers. Surely, churches in which the Spirit is at work powerfully through gifts functioning effectively should not be characterised by inept leadership, like ships without skilled helmsmen. This, at least, points to the need for Pentecostals to rethink and broaden their charismatic self-understanding, moving away from a tenuous exclusiveness and towards an inclusiveness acknowledging the sovereignty of God in the realm of grace.

In this connection, it may be helpful to point to a further charisma which for Paul seems to be significant enough to be identified in 1 Corinthians 7:7 but which most Pentecostal writers ignore, namely celibacy. Presumably, this avoidance has to do with a certain preoccupation with the 'gifts of the Spirit' of 1 Corinthians 12 on the one hand and with a reluctance to acknowledge celibacy as a gracious endowment for fear of identifying with clerical practice in Roman Catholicism on the other. Admittedly, Paul does not explicitly state that celibacy is a charisma, but the context of 7:1–7 leaves no doubt whatsoever that this is precisely what he had in mind. In contrast to those who are married (vv.1–6), he points to himself, wishing that all were as he is. This he follows by the assertion that each person 'has his own gift (charisma) from God; one has this gift, another has that'.

Paul is not arguing, nor are we suggesting, that all singles are charis-
matically gifted with celibacy simply because they are single. Conversely, nothing is to be gained from arguing that all who are married
have 'that gift'.[29] Equally, there is no justification here for maintaining
that celibacy is an apostolic prerequisite for ministry. Nevertheless,
Paul clearly considers his own singleness a gracious endowment from
God. In the framework of chapter 7, what the apostle may have
intended to convey is that sexual continence (celibacy) and sexual
fulfilment (in marriage) need to be understood and practised in the
context of the new life in Christ, the life of the Spirit, in which even
one's lifestyle is brought into the realm of God's liberating and
empowering grace. Since Paul uses marriage elsewhere (Eph. 5:22–33)
to reflect microcosmically what the church is to be, it may be
reasonable to suggest that the same grace and Spirit that make the
church a dynamic community are also to affect the lifestyle of the
individual in the community of faith. Charismatic giftedness, therefore, cannot be restricted to strictly community-related functions but
needs to be seen, from Paul's perspective, as God's way of bringing
all of life, individually as well as corporately, into the realm of grace
where his Spirit empowers to live life to the fullest and thus to serve
him by serving the church with everything he has entrusted.

## Conclusion

The discussion of various features of Pentecostal interpretation of
Pauline pneumatology, especially with reference to the gifts of the
Spirit, shows the prevalence of an experience-based, pragmatic
approach to practising and even more to understanding giftedness.
Some of the pioneers of the movement were aware of the tension
between the interpretation of the text and praxis. During the decades
of consolidation of growth and of further expansion, the emphasis
came to rest upon maintaining what was deemed unique and
tradition overtook the earlier signs of sensitivity to the text. Only in
recent years has the Pentecostal movement begun to realise how
important it is to begin the task of self-critical evaluation of practices

---

[29] See S. Schatzmann, *A Pauline Theology of Charismata* (Peabody:
Hendrickson, 1987) 28f; Fee, *1 Corinthians*, 284f.

and belief structures. The task of Pentecostal Bible colleges and critically aware ministers is not to dismiss the experiential out of hand on account of the failures of the past, but to test and submit the broad range of the experience and practice of giftedness to the directives given mainly, though not exclusively, in the Pauline letters. The application of informed exegesis and hermeneutics to the practice of giftedness in all its diversity may remain for the next generation to work out. The acid test for their work will be how they interpret the dynamic interrelationship between text, Spirit and community.

Chapter Five

# The Baptism in the Holy Spirit: The Theological Distinctive

David Petts

When Pentecostals talk about the baptism in the Holy Spirit, they generally mean an experience of the Spirit's power accompanied by speaking in tongues as on the Day of Pentecost (Acts 2:4). The terminology is derived from Acts 1:5 when, shortly before his ascension, the risen Christ promised his disciples that they would be baptised with the Holy Spirit in a few days' time. The experience is usually closely associated with enduement with power for service (Acts 1:8) and is understood to be 'subsequent to and distinct from regeneration'.[1] In this

---

[1] See, for example D. Gee, *Wind and Flame* (Croydon: AOG, 1967), 7f. Donald Gee (1891–1966) was one of the founder members of the British Assemblies of God. He served as principal of the Assemblies of God Bible College and was involved in all the Pentecostal World Conferences until his death. Perhaps his major contribution was as founder and editor of the quarterly international review, *Pentecost*. Gee claims that the Pentecostal movement has consistently taught that speaking in tongues is the scriptural initial evidence of the baptism in the Holy Spirit (*Wind and Flame*, 8). This is, however, an over-simplification. Not all Pentecostals insist on tongues as the 'initial evidence'. Elim, for example, does not, though it would appear that the majority of Elim pastors do expect tongues when a person receives the baptism in the Spirit. This statement was made in my hearing by T.W. Walker – then the Secretary-General of the Elim Churches – on November 18th 1986 in Cobham, Surrey. Certainly, Hathaway and Brewster (both early Elim writers) endorse the view that tongues should accompany the experience (W.G. Hathaway), *A Sound from Heaven* (London: Victory Press, 1947), 64; P.S. Brewster, *Pentecostal Doctrine* (Cheltenham: Elim, 1976), 34).

chapter, I purpose to consider this doctrine and some of the challenges to it in the light of the New Testament. In particular, I shall pay attention to the issues of subsequence (the view that the baptism in the Spirit is subsequent to regeneration) and of evidence (the view that speaking in tongues is the evidence to be expected when a person is baptised in the Spirit). In so doing I shall summarise the doctrine as usually presented by Pentecostals; identify some of the challenges that have been made to it and offer a response to those challenges; and suggest pastoral guidelines as to how the doctrine should be applied in practice.

## Subsequent to Regeneration

Pentecostal writers are generally agreed that the baptism in the Spirit is distinct from the new birth.[2] The main argument is drawn from the Book of Acts and may be summarised as follows. The disciples on the day of Pentecost were already, by our present understanding and use of the term, Christians. They had already confessed Jesus as the Christ (Matt. 16:16), been pronounced clean (John 15:3), been told that their names were written in heaven (Luke 10:20), and had forsaken all to follow him (Matt. 19:27). Thus, their reception of the Spirit at Pentecost is seen as subsequent to their regeneration.

Further evidence is adduced from the case of the Samaritans in Acts 8 who had received the word of God (v.14),[3] and who had been baptised

---

[1] *(continued)* Moreover, the tongues as initial evidence view is certainly the position adopted by the vast majority of Pentecostal groups. For a convenient summary of the Statements of Faith of several major Pentecostal denominations, see W.J. Hollenweger, *The Pentecostals* (London: SCM, 1972), 513–522.

[2] Gee, *Wind,* 7; A. Linford, *Baptism in the Holy Spirit* 5–13; Hathaway, *A Sound,* 18; T.W. Walker, 'The Baptism in the Holy Spirit', in Brewster, *Pentecostal Doctrine,* 27; M. Pearlman, *Knowing the Doctrines of the Bible* (Springfield: Gospel Publishing House, 1937), 311–312; C. Brumback, *What Meaneth This?* (Springfield: Gospel Publishing House, 1947), 183; E.S. Williams, *Systematic Theology* (Springfield: Gospel Publishing House, 1953), 45; H.M. Ervin, *These are not Drunken as Ye Suppose* (Plainfield: Logos, 1968), 57; R.M. Riggs, *The Spirit Himself* (Springfield: Gospel Publishing House, 1949), 47–61.

[3] A. Linford (*Baptism,* 7) sees this as an almost technical expression for conversion and cites Acts 11:1;1 Thess. 1:6, 2:13.

in the name of the Lord Jesus, but upon whom the Spirit had not yet fallen (v.16). Saul of Tarsus is seen as having been converted on the Damascus Road – it is there he first called Jesus 'Lord'. Later, Ananias referred to him as brother (Acts 9:17) before praying for him to receive his sight and be filled with the Holy Spirit. This is interpreted as meaning that Saul received the baptism in the Holy Spirit through the laying on of Ananias' hands after his conversion on the Damascus Road.

The final example from Acts is that of the twelve Ephesians upon whom the Spirit came when Paul laid his hands on them (Acts 19:6). This appears to have followed their water baptism, and therefore, by definition, their regeneration. Ephesians 1:13 is seen as confirmation of this.

In addition to this brief summary, however, two further points need to be made. First, despite their arguments for the subsequence of the baptism in the Holy Spirit, many Pentecostals hold a view of what I have called elsewhere immediate subsequence.[4] That is to say, the baptism in the Spirit is seen as ideally taking place as soon after conversion as possible, so much so that it might well be viewed as part of the conversion process, although distinct from regeneration. This is a view I share.

Secondly, the Pentecostal argument for distinctiveness is not merely based on subsequence (i.e. that in certain passages in Acts there appears to be a delay in timing between regeneration and the baptism in the Spirit) but on the grounds that Acts reveals a distinctive purpose (enduement with power) and a different manner of reception (including, sometimes, the laying on of hands, and, invariably, speaking in tongues) for the baptism in the Holy Spirit.[5] Indeed, because of this, the term 'separability' is probably to be preferred to 'subsequence'.

The understanding that the baptism in the Spirit is an enduement with power is based on a comparison of Acts 1:5 and Acts 1:8.[6] Being

---

[4]  See my MTh dissertation 'The Baptism in the Holy Spirit in Relation to Christian Initiation' (Nottingham University, 1986), 21–29.
[5]  For a more detailed development of this, see my MTh Dissertation 'The Baptism', 8–29.
[6]  Luke employs a variety of interchangeable expressions to describe this 'coming upon' of the Spirit. These include 'being baptised with the Spirit' (Acts 1:5, 11:15 f.), 'being filled with the Spirit' (Acts 2:4, 9:17), and 'receiving (the gift of) the Spirit' (Acts 2:38, 8:15, 17ff., 10:45, 11:17, 19:2).

baptised with the Holy Spirit (v.5) is seen as equivalent to having the power of the Spirit come upon (v.8),[7] the Christian, the promise of the risen Christ being fulfilled primarily on the Day of Pentecost (Acts 2) and subsequently on other occasions which are all linked in Greek by the use of the preposition 'epi' (on) in connection with the Spirit's coming (Acts 1:8, 2:17, 8:16, 10:44, 19:6). It may, and indeed should, be repeated in the experience of every Christian ever since Pentecost. These passages reveal a pattern which indicates what should be expected whenever the baptism in the Spirit is experienced.

Furthermore, the baptism in the Spirit may be distinguished from regeneration, not only because its purpose is distinct and because a delay in timing may be observed in certain passages in Acts, but also because it appears to have been received in a different manner. In Acts 8:17 and 19:6 at least,[8] the baptism in the Spirit was received through the laying on of hands and it is questionable whether the imposition of hands should be understood to be a part of regeneration. Further, since speaking in tongues is recorded as having accompanied the baptism in the Spirit (Acts 2:4, 10:46, 19:6), and since few, if any, would wish to insist that tongues is a part of regeneration, a distinction between regeneration and the baptism in the Spirit is clearly necessary. But that leads us naturally to the issue of evidence.

## The Initial Evidence

The Pentecostal belief that tongues should accompany the baptism in the Spirit is taken largely from certain passages in Acts (2:1–21, 8:5–24, 10:34–48, 19:1–7). The table at the end of the chapter may prove useful as a summary of the position held by most Pentecostals. It illustrates how Jesus' promise in Acts 1:8, 'You will receive power

---

[7] I have argued in my MTh Dissertation (51) that in his book *Baptism in the Holy Spirit* (London: SCM, 1970), J.D.G. Dunn has paid inadequate attention to the relation between Acts 1:5 and Acts 1:8. Yet this is crucial to the Pentecostal understanding of the baptism in the Holy Spirit. Cf. William Atkinson's comments which are supportive of my position ('Pentecostal Responses to Dunn's "Baptism in the Holy Spirit": Luke–Acts,' *Journal of Pentecostal Theology*, 6 (1995), 87–131, esp. 105).

[8] Acts 9:17 might also be cited.

when the Holy Spirit comes on you', was fulfilled not only at Pentecost, but also in the experience of the Samaritans, the household of Cornelius, and the Ephesians. It also shows how Luke uses a variety of interchangeable expressions (including 'baptised in the Holy Spirit') to refer to the same experience and how speaking in tongues was the one consistent manifestation immediately following it.

All Pentecostal writers on this subject deal with these passages, and generally speaking the exegesis is fairly similar. Brumback, for example, argues that the Day of Pentecost is to be seen as a pattern.[9] It was the phenomenon of glossolalia that caused the gathering to ask, 'What does this mean?' (Acts 2:12) to which Peter replied, 'This (i.e. glossolalia) is that which was spoken by the prophet Joel . . . In the last days, says God, I will pour out my Spirit' (Acts 2:16–17). Thus, for Brumback, speaking in tongues is the sign of the outpoured Spirit at Pentecost and this is the pattern for subsequent 'baptisms' with the Spirit.[10] Acts 11:15 and 15:8 ('as on us at the beginning') are adduced as evidence of this.

Concerning the passage in Acts 8 where critics have pointed out that tongues are not specifically mentioned, Brumback quotes no fewer than twenty-two non-Pentecostal commentators who agree that there was a visible and miraculous manifestation when the Samaritans received the Spirit and who nearly all agree that that manifestation was almost certainly tongues.[11] I shall argue later, however, that an even stronger case can be made for the Pentecostal view.

With regard to the passage in Acts 10, Brumback, along with most Pentecostal writers, is quick to stress verse 46. The Jews who came with Peter to the household of Cornelius knew that the gift of the Spirit had been poured upon the Gentiles, 'for they heard them speaking in tongues and magnifying God'.[12] This verse clearly appears to support the view that the tongues at Pentecost were a pattern for subsequent outpourings of the Spirit and is certainly of great importance to the Pentecostal understanding of the baptism in the Spirit.

---

[9]   Brumback, *What Meaneth This?*, 191–246; D. Petts, *The Dynamic Difference* (Springfield: Gospel Publishing House, 1976), 20–23.
[10]   Brumback, *What Meaneth This?*, 26, 191, 198ff.
[11]   *ibid.*, 205–214.
[12]   *ibid.*, 219–222.

Brumback's comments on the passage in Acts 19:1–7 are largely confined to a defence of his position that 'they spoke in tongues and prophesied' (v.6) means that all twelve men both spoke in tongues and prophesied rather than meaning that some spoke in tongues and some prophesied.[13] Grammatically, however, it seems clear that the verse can bear either interpretation, although a case might be made for the Pentecostal view by arguing that it is significant that tongues is mentioned before prophecy in this passage. Certainly, Pentecostals see in this passage another example of tongues accompanying the baptism in the Spirit.

In summary, the Pentecostal understanding of the four passages in Acts which are seen as instances of the baptism in the Spirit is that since tongues is the one repeated phenomenon in Acts 2, 10, and 19, and since it was 'almost certainly' the phenomenon that Simon saw (Acts 8:18), speaking in tongues should be viewed as the initial evidence of the baptism in the Spirit.

## Challenges – and a Response

The Pentecostal belief that the baptism in the Spirit is an experience which is both distinct from regeneration and accompanied by tongues has been challenged, on both counts, from a variety of perspectives. In this section, I shall seek to identify the major challenges to the doctrine and to offer a reasoned and biblically based response. Broadly speaking, challenges fall into two categories, hermeneutical and exegetical, and I shall deal with these in turn.

### Hermeneutical Challenges

As we have already noted, Pentecostals derive their doctrine of the baptism in the Spirit largely from the Book of Acts where a pattern is seen to emerge from a series of select passages. The underlying assumption is that contemporary experience should be identical to apostolic Christianity.[14] The experience of the disciples in Acts 2:4 is

---

[13]   *ibid.*, 223–227.

[14]   see R. Stronstrad, 'Trends in Pentecostal Hermeneutics', *Paraclete*, 22. 3. (1988), 1–12.

thus the pattern for believers for the whole church age.[15] But what if it can be shown that Acts is not suitable as a source of Christian doctrine and that any 'pattern' detected there is not a legitimate basis for our expectations today? Would this not throw serious doubt on the Pentecostal understanding of the baptism in the Spirit?

Before seeking to answer these questions, it is important to note that in recent years, Pentecostal scholars have sought to address these issues at some length but space allows for only the briefest summary of the individual positions advanced.[16]

I shall consider first the assertion that Acts is unsuitable as a source for doctrine. This is frequently advanced as a major plank in the argument of those who seek to attack the Pentecostal position.[17] It is, however, easily countered on the following grounds.

The first relates to the nature of doctrine itself. The word 'doctrine' essentially means teaching; Christian doctrine is therefore that which the Christian church may legitimately teach. And what the church teaches is that which Christians ought to believe and practise. In short, if doctrine relates to faith and practice, there is no self-evident reason why we cannot glean doctrine from Acts. Acts is a revealing account of

---

[15]  Brumback, *What Meaneth*, 192.

[16]  For further discussion of hermeneutical trends in Pentecostalism see: G.I. Anderson, 'Pentecostal Hermeneutics: Part 1', *Paraclete*, 28. 1. (1994), 1–11, 'Pentecostal Hermeneutics: Part 2', *Paraclete*, 28. 2. (1994), 13–22; G.D. Fee, *Gospel and Spirit: Issues in NT Hermeneutics* (Peabody: Hendrickson, 1991); R.D. Israel (*et al.*), 'Pentecostals and Hermeneutics', *Pneuma*, 15. 2. (1993), 137–162; M.D. McClean, 'Towards a Pentecostal Hermeneutic', *Pneuma*, 6. 2. (1984); R.P. Menzies, 'The Distinctive Character of Luke's Pneumatology', *Paraclete*, 25. 4. (1991), 17–30; W.W. Menzies, 'The Methodology of Pentecostal Theology; an Essay on Hermeneutics' in *Essays on Apostolic Themes*, P. Elbert (ed.) (Peabody: Hendrickson, 1985); Stronstrad, 'Trends', 1–12, 'The Hermeneutics of Lucan Historiography', *Paraclete*, 22. 4. (1988), 5–17, *The Charismatic Theology of St. Luke* (Peabody: Hendrickson, 1984), 'The Biblical Precedent for Historical Precedent', *Paraclete*, 27. 3. (1993), 1–10; see also Fee's response in the same volume, 11–15.

[17]  I have frequently encountered this rather unsophisticated approach when answering students' questions after teaching on the baptism in the Spirit in universities and colleges. It possibly reflects the position adopted by John Stott in *The Baptism and Fullness of the Holy Spirit* (Leicester: IVP, 1975, 15–17), although Stott has subsequently clarified his position; see John R.W. Stott, *The Message of Acts* (Leicester: IVP, 1990), 11f.

what the early church believed and how it conducted its affairs and to suggest that the church today may not learn from its example is clearly absurd. Indeed, it is probably true that most people learn more from example than they do from instruction and, if that be the case, it might well be argued that Acts could be more instructive than the epistles.

Furthermore, our understanding of the terminology in the epistles is considerably enlightened by the narrative passages in Acts. Our understanding of Paul's teaching on water-baptism as burial,[18] for example, is enhanced by passages such as Acts 8:38–39 which clearly indicate immersion. Viewed this way, Acts may be understood as a kind of literary visual aid which, far from being unsuitable as a source of doctrine, may well be the key to a right understanding of the teaching in the epistles. If I am right in thinking this, then we may only fully understand what Paul meant when he told the Ephesians to be filled with the Spirit (5:18) by 'watching' what it's like to be filled with the Spirit from the accounts in the Book of Acts.[19]

Moreover, those who teach that you cannot get doctrine from Acts usually tell us that you can, indeed must, get it from the epistles. Yet the epistles themselves indicate that all scripture is profitable for doctrine (2 Timothy 3:16). In the light of this, the burden of proof must surely rest with those who assert that Acts is unsuitable as a source for doctrine. It seems to me that there is no rational or biblical basis for such an assertion.

Finally, it is well worth pointing out that recent contributions to Lucan scholarship suggest very clearly that Luke was no mere historian, but rather a theologian who presented his message by means of narrative.[20] In other words, Luke was not simply telling the

---

[18]   Romans 6:1ff.

[19]   I have argued this at greater length elsewhere in *The Dynamic Difference*, 14–27.

[20]   S.G. Wilson, *The Gentiles and the Gentile Mission in Luke – Acts* (Cambridge: Cambridge University Press, 1973). According to Wilson (59), since the publication of Conzelmann's *The Theology of St. Luke*, 'it has become a byword of New Testament studies that Luke is a man with a theological axe to grind'. See also I.H. Marshall, *Luke, Historian and Theologian* (Grand Rapids: Zondervan 1970); Menzies, '*Luke's Pneumatology*;' M.M.B. Turner, 'Luke and the Spirit: Studies in the Significance of Receiving the Spirit in Luke – Acts' (unpublished PhD thesis, Cambridge University, 1980).

story of the early church. He had theological points to make! The argument that Acts is unsuitable as a source of doctrine should therefore be rejected not only for the reasons that I have outlined above, but also because it is contrary to the understanding of current biblical scholarship.

Having, therefore, argued that Acts is suitable as a source of Christian doctrine, it is now appropriate to ask how doctrine may be derived from it. The major issue here is the use of historical precedent. To what extent is it legitimate to see in Acts a pattern for the church today? In this connection, Fee[21] offers three principles:

1. The use of historical precedent as an analogy by which to establish a norm is never valid in itself.
2. Although it may not have been the author's primary purpose, historical narratives do have illustrative, and sometimes 'pattern' value.
3. In matters of Christian experience, and even more so in Christian practice, biblical precedents may be regarded as repeatable patterns – even if they are not to be regarded as normative.

Although I am broadly in agreement with these principles, it is important that they are applied with care. It is clear, of course, that we cannot take a single historical incident and insist that all Christian experience must conform to it in every detail. To argue that because the Christians in Acts 2 received the Spirit in Jerusalem, therefore all Christians must go to Jerusalem to receive the Spirit, would be absurd! Thus Fee is right in saying that the use of historical precedent as an analogy by which to establish a norm is never valid in itself. But that does not mean that frequently repeated historical incidents may not be understood to be normative.

Perhaps the point I am trying to make is best clarified by use of the distinction between what is descriptive and what is prescriptive. I concede that when I describe an incident I am not necessarily

---

[21] G.D. Fee, 'Hermeneutics and Historical Precedent: a Major Problem for Pentecostal Hermeneutics' in *Perspectives on the New Pentecostalism*, R.P. Spittler (ed.) (Grand Rapids: Baker, 1976), 128–129; see also G.D. Fee, 'Acts: the Problem of Historical Precedent' in G.D. Fee, D. Stuart, *How to Read the Bible for All it's Worth* (Grand Rapids: Baker, 1982), 87–102; G.D. Fee, 'Baptism in the Holy Spirit: The Issue of Separability and Subsequence', *Pneuma*, 7. 2. (1985).

prescribing a course of action. But when I am in a teaching situation and I describe not just one event, but several, and all those events have certain features in common, my students may legitimately assume that my intention is not just descriptive but also prescriptive. For example, if I relate how I handled certain cases in the course of my pastoral ministry, and in connection with each case I mention that I prayed for guidance in that situation, my students would be right to assume that my intention is to teach them that they too should pray in similar situations. I am, in effect, teaching by example. This is a powerful didactic method which may well be far more effective than straight instruction. What I am arguing here is that, if we accept the premise that Luke's intention in Acts is theological, that he is intending to teach us something, then the understanding that Luke's narrative must be viewed in a teaching context will radically affect our exegesis of Acts.[22]

Accordingly, it seems to me, Fee's statement that biblical precedents may be regarded as repeatable but not normative is too general and consequently too weak. Indeed, if a precedent is consistently repeated in a didactic narrative, then the precedent ought to be considered normative. To illustrate, I consider the phenomenon of the sound of a violent wind at Pentecost (Acts 2:2) to be repeatable, but not normative. But that speaking in tongues should be expected as evidence of the baptism in the Spirit, I consider to be normative because of the consistency with which Luke refers to it.

In this connection, I believe that the case for the Pentecostal position is far stronger than is usually allowed. It is usually argued that the case for tongues is based on three out of five incidents in the Book of Acts. But to argue this is to ignore two important facts. First, it is clear from the context in Acts 8 (where tongues is not mentioned) that the passage is not a full description of what took place. (We are told that Simon saw that the Spirit was given through the laying on of the apostles' hands, but we are not told what he saw. The passage itself makes clear that it is not a complete description of events.) The same is true of the account of Saul's conversion in Acts 9. We are told that Ananias came that Saul might be filled with the Spirit, but there

---

[22] See also Johns' helpful comments with regard to narrative theology (D.A. Johns, 'New Directions in Hermeneutics', in G.B. McGee (ed.), *Initial Evidence* (Peabody: Hendrickson, 1991), 153–156.

is no description of Saul's reception of the Spirit. If these two passages were intended to be full descriptions (which they clearly are not) and if as full descriptions they failed to mention tongues, then the Pentecostals' case for insisting on tongues would be disproven. But these passages are not full descriptions[23] and this fact actually strengthens the Pentecostals' position. For wherever there is a fuller description of events in connection with the baptism in the Spirit, the first recorded manifestation is speaking in tongues (Acts 2:4, 10:46, 19:6). But this leads to my second point.

The argument that the Pentecostal position is based on three out of five cases is also fallacious because it considers occasions rather than individual baptisms in the Spirit. The precise numbers are not important, but it is usually assumed (on the basis of Acts 1:15) that there were some 120 disciples present on the Day of Pentecost. If that be the case, then Acts 2:4 describes 120 baptisms in the Spirit. All 120 were filled with the Spirit and all 120 spoke in tongues. Similarly in Acts 10:44–46, the Spirit fell upon 'all who heard the message' (v.44) and they spoke in tongues and magnified God (v.46). In Acts 19:6–7, we are told that the number of Ephesians upon whom the Spirit came and who spoke in tongues and prophesied as a result was about twelve. This means that in the three passages in Acts where there is a fuller description of people being baptised in the Spirit, some 150 people received the Spirit, and on each occasion, the first phenomenon Luke records is speaking in tongues. In the light of these considerations, if we accept as I have already argued that Luke's intentions were didactic, we must conclude that tongues is to be viewed as the normative accompaniment to the baptism in the Spirit. But we must now consider challenges made to the doctrine on the basis of exegesis.

### Exegetical Challenges

From the exegetical perspective, the Pentecostal understanding of the baptism in the Spirit is usually challenged by arguing, first, that the

---

[23] I wish to make it clear here that my argument is not circular. I am not arguing that because tongues are not mentioned, the passages are not full descriptions. The passages themselves make it clear that they are not full descriptions.

Pentecostal exegesis of certain passages in Acts is incorrect and that, second, there are passages in the epistles which contradict the Pentecostal understanding of Acts. I shall deal with each of these points in turn.

With regard to Acts, I shall confine attention to the passage in 8:4–25 because it highlights the difficulties found by many with regard to the Pentecostal position. Pentecostals see Acts 8 as clear evidence that it is possible to be a Christian and yet not to have been baptised in the Spirit.[24] Philip had preached Christ to the Samaritans (v.5). As he preached 'the good news of the kingdom of God and the name of Jesus Christ' they believed and were baptised (v.12). When the apostles in Jerusalem heard that they had 'accepted the word of God', they sent Peter and John to them to lay hands on them and pray that they might 'receive the Holy Spirit' (v. 14–15). This was because so far the Spirit had 'come upon' none of them; they had simply been baptised into the name of the Lord Jesus (v.16).

Now the clear implication of all this is that it is possible to be a believer – indeed a baptised believer – and yet not to have 'received the Spirit' in the Lucan sense of being baptised in the Spirit or having the Spirit come upon you (cf. v. 15 and 16) as an enduement with power for service.[25] However, this understanding has been robustly challenged, either by claiming that the Samaritan situation was

---

[24]  It is not my intention to suggest that Christians who have not been baptised in the Spirit have no experience of the Spirit at all, for regeneration is itself a work of the Spirit (John 3:5, Titus 3:5, cf. Romans 8:9). However, Luke uses the phrase 'receive the Spirit' synonymously with 'being baptised in the Spirit' which he understands as being empowered for service. It is in this sense that some Christians have not yet 'received the Spirit'.

[25]  The passage in Acts 19:1–6 conveys the same idea. The Ephesians did not receive the Spirit until after they came to faith in the Lord Jesus and were baptised into his name. The phrases 'receiving the Spirit' and 'having the Spirit come upon you' are also seen to be synonymous in this passage (cf. v. 2 and 6). Furthermore, Paul's very question, 'Did you receive the Holy Spirit when you believed?' (v.2) implies that it is possible to have believed without having received the Spirit. The genuine difficulty of envisaging some Christians as not 'having received the Spirit' is resolved by the understanding that in Luke the phrase 'receive the Spirit' means receiving the baptism in the Spirit. This is illustrated in the table at the end of the chapter.

exceptional, or by arguing that the Samaritans were not really Christians at all.[26]

The claim that the Samaritan situation was exceptional and should therefore be disregarded is, however, fraught with difficulty. It must be rejected, first, because those who advance the claim want us to believe that Christians have been baptised with the Spirit simply by virtue of being Christians. But if that be the case, to argue that the Samaritans were exceptions does not really help, for it takes only one exception to disprove a rule! If it really is impossible to be a Christian without having the Spirit, then even the Samaritans can be no exception!

Secondly, those who advance this hypothesis must answer the question, 'But how do we know that the Samaritans were exceptions?' There is no clear biblical evidence that Luke intends us to understand that the Samaritan situation was exceptional. Indeed, nothing in the text supports such a view for Luke regularly separates the baptism in the Spirit from baptism in water (Acts 1:5, 9:17ff., 10:44ff.). Thus, the burden of proof must surely rest with those who argue that the Samaritan situation was exceptional.

Thirdly, the view that the Samaritans were exceptions is unnecessary. Pentecostals do not want to argue that the Samaritans did not have the Spirit at all, but rather that, as Luke tells us, until the apostles laid hands on them, the Holy Spirit had not yet 'come upon' any of them. That is to say, in Lucan terminology, they had not yet been endued with power for witness (Acts 1:8). There is no suggestion that they were complete strangers to the gracious working of the Holy Spirit bringing them to conversion, for how else would they have come to faith in Christ?

Another basis for rejecting the Pentecostal understanding of Acts 8 is the view that the Samaritans were not Christians at all. The Samaritans are seen as having understood Philip's message in terms of their own nationalistic expectations of the Messiah and the phrase 'they believed Philip' (rather than 'in the Lord') is taken to indicate that the Samaritan response was mere intellectual assent rather than genuine faith. However, there is nothing in the passage to suggest that there was anything lacking in either Philip's presentation of the Gospel

---

[26] Dunn, *Baptism in the Spirit*, 55ff.

or the Samaritans' understanding of it.[27] He proclaimed 'the Christ' (v.5)[28] and preached 'the good news of the kingdom of God and the name of Jesus Christ' (v.12). If such terminology does not reflect an adequate proclamation of the Gospel, it is difficult to imagine what does! Indeed, if there had been any deficiency in Philip's message, we might expect the apostles to have remedied this by further teaching, any reference to which is conspicuously absent.

Furthermore, the argument that the Samaritans' faith was defective really fares no better. Acts 16:14 reveals that for Luke, belief in the evangelist's message indicates faith in God and the statement that the Samaritans had 'accepted the word of God' (8:14) is parallel to the report of the conversion of Cornelius (Acts 11:1). There is thus no sound reason to suggest that the Samaritans were not really Christians at all. The passage undoubtedly supports the Pentecostal conclusion that to be a Christian does not automatically mean that one has received the baptism in the Spirit.

But that leads us to our next question. Are there not passages in the epistles which appear to contradict the Pentecostal understanding of Acts? In this connection, I shall consider two passages in 1 Corinthians, the first relating to subsequence (1 Corinthians 12:13), the second to evidence (1 Corinthians 12:30), but first a brief preliminary comment is appropriate with regard to the relationship between the theology of Paul and that of Luke. It needs to be recognised, first, that each author has his own distinct emphasis and that Paul's writings possibly reveal a more developed theology of the Spirit than those of Luke.[29] However, that need not imply that Paul did not also embrace Luke's charismatic theology of the Spirit. There need be no contradiction between the two. Indeed, if our understanding of each writer

---

[27]  H.M. Ervin, *Conversion – Initiation and the Baptism in the Holy Spirit* (Peabody: Hendrickson 1984), 28 ff.; Menzies, 'Luke's Pneumatology', 23ff.

[28]  Menzies (*ibid.*, 24) points out that the phrase 'the Christ' appears frequently in Christian proclamation in Acts and with reference to the central elements of the kerygma, Christ's death (3:18) and resurrection (2:31).

[29]  The case for a distinct Lucan theology of the Spirit has recently been well made by Menzies ('Lukes Pneumatology', 17–30); see also his PhD thesis 'The Development of Early Christian Pneumatology with Special Reference to Luke – Acts' (University of Aberdeen 1990).

results in a contradiction, then our understanding must be modified. If, for example, Paul's teaching plainly contradicts the Pentecostal understanding of Acts, then that understanding must be rejected. But I shall argue that Paul's teaching does not contradict that understanding and that his theology of the Spirit is in complete harmony with that of Luke and with the Pentecostal understanding of Acts. In defending the Pentecostal position, therefore, I shall not resort to emphasising the distinctiveness of Lucan pneumatology, although I recognise Luke's unique contribution to our understanding of the Spirit's work. I shall rather seek to show, with particular reference to the 'proof-texts', which are usually quoted against the Pentecostal position, that there is no contradiction between Paul's teaching and the Pentecostal understanding of what Luke is saying in Acts. But that brings us to the 'proof-texts' in question.

In the NIV, the first part of 1 Corinthians 12:13 is translated, 'For we were all baptised by one Spirit into one body'. On the basis of this verse, it is frequently argued that the Pentecostal understanding that the baptism in the Spirit is separate from regeneration must be rejected. The verse is interpreted as meaning that all Christians were 'baptised in the Spirit' when they were born again. This understanding is based on the following reasoning. The phrase 'into one body' is seen as identifying the event referred to as regeneration when we become members of the body of Christ, the church. The phrase 'by one Spirit' is correctly interpreted as 'in one Spirit'[30] and the event referred to is thus baptism in the Spirit. The word 'all' is stressed as referring to all Christians. Thus, all Christians are baptised in the Spirit when they come into the Body at regeneration. Therefore, baptism in the Spirit is assumed to be synonymous with regeneration and the Pentecostal understanding of Acts is deemed to be wrong.

There are, however, a number of problems with this analysis. First, it does not take sufficient account of the context in which the verse is set. Paul is not discussing the Corinthians' conversion, but rather their use of charismatic gifts, especially tongues, within the context of the church. An interpretation which understands the verse within this charismatic context is, therefore, more likely to be correct.

Secondly, this analysis reads an entirely different understanding into Paul's use of 'baptised in the Spirit' from that of Luke. The plain

---

[30]    The Greek 'en' may be translated as either 'by' or 'in'.

sense of Luke's use of the term is enduement with power for service (cf. Acts 1:5, 8) and it is not just the Pentecostals who have to reconcile Paul's terminology with Luke's! Even allowing for the possibility of differences of emphasis between the two writers to which I have already referred, I find it inconceivable that Luke, as one of Paul's travelling companions, should have such a radically different understanding of what it means to be baptised in the Spirit.

Finally, there simply is no need to interpret the verse this way. As I shall demonstrate below, it is possible to interpret the verse in full harmony with the immediate charismatic context of the passage in which it is set, and without reading into Paul's use of the terminology a different understanding from that of Luke. Such an interpretation can only be gained, however, by a fresh translation of the verse.

The problems we have referred to above disappear if we translate the first part of 1 Corinthians 12:13 as follows 'For we have all been baptised in one Spirit for (i.e. for the purpose or benefit of) the one body'. The essential difference with this perfectly legitimate translation of the Greek text is twofold. First, the preposition 'en' has been translated as 'in' instead of 'by'. This should cause no difficulty for the opponents of the Pentecostal position as they too interpret the verse as referring to baptism in the Spirit.

Secondly, and more importantly, is the translation of 'eis' as 'for' rather than as 'into'. This may be justified on the following grounds. Although 'eis' frequently bears the meaning 'into', this is by no means its only meaning. It also conveys the idea of purpose as, for example, when used with the articular infinitive, and thus may also mean 'for'. The Greek expression 'eis polemon', for example, is used in the context of preparing for war and the phrase 'eis ti' means 'for what' or 'why'. A highly significant example of this use is found in Matthew 3:11 where baptism in the Spirit is contrasted with baptism in water. Here 'eis' does not carry the force of 'into', for repentance was required before John would baptise, as the preceding verses make clear. Accordingly, the NIV translates it as 'I baptise you in water for repentance'. By analogy, the baptism in the Spirit no more puts a person into the body than baptism in water puts them into repentance.

More importantly still, we know that Paul himself understood and used 'eis' with this force as is demonstrated by the NIV translation of 'eis' as 'for' in 1 Corinthians 8:6, and, as I have already suggested, the immediate context of 1 Corinthians 12:13 would not lead us to expect

Paul to discuss entrance into the body, but our function or purpose within it. If Paul, as I believe, understood with Luke that the baptism in the Spirit was a charismatic enduement of supernatural power accompanied initially by speaking in tongues, the verse may be understood as reminding the Corinthians that the charismatic gifts they had received as a result of being baptised in the Spirit were not given for their own selfish ends, but for the edifying of others. Understood this way, the verse may be taken to be underlining what Paul has already said of charismatic gifts in verse 7 – that the manifestation of the Spirit is given to each person for the common good. This interpretation is much more in keeping with Paul's overall teaching in chapters 12–14 and on these grounds alone is to be commended.

In short, the simple understanding that 'eis' need not mean 'into' dismisses the charge that 1 Corinthians 12:13 contradicts the Pentecostal understanding of the Baptism in the Spirit. When the verse is understood correctly in its context it actually confirms it.[31] But we must now turn briefly to 1 Corinthians 12:30 which is often cited in objection to the Pentecostal understanding that tongues is to be expected at the baptism in the Spirit.

In 1 Corinthians 12:30, Paul asks the rhetorical question, 'Do all speak in tongues?'. Since he was clearly implying that all do not, this verse, at first sight, appears to conflict with the Pentecostal insistence that all should speak in tongues as a result of being baptised in the Spirit.[32] However, our understanding of this verse must be set in the context of Paul's overall teaching on tongues which indicates that he recognised two distinct functions of speaking in tongues, one private and the other public. We see in 1 Corinthians 14:18 that Paul valued very highly his ability to speak in tongues, yet 'in the church' (v.19),

---

[31]   For further discussion of this theme and for an alternative Pentecostal rebuttal of the charge, see my article 'Baptism in the Spirit in Pauline thought', *EPTA Bulletin*, 7.3 (1988), 88–94.

[32]   I shall make certain practical observations with regard to this in a later section. Criticism of the Pentecostal position is, in my view, often rooted in practical rather than exegetical or theological considerations. However, my purpose, for the present, is simply to show that a correct understanding of 1 Corinthians 12:30 does not contradict the view that tongues is the initial evidence of Spirit baptism.

he preferred not to use it because he recognised that his teaching ministry was of far greater importance. We must therefore conclude that he used it in private. Nevertheless, Paul saw a place for tongues in church provided that they were interpreted so that the church might be edified (v. 5, 13).

There are thus, according to Paul, two distinct functions of speaking in tongues. One is private, as prayer 'with the spirit' (14:14), which does not require interpretation since only God is the hearer. The other is public and requires interpretation since it is heard by the whole church that will remain unedified unless the tongue is interpreted.

Now to return to Paul's rhetorical question in 1 Corinthians 12:30, it is clear from the context that the apostle is referring to the bringing of a public utterance in tongues and not to the ability to speak in tongues privately. This is indicated by the question which immediately follows, 'Do all interpret?', by the overall context of the chapter in which Paul is discussing the functions of the body,[33] and by the immediate context of the list of gifts and ministries (v. 28–30) which Paul cites as evidence of the multiplicity of functions within the body of Christ, the church.

The question 'Do all speak in tongues?' therefore refers to the public use of tongues within the church when the body is gathered together and need not be taken to refer to the private use of tongues as prayer with the spirit. Understood in this way, the verse does not conflict with the Pentecostal view that tongues should be expected at the baptism in the Spirit. Indeed, all should speak in tongues privately! How else will they pray with the spirit? But not all will speak in tongues publicly as Paul's question clearly implies.


## Pastoral Guidelines

If the above analysis is correct, and the Pentecostals are right in their understanding that the baptism in the Spirit is an enduement with power, distinct from conversion, and that the experience should be evidenced by speaking in tongues, certain practical issues arise, especially with regard to Christians who have not spoken in tongues. These

---

[33] Note the repeated references to the body in verses 12–27.

fall into three main categories, namely, those who claim to have been baptised in the Spirit, but have never spoken in tongues; those who, despite prayer for the baptism in the Spirit, have not yet spoken in tongues; and those who have exercised spiritual gifts, but have never spoken in tongues

### Those who Claim to Have Been Baptised in the Spirit, but Have Never Spoken in Tongues

Traditionally, those who hold the Pentecostal view that speaking in tongues is the initial evidence of the baptism in the Holy Spirit have tended to say that if a person has not spoken in tongues, they have not yet been baptised in the Spirit. Those who have experienced the Spirit in some other way have been told that they have received 'an anointing but not the baptism'!

There are, however, great difficulties with this view, not least because in the New Testament there are no examples after Pentecost of anyone receiving 'an anointing but not the Baptism'.[34] A more helpful way forward, in my view, is to make two clear distinctions. First, we must distinguish between the experience of the Spirit coming upon one (i.e. the baptism in the Spirit) and the subsequent result of that experience, speaking in tongues. It is noteworthy that in the New Testament it is the Spirit who comes upon the Christian, but it is the Christian (not the Spirit) who speaks in tongues.[35] It is, therefore, presumably possible for the Spirit to come upon a Christian without that Christian responding by speaking in tongues. It is, in my view, because of this human element in glossolalia that not all present-day 'baptisms in the Spirit' conform to the biblical norm.

But that leads us to the second distinction that needs to be made, namely between what the New Testament teaches us and what we actually experience today. Perhaps some Christians may experience a

---

[34] It might, of course, be argued that people who experienced the Spirit's power before Pentecost received 'an anointing but not the Baptism', but this is not relevant to the present discussion since Pentecost was a turning point in the Spirit's dealings with mankind (John 7:37–39).
[35] Of course, it is the Spirit who enables speaking in tongues, but wherever speaking in tongues is mentioned in the New Testament, it is the Christian who does the speaking.

'baptism in the Spirit' without speaking in tongues. But that does not mean that they could not or should not speak in tongues. Indeed, the Spirit has come upon them and in so doing has enabled them to do so. Any failure to do so may be through lack of understanding or even a lack of desire. What I must not do as a result of any person's experience (or lack of it!) is modify my doctrine accordingly. Doctrine must be based on Scripture, not on experience. I continue to teach that speaking in tongues is the initial evidence of the baptism in the Spirit, but when told that someone has been 'baptised in the Spirit' without speaking in tongues, I do not tell them that they have 'not received the baptism', but rather that, if they really have, they can and should speak in tongues.

### Those who, Despite Prayer for the Baptism in the Spirit, Have Not Yet Spoken in Tongues

Space does not allow detailed comment on this important matter.[36] However, I have discovered in my pastoral experience that, if right teaching is given early on in a Christian's experience, this situation rarely arises. If we have understood correctly the doctrine of the immediate subsequence of the baptism in the Spirit (i.e. that it should occur at or immediately after regeneration), then we will encourage all who come to Christ for salvation to repent, to be baptised (in water), and to receive the gift of the Holy Spirit (Acts 2:38) right at the start of their Christian experience. Young converts, when instructed aright, have the simplicity of faith to receive the gift that the Father has promised. And even those who hear of the baptism in the Spirit relatively late in their Christian experience, once misunderstandings are removed by clear biblical teaching, will receive in the same way. Finally, it is noteworthy that some are especially gifted at leading others into the baptism in the Spirit.[37] Pastors without this gift should not hesitate to enlist the help of those who have it.

---

[36] For more detailed teaching with regard to how to receive the baptism in the Spirit, please consult my earlier work on this subject, *The Dynamic Difference*, chapter 3.

[37] Compare Peter and John's ability to impart the Spirit to the Samaritans with Philip's apparent inability, despite his many other gifts (Acts 8:5–17).

# Table summarising the Pentecostal view of the Baptism in the Spirit

This table shows (1) the interchangeability of such expressions as *the Spirit coming upon* and *being baptised in the Spirit*; (2) the identity of the events described in the four passages in question; and (3) that wherever Luke provides a fuller description of the baptism in the Spirit, speaking in tongues is the first subsequent manifestation recorded. This covers some 150 baptisms in the Spirit.

| Terminology used | The Disciples at Pentecost | The Samaritans | Cornelius etc. in Caesarea | The Ephesians |
|---|---|---|---|---|
| **The Spirit coming on or upon** (The use of the Greek preposition *epi* clinches the identity of all these events.) <br><br> **Compare Acts 1:8** *You will receive power when the Holy Spirit comes on you.* | **Acts 2:16–17** *This is what was spoken by the prophet Joel, 'In the last days, Gods says, I will pour out my Spirit on all people.'* <br><br> cf **Acts 11:15** *The Holy Spirit came on them as he had come on us at the beginning.* | **Acts 8:16** *The Holy Spirit had not yet come upon any of them.* | **Acts 10:44–45** *The Holy Spirit came on all who heard the message . . . poured out on the Gentiles.* <br><br> cf **Acts 11:15** *The Holy Spirit came on them as he had come on us at the beginning.* | **Acts 19:6** *The Holy Spirit came on them.* |
| **Receiving (the gift of) the Holy Spirit** | **Acts 1:4** *Wait for the gift my Father promised.* <br><br> **Acts 2:38** *You will receive the gift of the Holy Spirit.* <br><br> **Acts 11:17** *God gave them the same gift as he gave us.* | **Acts 8:15** *They prayed for them that they might receive the gift of the Holy Spirit.* <br><br> **Acts 8:17** *Peter and John placed their hands on them and they received the Holy Spirit.* <br><br> **Acts 8:18** *The Spirit was given at the laying on of the apostles' hands.* | **Acts 10:45** *The gift of the Holy Spirit had been poured out on the Gentiles.* <br><br> **Acts 11:17** *God gave them the same gift as he gave us.* | **Acts 19:2** *Did you receive the Holy Spirit when you believed?* |
| **Being baptised in (or with) the Holy Spirit** | **Acts 1:5** *You will be baptised with the Holy Spirit.* <br><br> **Acts 11:15–16** *As I began to speak the Holy Spirit came on them as he had on us at the beginning. Then I remembered what the Lord had said, ' . . . you will be baptised with the Holy Spirit '.* | | **Acts 11: 15–16** *As I began to speak the Holy Spirit came on them as he had on us at the beginning. Then I remembered what the Lord had said, ' . . . you will be baptised with the Holy Spirit '.* | |
| **First manifestation recorded after receiving baptism in the Spirit** | **Speaking in tongues** – 120(?) people involved **Acts 2:1–4** | Incomplete description – manifestation not recorded. | **Speaking in tongues** – a household involved. **Acts 10:44–46** | **Speaking in tongues** about 12 people involved. **Acts 19:1–7** |

### Those who Have Exercised Spiritual Gifts, but Have Never Spoken in Tongues

Pentecostals have sometimes taught that the baptism in the Spirit is the gateway to the exercise of the spiritual gifts referred to in 1 Corinthians 12:8–10.[38] Indeed, if the exegesis of 1 Corinthians 12:13 that I offered earlier in this chapter is correct, Paul is teaching here that Christians have been baptised in the Spirit in order that, inter alia, they may edify the Body (the church) by the exercise of such gifts. Indeed, since Christians in Acts appear to have been baptised in the Spirit and spoken in tongues at or even before the time of their baptism in water, it is inconceivable that any of them would have exercised spiritual gifts before being baptised in the Spirit.

Yet this teaching is challenged by the experience of those who claim, for example, to have prophesied, and yet not to have spoken in tongues. My response to this is broadly similar to my comments above. Doctrine must be derived from Scripture, not from experience. Accordingly, I would not encourage people to exercise spiritual gifts until after they have been baptised in the Spirit. But neither do I say that a person's gift is not genuine if they have not first spoken in tongues. Indeed, I have already indicated that, largely because of lack of understanding (due often to a lack of clear teaching), our experience today does not always conform to the biblical norm. But that does not stop me teaching what I believe the Scripture teaches. Quite the opposite! For it is only by clear biblical teaching that Christian experience will be brought into line with biblical norms.

---

[38] *The Dynamic Difference*, chapter 4; this assumption is also implicit throughout Harold Horton's classic *The Gifts of the Spirit* (Luton: AOG, 1934), esp. 227f.

Chapter Six

# Eschatology: A Clear and
# Present Danger – A Sure and Certain Hope

James J. Glass

## Preface

There was silence. The crowd of thousands was momentarily dumb.
Not a sound could be heard, save for the flapping of the flags in the
gentle summer breeze. The many purpled sky adorned in sunset
grandeur seemed silent too. It was as though our lack of words not
only marked respect for those who had sacrificed their lives for
generations yet unborn, but also expressed, more powerfully than
words could ever do, our deepest yearnings that the hope which
sprung from that sacrifice was not vain.

There is something in us as human beings which cries out for a better
day, a new order, a fundamental change in the structure of earthly
existence. It finds expression in political theory, philosophy and religion. And even the moments of silence at a V-E Day celebration, as
described above, cause one to reflect on the hope that a 'New Jerusalem'
would come about in Britain at the end of the Second World War.

In many ways, Pentecostal eschatology addresses this hope which
we sometimes cherish, and articulates an understanding of Scripture
which says, 'Yes, one day there will be peace on earth, one day there
will be justice, one day we will no longer have to live with the
disillusionment of quashed hopes norlabour in vain to bring about a
harmonious social and political order'.[1]

---

[1]  In an article on 'The Millenium', J.W. Montgomery writes: 'Secular
Utopianism is a theme in the history of ideas correlative with the millenial

Eschatology is a vast and complex subject. It is not always easy to do it justice and at the same time correlate it with the emergence of a religious movement. In this chapter, I have deliberately avoided giving a detailed biblical analysis of Pentecostal eschatology. Nor have I sought to chart its pre-Pentecostal theological history. What I have attempted to do is to try to understand why Pentecostals embraced the eschatology they did, and how this has affected the Pentecostal movement. I have tried to explore these questions within the theological and historical milieu in which the Pentecostal movement had its genesis.

It also seemed necessary to try to evaluate contemporary developments in and challenges to Pentecostal eschatology and to make some suggestions as to approaches to eschatology which would enable Pentecostals to embrace the current insights of New Testament theology whilst at the same time remaining true to their roots. In so doing, I express personal opinions and do not claim to speak for the Pentecostal movement or sections within it.

Whilst I believe it is important to integrate the best findings of scholarship into Pentecostal theology, I do not believe that this necessarily means jettisoning the past; Pentecostals will have a better understanding of where they are going when they have better understood where they have come from. Tradition, when handled properly, can be as liberating as it is stifling when given an improper place in the life of faith. Nor do I wish to criticise those who had a formative theological influence on Pentecostal theology. I have no doubt that their ultimate aim was to be faithful to God's Word. Their theology in general and eschatology in particular must be seen, above all else, as an attempt to achieve that aim. Whatever conclusion one reaches concerning the merits or demerits of Pentecostal theology, it was theology done from a believing heart and a sanctified mind. This, at least, must be seen as commendable.

My information and analysis are not based solely on academic research. Pentecostal theology is more of an oral tradition than a literary one. It was and is mainly disseminated by preachers and

---

1 *(continued)* hope, and it is instructive to note that where Christian millenial expectation has been absent or down-played, its Utopian counterpart has entered the breach' (in C.E. Armerding and W. Ward Gasque (eds.), *A Guide to Biblical Prophecy* (Peabody: Hendrickson, 1962).

pastors. Coming from a family which has been connected with the Pentecostal movement for four generations, my perspective on Pentecostal theology has been acquired through sermons, discussions and the romantic legends that become attached to great spiritual movements.

Any attempt to understand Pentecostalism necessarily entails consideration of the eschatological outlook which to a great extent still characterises those denominations which might be termed 'classically Pentecostal'.[2] Such a study will not only take into account formal statements of eschatological positions, but will also consider the ethos of Pentecostalism, for classically and elementally, Pentecostal ethos and eschatology can best be understood when studied in relation to one another. The Pentecostal psyche took shape under the influences of the most fixed and biblically clear principles of its eschatology and as Pentecostalism spread, its more distinctive eschatological beliefs were to some degree engendered by the corporate soul of a movement acutely aware of the imminence of Christ's return.

## Conservative Evangelical Alternatives to Pentecostal Eschatology

As a prelude to a consideration of specifically Pentecostal eschatology, it might be helpful to outline the two alternative schools of prophetic interpretation adhered to by conservative evangelical Christians, namely amillenialism and postmillenialism.

### Amillenialism

Amillenialism understands the thousand-year period of Revelation 20 as nonliteral. For the amillenialist, the millenium is little more than a symbolic reference to the gospel age. It is this nonliteral, symbolic approach to biblical interpretation, or more accurately to interpretation of the prophetic scriptures, that distinguishes it from premillenialism.

---

[2]   Robert Anderson and David Faupel see eschatology as the integrating factor of Pentecostalism (cited by D.W. Dayton, *Theological Roots of Pentecostalism* [Metuchen: Scarecrow Press, 1987], 143)

The amillenialist sees many Old Testament scriptures fulfilled in the New Testament. Hence, those of the amillenialist persuasion do not regard the rebirth of Israel as a nation as having prophetic significance, since for them Israel is no longer to be considered God's chosen nation. God has rather raised up a new nation, the church, which includes Jews and Gentiles, through his Son, Jesus. It is this that may be defined as the Israel of God.

Amillenialists are sometimes accused of teaching 'replacement' theology, in which the Jews are displaced as the people of God and replaced by what has become a largely Gentile church. In fairness, though, this is a disingenuous criticism of amillenialism (or postmil-lenialism, since it is criticised in the same manner) and is to my mind a shameless, if covert, allegation of anti-Semitism. One has only to read amillenialist commentators to realise that they are not claiming that God has replaced Israel, but that he has extended his covenant to the whole of humanity through the death and resurrection of Christ.

The rule of Christ is likewise understood in a spiritual rather than in a political or concrete manner. Christ has now sat down at the right hand of God and exercises his rulership in the heavenly realms. The splendour of Christ's rule is now seen in his church and will one day be witnessed by all the world when he returns as judge and king. The second coming will not, in the eyes of the amillenialist, usher in the millenium but the last judgement, the new heavens and the new earth.

The symbolic or spiritual interpretation of scripture pervades amillenialism. The book of Revelation, for example, is not seen as a prophetic timetable of future events. It is more often considered to refer to events contemporary to those who read it in the first century. As a result, the great tribulation and the revelation of Antichrist are often seen as having been fulfilled in the first century.

For the amillenialist, many prophecies which are not interpreted spiritually or symbolically have already been fulfilled. Thus, for exam-ple, the Olivet Discourse (Mark 13; Matt. 24) is largely taken to have been fulfilled in AD 70 when Jerusalem was besieged by the armies of Rome. Old Testament prophecies are similarly handled. The promise of the land to Abraham's descendants is seen as fulfilled in the conquest of Canaan, while the future blessing prophesied by the pre-exilic and exilic prophets is held to have come to pass during the period of restoration under Ezra and Nehemiah. With regard to the world situation immediately prior to the Lord's return, most amillenialists would perceive evil escalating. Some, on the basis of Romans 11, look for the conversion of natural Israel. Apart from such general developments, the amillenialist school offers no timetable of events leading up to the return of Christ.

The strength of amillenialism is that it appears to do justice to the broad sweep of New Testament revelation. Its understanding of the millenium is not based solely on Revelation 20 and, whilst it is not unsound to argue for a political, earthly kingdom on the basis of that passage, one can understand amillenialist reluctance to develop an understanding of the millenium not explicitly set forth anywhere else in the New Testament.

The weakness of amillenialism, in my view, is a failure to do justice to the text of Revelation 20. For example, the amillenialist identifies the binding of Satan in Revelation 20:2 with Luke 11:21–23. However, the binding of Satan in Revelation 20 seems more far-reaching than that mentioned in Luke 11.

Amillenialism has generally been popular in Reformed circles: Augustine, Luther and Calvin were all amillenialist. In more recent times, William Hendriksen, Stephen Travis and Michael Wilcox have also espoused it.[3]

## Postmillenialism

Postmillenialists approach the prophetic scriptures in much the same way as amillenialists. However, as the prefix 'post' implies, those of this school believe that Christ will return to earth after the millenium. According to postmillenial teaching, the church will continue to grow and society will become more and more influenced by the gospel. An age of peace and righteousness will gradually come about on earth as society yields to the impact of godly principles presented through the preaching of the gospel. This is what postmillenialists see as the millenium, and it provides for them a fulfilment not only of Revelation 20 but also of Old Testament prophecy. Postmillenialism takes the hermeneutic approach of amillenialism and combines it with the hope of future glory on earth that is characteristic of premillenialism.

---

[3]   For a more detailed exposition of amillenialism, see A.A. Hoekema, *The Bible and the Future* (Grand Rapids: Eerdmans, 1979); O.T. Allis, *Prophecy and the Church* (Philadelphia: Presbyterian & Reformed, 1945).

The major strengths of postmillenialism are its confidence in the power of the gospel and its attempt to do justice to the prophecies of future blessing for the church. Unlike premillenialism, it does not relegate the latter to a postparousia millenium. Nor does it 'spiritualise' them away as amillenialism sometimes appears to do.

One of the great weaknesses of postmillenialism, however, is its failure to adequately exegete those passages of the New Testament which speak of moral decline before the Lord's return. It should be said that, even for the postmillenialist, the time before the Lord's return must be one of falling away, since this is how Revelation 20 describes the end of the millenium. Secondly, postmillenialism has, on occasions, been hijacked by those who preach a social gospel. This vulnerability to liberalism has made it a bête noire of eschatology for some conservative evangelicals.

Like amillenialism, postmillenialism has its main supporters in Reformed circles. Many of the Puritans were postmillenialist, as were B.B. Warfield and A.H. Strong. Among the ranks of contemporary postmillenialists are Iain H. Murray and John Piper.[4]

## Pentecostal Hermeneutics: The Basis of Pentecostal Eschatology

What beliefs made Pentecostalism distinct? Before listing the general points of Pentecostal eschatology, something should be said about the hermeneutics of Pentecostalism. The eschatology of Pentecostalism had at its foundation a literalist approach to the interpretation of Scripture. In that sense, Pentecostalism was (and is) a fundamentalist movement. That is not to say that Pentecostals slavishly interpreted every detail of biblical revelation literally. It does mean, however, that if a particular passage was open to a symbolic interpretation, but other passages could be adduced which gave plausible reason for a literal interpretation, then Pentecostals opted for the latter. The rationale of such an approach was to ward off any line of interpretation which might diminish the status, veracity or power of God's written word.

---

[4] For a more detailed exposition of postmillenialism, see Boettner, *The Millenium* (Philadelphia: Presbyterian & Reformed, 1957); I.H. Murray, *The Puritan Hope* (London: Banner of Truth, 1971).

This was not only intended as a safeguard against the theological liberalism of the early 1900s but also against the 'abstraction' of revelation which, to many Pentecostals, was all too evident in some evangelical churches and institutions. In fact, it might be more accurate to describe the Pentecostal hermeneutic as 'concrete' rather than 'literal'; God had said and was saying something concrete to the world as opposed to something abstract.

It was this kind of interpretative grid that the early Pentecostals imposed on the prophetic scriptures. It yielded the eschatological dogma which eventually found formal definition in Pentecostal statements of belief and popular exposition at conventions, conferences and, above all, evangelistic outreaches. Although Pentecostals were zealous students of the Bible, it must be said that many people came into the Pentecostal movement with their doctrinal views on a wide range of issues already fixed. This is particularly true with regard to eschatology.

If one examines the ecclesiastical soil in which Pentecostalism took root, one will find that Brethrenism provided a major source of ideas and personnel.[5] The result was that some Pentecostals were in fact Brethren who had grafted the baptism and gifts of the spirit onto their Brethrenism.[6] Dispensationalism was, therefore, theologically generative in early Pentecostalism. Though it might be argued that Pentecostals simply embraced dispensationalism, I would argue that, firstly, some Pentecostals were of that outlook because they had come from that school of thought and did not see it as conflicting with the Pentecostal teaching on the Holy Spirit which they had embraced (and experienced). Secondly, Pentecostals who were not of that school found it attractive because of their convictions about the Bible and its interpretation, in particular conviction that it was God's inspired word

---

[5]    contra Dayton, *Theological Roots*, 145–6. I think Dayton's views might be more pertinent to American Pentecostalism.

[6]    The influence of J.N. Darby, the leading apostle of Brethrenism, was not limited to that dissenting circle. Darby was an extremely influential figure in the prophetic conferences of the early 1800s attended by eminent Anglican evangelicals. This is important from a Pentecostal perspective, since British Pentecostalism had its beginnings in the Anglican Church (see I.S. Rennie, 'Nineteenth Century Roots' in Armerding and Ward Gasque, *A Guide*, 57).

and that it should be interpreted in a concrete manner, wherever it was natural to do so or when internal corroboration was possible.

## Pentecostal Eschatology: An Overview

That the Lord Jesus Christ will return to earth in glory is the bedrock of Pentecostal eschatology. Whilst there is discussion as to the manner of Christ's return and the events leading up to it, the fact of his return is beyond dispute. The biblical basis of the second advent is found in the words of the Lord himself and in the teaching of his apostles. In Matthew 24:30, Jesus declares that 'At that time, the sign of the Son of Man will appear in the sky, and all the nations of the earth will mourn. They will see the Son of Man coming on the clouds of the sky with power and great glory.' Similarly, 1 Thessalonians 4:15 states that 'The Lord himself will descend from heaven' while Peter reassures his readers that the Lord will keep his promise to come again (2 Peter 3:3–10). For the Pentecostal, scriptures such as these are the foundation of their hope that Christ will personally return to the earth as a potentate. Everyone will witness that coming and all, including the most powerful, will have no option but to recognise him as Lord (Phil. 2:10–11).

This is the foundation of Pentecostal eschatology and the central hope of Pentecostalism. It is the hub from which other aspects of eschatology protrude like spokes, joining the hub to current events and issues and also to issues that are postparousia.

### The Restoration of Israel

For many Pentecostals, one of the most significant unfulfilled prophecies concerned the restoration of the Jews to the promised land.[7] The basis for this was Old Testament scriptures such as Isaiah 66 and Zechariah 14 which indicated that one day God's people would be regathered to the land that God had promised them. Such scriptures, it was felt, need to have a temporal, political application to fully do

---

[7] W.J. Maybin, 'Bible Prophecy', in P.S. Brewster (ed.), *Pentecostal Doctrine* (Cheltenham: Elim, 1976), 221–222.

justice to them.[8] To interpret the prophesied restoration as applying to the church is thus exegetically inadequate. Furthermore, if the prophecies that applied to the restoration recorded in Ezra, Nehemiah and some of the minor prophets had a concrete application, then so must other prophecies couched in similar language and spoken by the same prophets. Not only that, but it was understood that God had given the promised land to his chosen people as an eternal possession. Therefore to 'spiritualise' away prophetic promises betrays an inconsistent exegesis of the prophetic corpus in Scripture. This issues in a disharmonisation of the teaching of the prophets with what had been taught in the Law concerning that which God had covenanted to Israel as a whole, and with what had been taught in the historical writings, especially the record of God's eternal covenant with David. The implications of a 'spiritual' approach were even more serious than mere exegetical imprecision: it made God out to be less than serious when he promised the land as an everlasting possession, and when he, through his prophets, promised restoration to the land. Scripture would therefore be seriously undermined in its claim to be divinely inspired. By dint of such reasoning, the restoration of the Jews to Palestine became an important component in 'signs of the times' teaching.[9]

However, the promised restoration took on even greater significance in the popular exposition of Pentecostal eschatology. In Matthew 24:32–34, Jesus used the example of the fig tree, reminding his hearers that one can tell the approach of summer by the emergence of its leaves. He then added that 'this generation' would not pass away until all that he had spoken of was fulfilled. Some teachers interpreted the fig tree as a reference to Israel: flourishing fig tree = flourishing Israel. This was then seen as a reference to the restoration, while 'this generation' was understood as the generation that would witness the restoration and see the Lord's return. One can imagine the excitement caused when Israel became a nation once again in 1948. It goes a long way to accounting for books with titles such as 'Christ Returns By 1988'.

---

[8]    For example, J.C. Smyth, 'The Signs of the Times' in Brewster, *Pentecostal Doctrine*, 386.

[9]    Pentecostals may not have presented their teaching in this way, but it is implicit in their approach and borne out by their high view of scripture.

The major criticism that can be levelled against this line of interpretation is that an image has been figuratively deconstructed and has become a prophetic statement in itself. It seems odd that a scheme of prophetic interpretation so committed to a concrete understanding of God's word should 'spiritualise' a statement and hang its hopes on it.

Israel's restoration is held by many to be the prophetic catalyst which prepares the world for the coming to pass of a series of other prophecies.[10] One of these is directly connected to the restoration of Israel: the conclusion of the period known as the 'times of the Gentiles'. In Luke 21:24, Jesus said that Jerusalem would be trampled on by the Gentiles 'until the times of the Gentiles be fulfilled'. Israel's presence in Jerusalem once again as a result of gains in the Yom Kippur war was seen as a fulfilment of this prophecy.

## The Rapture

The next prophecy awaiting fulfilment is held to be the rapture of the church. This point is controversial. Most Classic Pentecostals believe that the church is 'raptured' or snatched away (sometimes the word 'translated' is used) from the earth upon which God then pours his judgement. The term 'rapture' is not used in Scripture, but, it is urged, the concept is evident in a number of passages. I Thessalonians 4:13–18 is the primary textual basis for the concept of the rapture, in particular verse 17 which says 'We who are still alive and are left will be caught up together with them (those who have been resurrected) in the clouds to meet the Lord in the air. And so will we be with the Lord forever.' It is the verb 'caught up' (*harpadzo*) that is the focus for Pentecostal theologians. The thrust of the passage to them appears to be that of meeting the Lord in the air.

Pursuing the logic of a concrete hermeneutic rules out the identification of the events of this passage with the second coming of Christ, since what we have here is descriptive not of a coming to earth, but to air, and not of a coming to judge the world but to deliver the church. Adherents of this view are classed as 'pretribulationists' in that they believe Christians are taken up from the earth to meet the Lord

---

[10] For example, Maybin, 'Bible Prophecy', 221.

before the onset of the great tribulation. This is the majority view in Classical Pentecostalism.[11]

Others have believed that the Scriptures teach a midtribulation rapture, while others prefer a posttribulation rapture.[12] The main attack on pretribulationalism is that firstly, the second advent is not pictured elsewhere in scripture as a two-stage event, while secondly, it is nowhere recorded that the church will be taken from the world before the Lord comes again.

One main assumption of pretribulationism is that the church, since there is no mention of it being on the earth from chapter four of Revelation onwards, must therefore have been raptured. This interpretation of Revelation is facilitated by understanding the address to the seven churches in Asia Minor not simply as an address to seven local churches but also as an address to the universal body of Christ in seven different ages.[13] Those outside of the pretribulationist camp see this as an unwarranted argument ex silentio, a dogmatic pronouncement based on eisegesis rather than exegesis.

Discussing the sequence of events leading up to the coming of the Lord is to tread a theological minefield. We have already seen that the timing of the rapture is controversial. To a certain extent, one's understanding of the rapture will determine whether one is a futurist or a historicist; conversely, one's futurism or historicism will affect one's understanding of the rapture.

Futurism or futurist premillenialism in essence holds that most of the events prophesied by Jesus in the Olivet discourse (Matt. 24; Mark 13; Luke 21) are yet to be fulfilled or are in the process of fulfilment in the twentieth century. Religious deception, worldwide conflict, famine and earthquakes, it is argued, are more prevalent now than ever (Matt. 24:4–7). We are, therefore, living in the time known as 'the beginning of birth pains' (Matt. 24:8). In Matthew 24:15, Jesus speaks of the 'abomination that causes desolation', (a term used by Daniel in Dan. 9:27; 11:31; 12:11) and says that the aftermath of that will be a time of

---

[11]   For a Classic Pentecostal exposition of this view see I.W. Lewis, 'The Rapture of the Church', in Brewster, *Pentecostal Doctrine*, 259–271.

[12]   I am not aware of any Pentecostal writer or theologian who has put his posttribulation views in print. However, I do know of an increasing number of Pentecostal preachers who hold this view.

[13]   For example, see Maybin, 'Bible Prophecy', 218f.

great distress (v.21) or 'great tribulation' (AV). Historicism or historical premillenialism, on the other hand, sees much of what Jesus prophesied in the Olivet discourse as referring to the fall of Jerusalem in AD 70.

Pentecostals have, in the main, taken a futurist view of the Olivet discourse and, for that matter, of other prophetic passages of the New Testament. Historical premillenialism might become more attractive to those who have been influenced by the theology of G.E. Ladd[14] and the philosophy of ministry propagated by charismatic renewal leaders such as John Wimber,[15] who feel that a dispensational hermeneutic cannot be reconciled with a theology of signs and wonders which has, as a central dynamic, the kingdom of God as a present reality.[16]

### The Great Tribulation and the Return of Christ

The great tribulation is held to be seven years in duration (Rev. 7:14; 13:5; Dan. 7:25; 9:27). At the outset of the tribulation, Antichrist is revealed. His accession to world power initially heralds peace and prosperity for the world but unparalleled woe for the 144,000 Jews whom God supernaturally turns to Christ (Rev. 7:8 ff). Conditions gradually degenerate as God pours out his judgement (Rev. 6; 8; 9) and the peace initiated by Antichrist is eventually shattered and the nations of the earth converge on the plain of Megiddo for the battle of Armageddon (Rev. 16:16). It is then that the Lord returns to earth and inaugurates his millenial reign (Isa. 11; Rev. 20). Satan is bound for one thousand years (Rev. 20:2) and at the end of the thousand years, he is loosed and the nations rebel against the Messiah

---

[14] G.E. Ladd, *The Blessed Hope* (Grand Rapids: Eerdmans, 1956); *New Testament Theology* (Cambridge: Lutterworth, 1974).

[15] Two leading biblical scholars connected with Wimber and the Vineyard Movement, Peter Davids and Wayne Grudem, are both premillenialist; see P. Davids, *More Hard Sayings of the New Testament* (London: Hodder & Stoughton, 1992), 294; W. Grudem, *Systematic Theology* (Leicester: IVP, 1994), chapter 55. This seems to me to be important given the criticism that has been directed at Wimber for an over-emphasis on realised eschatology.

[16] Grudem (*ibid.*, 860) draws attention to a variation on dispensationalism known as progressive dispensationalism. Briefly, progressive dispensationalists do not believe that God has two separate purposes, but only one- the establishment of his kingdom. However, they do see the OT prophecies concerning Israel being fulfilled by natural Israel.

(Rev. 20:7–8), though fire from heaven destroys them (v.9). The second resurrection then takes place and the unrighteous dead are raised to stand before God (v. 5, 11–13a), judged and cast into the lake of fire along with Satan (v. 13b–15). The earth is finally destroyed and a new heaven and earth are brought into existence (21:1).

The outline above may be understood as a fair portrayal of the views of most Pentecostals. This kind of eschatology is similar to that found in many evangelical churches. It might be noted, however, that it is adherence to such an eschatology which has distinguished Pentecostalism from the renewal/charismatic movement in which eschatology does not seem to have held such a defining position. Those evangelicals, on the other hand, whose theological spectacles have dispensationalist lenses have however, often been the most opposed to a charismatic/Pentecostal understanding of spiritual gifts.

## Influences on Pentecostal Eschatology

Why Pentecostalism embraced the kind of eschatology it did has already been alluded to. We have seen that Pentecostals hold a high view of Scripture and interpret Scripture accordingly. We have also seen that early Pentecostals were influenced by dispensationalist teaching because some early Pentecostals had come from Brethren churches.

However, that is not the whole story. There are a number of other factors that need to be taken into account. First, one needs to account for the other streams besides Brethrenism which refreshed early Pentecostalism. One major source of influence was the Holiness movement. In many ways, the Pentecostal movement is the natural heir of the nineteenth century Holiness movement, which in turn is rooted in the Methodism of John Wesley. The emphasis of the latter on the baptism in the Spirit as a crisis experience distinct from regeneration is similarly fundamental in Pentecostal theology, and it is the experience of baptism in the Spirit that essentially defines one as Pentecostal as opposed to non-Pentecostal.[17]

---

[17]    In his preface to *Joy Unspeakable* Christopher Catherwood recalls being asked if his grandfather had become a Pentecostal. The question seems to have arisen in connection with Lloyd-Jones' emerging views on Spirit baptism (D.M. Lloyd-Jones [Eastbourne: Kingsway, 1984]).

It seems that there was not a uniform eschatological outlook in the Holiness movement. Postmillenialism and premillenialism were both espoused by proponents of Holiness teaching. It does seem, however, that in the early part of the nineteenth century, postmillenialism held sway (as it did in evangelicalism generally; the nineteenth century missionary movement was fuelled by postmillenialist expectations). Towards the end of the century, premillenialism was becoming increasingly accepted. By the first decades of the twentieth century, postmillenialism was considered at best naïve optimism, at worst an aberration of exegesis that was ultimately connected with liberal theology and the social gospel. Undoubtedly, the shift had something, perhaps much, to do with changing social conditions and the increasing antagonism that orthodox Christian theology generated in circles of social, religious and academic sophistication. By the time of the Great War, postmillenialism appeared to be dead and buried as a valid option in Holiness/evangelical eschatology.

The Holiness influence on Pentecostalism might not simply have been a straightforward doctrinal influence, for Pentecostalism inherited to a large degree the ethos of the Holiness movement evidenced in, amongst other things, the crusading zeal which was and is a hallmark of Classical Pentecostalism. The Holiness movement was a radical movement, much more so than other streams of nineteenth century evangelicalism. It was a movement of crisis; the crisis of conversion; the crisis of baptism in the Spirit. It was a movement of revival that expected God to break into people's lives, and even the whole of society. Its eschatology both in post- and premillenial expressions was similarly radical. God would 'rend the heavens' and rule the earth either by means of the church or by the personal advent of Jesus to establish his kingdom. Pentecostalism too is what might be termed a radical evangelical movement and, at its inception, embraced an eschatology appropriate to its ethos.

## Theology and Ethos of Pentecostalism

The relationship between the theology of Classical Pentecostalism and its ethos is a complex one. That being so, it is, not surprisingly, sometimes difficult to determine whether Pentecostal eschatology was the stimulus to Pentecostal practice or whether Pentecostal practice

made Pentecostal eschatology a necessity.[18] At the beginnings of the
movement, it would seem that the desire for an authentic and dynamic
experience of the Holy Spirit was the common denominator amongst
Pentecostals. Premillenialist eschatology became more prominent in
later years as the movement became less associated with Alexander
Boddy and Anglicanism and took an increasingly nonconformist and
fundamentalist direction. The ministries of George and Stephen
Jeffreys played a crucial role in the spread of premillenialism. As the
earliest major Pentecostal evangelists in Britain (along with Smith
Wigglesworth), their preaching not only included the call to salvation
and the declaration that Christ could save and heal, but also that Christ
was coming again and that salvation and judgement were at hand. For
those who were strangers to Pentecostalism, the preaching of the
Jeffreys brothers must have represented in essence what Pentecostals
believed. If the above thesis is correct, it might be argued that by the
time of the Great War, eschatology was becoming more and a more
a feature of Pentecostalism while at the same time the Anglican links
were becoming more and more tenuous.[19]

The actions of some leading Pentecostals in the Great War serve
to highlight how radical Pentecostalism was becoming. At a time
when many Christians were rallying to king and country, Pentecostal
believers such as Howard Carter and Donald Gee felt service in the
war incompatible with their Christian convictions.[20] The former spent
the war in Wormwood Scrubs, the latter on a farm.[21] Pentecostalism
was becoming not only nonconformist in ecclesiastical terms but also
in terms of political dissent.

Was this a result of the eschatological consciousness of the movement
or was the burgeoning eschatology a result of a growing feeling of acute

---

[18]   It seems that premillenialism and ecclesiastical primitivism go hand in
hand. Pentecostalism stands in the restorationist tradition of ecclesiastical
primitivism and premillenialism.
[19]   W.J. Hollenweger, *The Pentecostals* (London: SCM, 1972; reprint,
Peabody: Hendrickson, 1988), 185.
[20]   Not all Pentecostals were conscientious objectors. I have heard of a late
Elim pastor who had fought in the Great War. All his comrades sought to
stay near him in battle because of his faith in the promise, 'A thousand may
fall at your side, ten thousand at your right hand, but it will not come near
you' (Ps. 91:7).
[21]   C. Whittaker, *Seven Pentecostal Pioneers* (London: Marshalls, 1984).

alienation from the world and the apocalyptic landscape of modern warfare? It is difficult to tell. In my view, the time of the Great War was the period when Pentecostalism took the shape that it still retains today. In an indirect way, the War further strengthened premillenialist convictions for it appeared to demolish any remaining hopes of a kingdom established through the church; the kingdom of God would only be established through the coming of Christ. In the aftermath of the War, Pentecostals were left with a message of hope for a nation devastated by war and in economic decline. The social conditions of the day and the recent war validated the Pentecostal assertion that things would grow worse and that the second coming was at hand.

The ministry of Stephen Jeffreys helps us to see another aspect of Classical Pentecostalism. In his ministry, more than in that of any other early leader, the strongly prophetic character of Pentecostalism can be seen.[22] Two instances are demonstrative of this. First, in a chapel in Llanelli, a few weeks before the outbreak of the Great War, there appeared a vision of a lamb on the wall behind the pulpit as Jeffreys was preaching. It became transformed into a vision of Christ. It remained there for a number of days and was witnessed by many whilst at the same time being taken as a portent of impending judgement.[23] The second example comes to us by way of Donald Gee.[24] Gee recalled how, whilst walking through London at the time of the Blitz, he remembered Jeffreys' pronouncement of doom on an unrepentant London in the late twenties. Experiences of this kind, though admittedly rare, must have given many Pentecostals additional reason to believe that God had raised up the movement to proclaim the near return of Christ.

Another factor in the embrace of premillenialism by Pentecostalism is frequently overlooked. Many commentators, to a certain extent rightly, perceive Pentecostalism as a movement of the Spirit. However, to see Pentecostalism as pneumatocentric is misguided. If anything,

---

[22] contra Dayton (*Theological Roots*, 158–160) who views premillenialism as a move away from the ethical prophetism of postmillenialism to a historical apocalypticism. I am not sure that the early Pentecostals would have seen it quite like that.

[23] D. Gee, *Wind and Flame* (Croydon: AOG/Heath Press, 1967), 91f.

[24] D. Gee, *These Men I Knew* (London: Evangel Press; Nottingham: AOG Publishing House, 1980), 53.

Pentecostalism is Christocentric. The kind of Word/Spirit tensions that can be seen in the charismatic movement do not seem to have surfaced in early Pentecostalism.[25] The emphasis on the person of Christ has been a shaping factor in Pentecostal eschatology. Eschatology is a Christological concern. The high Christology of Pentecostalism may well have pushed Pentecostal eschatology in a literalist direction. One Pentecostal author goes so far as to say that anything less than a literal, earthly millenial kingdom undermines the incarnation.[26] In other words, if the thousand years of Revelation 20 are mythical in the theological sense of the term, then what is to stop us saying that the incarnation is similarly mythical? Whether or not the argument stands up, it certainly highlights the eschatology/Christology relationship. A nonliteralist eschatology may thus be viewed as being detrimental to the status of Christ; the more literal the eschatology, the more dignity and glory accorded to Christ.

Pentecostal Christology is not only a high Christology, it is also an experiential Christology. Classical Pentecostal preachers had four major themes: Christ the saviour; Christ the healer; Christ the baptiser in the Holy Spirit; Christ the coming king. This 'foursquare' gospel proclaimed a Christ who could be experienced. At the Second Coming, everyone would, in a sense, experience Christ whether they wished to or not.

With such a strong premillenialist eschatological emphasis in the early years of the movement, it is tempting to question why uncertainty concerning this hallmark of Pentecostal belief has crept in. The results of that shift and its scope can be seen most acutely in Elim. At one Elim Conference in the 1950s, an Elim minister raised the possibility of discussing various views on the millenium. The Secretary General asked him if he could subscribe unreservedly to the premillenial position set forth in the Elim fundamentals. He said that he could not, and his credentials as an Elim minister were withdrawn on the spot.[27] By 1994, premillenialism had been dropped from those same

[25]	M.S. Clark, H. Lederle, et al. *What is Distinctive about Pentecostal Theology* (Pretoria: University of South Africa, 1989), 115.
[26]	G. Canty, *In My Father's House* (Basingstoke: Marshall, Morgan & Scott, 1969), 126.
[27]	I owe this information to Robert Gilmore, for many years an elder in an Elim church.

fundamentals. These two scenarios serve to illustrate the strength of conviction with which premillenialism was originally held and give some idea of the kind of revolution needed to undermine faith in it.

Throughout the history of the Pentecostal movement there have always been those who have dissented from dispensationalist and premillenialist interpretations of prophecy, but they never formed a coherent enough body or held leadership positions sufficiently influential to affect denominational statements of faith. Nor were their preaching ministries populist enough to influence the thinking of the movement at grassroots level. However, the sort of Pentecostal who had abandoned premillenialism (usually for amillenialism) was often one who had read more widely than the standard dispensationalist texts and was to some degree influenced by Reformed theology.[28] In the light of recent theological debate and developments in Pentecostal education, it could well be argued that these men anticipated what was to happen in decades to come. They were a harbinger of a time when Pentecostal theology would be formulated taking into account broader theological developments and perspectives rather than on the anvil of a fundamentalist hermeneutic, itself fashioned as a reaction to the apparently unstoppable spread of modernism. Undoubtedly, the acceptance and promotion of theological education has had an affect on the shape of Pentecostalism. However, a feeling of eschatological uncertainty cannot be attributed to the development of theological education alone.

William Kay in his history of the Assemblies of God in Britain *Inside Story*, has said that the 1970s was a decade in which the Pentecostal movement had to choose between two options, one almost equal in pain to the other: reform or die.[29] This was not only true of the AOG but of Elim as well. Why had these expressions of

---

[28] I.H. Murray refers to an address by Lloyd-Jones given at the annual meeting of the Evangelical Library in 1963 which includes the following opinion: 'So, you see, there is this extraordinary change taking place. Some of the older denominations seem to be looking more or less in the direction of Pentecostal teaching, whereas the Pentecostals themselves are looking in the direction of Reformed theology' (Martyn Lloyd-Jones: *The Fight of Faith 1939–1981*, [Edinburgh: Banner of Truth, 1990] 481).

[29] W.K. Kay, *Inside Story* (Mattersey; Mattersey Hall Publishing, 1990), 349.

Pentecostalism come to this kind of crossroads and why did it affect Pentecostal eschatology?

Before giving possible reasons for this, it must be established that whatever was happening in the seventies raised questions regarding the existing stance on eschatology. As early as 1978, an AOG leader, Keith Munday, addressed the subject at a joint Elim/AOG Conference at Swanwick and reaffirmed the Classical Pentecostal premillenialist position. If the leaders of the respective denominations had not felt that an eschatological undercurrent was threatening the doctrinal moorings of Pentecostals, then the need to address the subject was questionable. If the issue was not addressed because of a perceived threat, a real threat soon did emerge. By 1985, it was a hot issue at the AOG Conference. At the 1987 Conference, David Allen restated the premillenialist position, basing his apologia on Scripture and the church fathers.[30]

A similar pattern could be seen in Elim. At the 1984 Conference, the theme was 'Kingdom Authority' followed by the text 'The kingdom of the world has become the kingdom of our Lord and of His Christ' (Rev. 11:15). In most of the Bible studies and sermons on kingdom authority, the kingdom was presented as a present reality. This flew in the face of dispensationalist teaching on the kingdom; dispensationalists say that the kingdom has been postponed until the millenium. The president of Elim for that year, Len Cowdery, gave a presidential address which had much in common with covenant theology and not much in common with dispensational premillenialism.[31]

As to the reasons for this trend, one needs to take into account the religious climate of the seventies. Firstly, it seems plausible to suggest that Pentecostal hopes of the imminent return of the Lord were in a sense dashed. At face value, the suggestion might appear extreme, but I believe it is the way some Pentecostals felt, even if they did not care to admit it. Not only had the first generation of Pentecostal leaders died out, the second generation was also beginning to pass away. It is hard to imagine the emotional impact this had on the soul of the movement. Many of these men and women

---

[30]  *ibid.*, 349.

[31]  L. Cowdery, 'Kingdom Authority and Revival', *Elim Evangel* (June 1984) 2.

did not expect to die, believing that the Lord would return in their life time.[32]

More than once the return of Christ seemed, at most, a few years away. The Second World War, the Suez crisis, the Cuban missile crisis, the Arab–Israeli conflict and the mediation of Henry Kissinger had all, in their moments, appeared to verify the Pentecostal understanding of prophecy that the coming of the Lord was at hand. Perhaps the death of the great men and women of God was causing some Pentecostals to think again. Perhaps emerging leaders had to consider how they might prepare for the future in the event of Christ not returning, aware that they could no longer rely on a revivalistic impetus to propel men into ministry. Perhaps there was a greater willingness and desire to confront the harsh realities of secular western civilisation and the role of the Pentecostal movement in these rather than to pursue and promote interpretations of Scripture which were sometimes speculative. This might account to some degree for the lower profile given to Bible prophecy in post-70s Pentecostalism.[33]

A major factor in the reconsideration given to many aspects of Pentecostal thought and practice in the 1970s (and '80s) must be the emergence of firstly, the Renewal movement and then, the Restoration house church movement. This is important for a number of reasons. First of all, the outpouring of the Spirit in the historic denominations undermined the notion that those denominations represented apostate Christendom, the Laodicean church of the last days that was beyond redemption. This attitude towards the established church was so embedded in Pentecostal thinking that it caused many Pentecostals to reject the moving of the Spirit in Renewal circles as the work of Satan. This thinking was, in part, engendered by the

---

[32] I remember accompanying my father on a visit to a Pentecostal evangelist who was on her death bed. She confessed that she had not expected to die, but rather 'to meet the Lord in the air', referring to the Rapture.

[33] There seems to have been a drift away from the kind of eschatological focus Pentecostals had been used to with the advent of the renewal movement. In N. Scotland's book, *Charismatics and the Next Millenium*, there is no single chapter devoted to eschatology nor is there a reference to the topic in the index (London: Hodder & Stoughton, 1995).

eschatological understanding of an increasingly corrupt church in the last days. The Pentecostals (amongst other evangelicals) found themselves in a dilemma; on the one hand, their understanding of the church of the end-times was that it was an apostate church and this had in previous decades been verified by evidence of increasing apostasy; on the other hand, contact with Renewal leaders and people who had been blessed by contact with the movement seemed to controvert the accepted eschatological line and furnish evidence of God doing a new thing.[34]

The Renewal movement was one thing, but the Restoration house church movement which it spawned was another. The Renewal movement never seriously threatened the place of Pentecostalism in the Christian community. Indeed, it did not set out to challenge the legitimacy of Pentecostalism. On the contrary, leaders within the Renewal movement respected the Pentecostals even if they did not always agree with them on doctrinal issues. The Restoration movement, on the other hand, was too close to Pentecostalism in theology and ethos for comfort. Its understanding of the baptism and gifts of the Spirit was nothing less than Pentecostal. Its personnel had the same kind of nonconformist roots as the early Pentecostal movement, and some of them had originally been Pentecostals. It sometimes seemed that some of the Restoration churches were more Pentecostal than the Pentecostal churches; tongues, prophecy, healing and exorcism were all present in this burgeoning neo-Pentecostal group.

The challenge from the Restoration movement came not only in terms of the apparent vibrancy of its spiritual experience in comparison with that of the average Pentecostal church. Restorationists were bold enough to challenge the right of denominations to exist at all. This was one of the perspectives that made for the radical nature of house church Christianity.[35] The problem with this radical anti-institutional stance for many Pentecostals was that they themselves viewed things similarly. It was also true that the early Pentecostal leaders had been opposed to denominationalism, emphasising the charismatic aspect of the church rather than the institutional.

---

[34]  H.W. Greenway grapples with this tension (*Pentecostal Doctrine*, 293–304).

[35]  A. Wallis, *The Radical Christian* (Eastbourne: Kingsway, 1983).

What may have proved as attractive as any of the above to many Pentecostals was the Restorationist outlook on the future of the church. In house church circles, there was not mention of the church growing steadily worse and waiting for the Rapture. Instead of doom and gloom there was to be glory and dominion. God would restore his church to her pristine New Testament condition and she would enjoy even greater missionary success than the first century church. Believers were no longer encouraged to stay away from what had been considered worldly professions such as those within the arts, media or politics. Rather, they were encouraged to take the message of the kingdom into every area of life. Pessimism gave way to optimism and talk of revival was in the air again. A 'Puritan Hope'-type eschatology, a governmental structure which advocated strong charismatic leadership and a stress on a Pentecostal type of spirituality was a potent mixture that sometimes was as appealing to a theologically informed Pentecostal as it was to a disgruntled Free Church believer.

The challenge here was not only ecclesiological, it was eschatological as well. The Restoration movement seemed to offer hope to the church at a time when many Pentecostals were expecting its demise. But that expectation of demise was inextricably connected to Pentecostal eschatology. Perhaps, too, the emergence of the Restoration movement brought to the surface an unresolved tension in Pentecostal theology which involved the expectation that the church would decline set against the Pentecostal instinct that God could revive it and would pour out the latter rain. The understanding of the future of the church in Restorationist theology was connected to another very important emphasis in Restorationist teaching: the kingdom of God as a present reality.

If the charismatic movement had one conversion for every time the word 'kingdom' has been mentioned in the last twenty years, we would be enjoying the greatest revival there has been for many years. Not only has there been an emphasis on the kingdom of God as a present entity, but 'kingdom' has come to be used adjectivally as well. Hence, we have terms such as 'kingdom power', 'kingdom authority', 'kingdom lifestyle', and even 'kingdom people.' Such terminology has come from an understanding of the kingdom that sees it as already present. The kingdom is the rule of God which God wants to extend throughout the world. The church is the vehicle by means of which the kingdom is brought into society today. God's rule or kingdom (or kingdom rule as some would have it) is extended when the gospel is preached, sinners are converted, the sick are healed or demons are cast out. It is also demonstrated in the lives of Christians as they live holy lives in the world. This concept of the kingdom of God is probably what has given birth to some of the emphasis on spiritual warfare; prayer is the people of God's kingdom wrestling with the forces of Satan's kingdom. The influence of 'kingdom teaching' is ubiquitous in charismatic theology and culture. In years to come, church historians may come to recognise it as a common denominator, along with a broadly Pentecostal understanding of the work of the Spirit in a movement of such multifarious expressions (and theology).

What some charismatics and evangelicals did not realise was that this teaching had much contemporary conservative scholarship on its side. Some of the accusations that have been (and still are) made about charismatic teaching on the kingdom have at best been theologically ill informed. It is to be noted that 'kingdom teaching' also fitted neatly into traditional evangelical eschatology.

This caused more problems for traditional Pentecostal eschatology. At a popular level, the kingdom of God was thought of as something which would come when the millenium was inaugurated. As a result, the kingdom was not generally thought of as a present reality. Those who had been initiated into the interpretative rites of dispensationalism would have said that the kingdom was postponed because the Jews rejected Jesus or, as a non-Pentecostal preacher put it, the prophetic clock had stopped.[36] Now there were groups of believers, in fact a whole movement, who were operationally Pentecostal yet believed that the kingdom was a present reality and even based their theology of signs and wonders on it.[37]

Not only was there pressure on traditional eschatology from outside the Pentecostal movement. Internal pressure built up as well. The pressure came not from people who wanted to abandon traditional Pentecostal eschatological positions. It came from pastors who had enjoyed church growth, some of whom had been blessed by contact with leaders in the Renewal and Restoration movements. This often

---

[36]   Harry Ironside cited by E.J. Young in *The Prophecy of Daniel: A Commentary* (Philadelphia: Banner of Truth, 1949), 194.
[37]   See A. Walker, *Restoring the Kingdom* (London: Hodder & Stoughton, 1987).

resulted in changes of structure in the local church, with the introduction of cell groups and encouragement of body ministry. It was
hard for such people to believe that God had finished with his church.

In addition to what was happening in Britain, news was continually
filtering through of outpourings of the Spirit in other countries. Paul
Yonggi-Cho, a South Korean Pentecostal, was seeing phenomenal
growth in Seoul. Rheinard Bonnke was witnessing thousands of
conversions as he preached the gospel in Africa. There were promising
signs for Pentecostalism in other countries and those who had seen
them were ready to share them with their brothers and sisters in
Britain. One of them, an American, Ralph Mahoney, preached at the
1979 AOG Conference. His message was one of hope for the church;
the tribulation and the Antichrist did not get a mention.[38]

Undoubtedly, the developments cited above gave many a Pentecostal believer a desire to see the Spirit outpoured in his or her own
church and provided an antidote to some of the depression stemming
from a combination of church life that had grown stale and pessimistic
eschatology. What most people were not conscious of was the
revolutionary theological implications of this kind of thinking.

Along with the charismatic movement, the evangelical church in
general has enjoyed a renaissance over the last three decades. The
growth of Christian literature alone bears eloquent testimony to this.
The evangelical theologian is no longer the academic poor relation.
Evangelicalism has been blessed with godly and able leaders like D.M.
Lloyd-Jones, Francis Schaeffer and John Stott to name but three. Men
like these have helped deliver evangelicalism from the ecclesiastical
ghetto which it seemed doomed to inhabit just before the last war. As
a result, evangelicals can more confidently take their message to their
society. This confidence factor plus a renewed interest in Reformed
theology has dispelled some of the dispensationalist despair. Add to
that the evangelical and charismatic growth in the Anglican Church
and the church does not seem as Laodicean as it did sixty or seventy
years ago.

Pentecostals, as evangelicals, have been affected by the new mood
of optimism. Once again, however, it is Classical Pentecostal eschatology which stands to lose out in this renaissance. This renaissance of
evangelicalism can be seen in the rise of evangelical scholarship. The

---

[38] Kay, *Inside Story*, 349.

younger generation of evangelical scholars is not afraid to challenge secondary tenets of scholarly and popular evangelicalism. Dispensationalism has not escaped scholarly critique and its status as the most valid interpretative approach to Scripture has been damaged. If its popularity continues to decline, then the shape of any movement's or denomination's eschatology which is based on it will be altered. Even the character of premillenialism will be changed if dispensationalism is removed from its foundation.

In some respects, the greatest threat to traditional Pentecostal eschatology came from dispensationalist teachers, both Pentecostal and non-Pentecostal.[39] So-called experts on biblical prophecy often made startling predictions and the study of the prophetic scriptures gave way to unbiblical speculation. This was especially true in the seventies and early eighties. Henry Kissinger, successive popes, and Anwar Sadat were all put forward as possible candidates for the role of Antichrist. The European Community was considered the beast of the Apocalypse. Although no-one ever claimed to know the day or the hour of the Lord's return, some reckoned they knew the year; 1962 was postulated as likely since the planets were to be in line that year (what this has to do with biblical revelation, I do not know) as was 1968. Prophetic teachers sometimes claimed that the Bible was as up to date as today's newspaper, yet some of their expositions were soon as out of date as yesterday's newspaper. This kind of sensationalism did and does great harm to the study of Bible prophecy and eventually produces frustration and disillusionment in those who follow such teaching. This might well explain a dearth of preaching on the Lord's return; the reaction against sensationalism may have been one against Bible prophecy as well.

Social changes must also be taken into account when trying to explain the reasons for the shift in Pentecostal eschatology. As society has become more middle class and better educated, so has Pentecostalism. It might be that the Pentecostal of today is not afraid to challenge the eschatological shibboleths of his or her forefathers. The education system has given the equipment to do just that.

Where does Pentecostalism go from here? Of the major Pentecostal churches in Britain, it seems that only Elim has removed

---

[39] J. McQueen, *Joel and the Spirit: The Cry of a Prophetic Hermeneutic* (Sheffield: Sheffield Academic Press, 1995), 96f.

premillenialism from its formal creed. Whether the other Pentecostal denominations will follow suit remains to be seen. It might be noted that, despite the fact that premillenialism has been retained in the various formal creeds, the working creed of not a few Pentecostals does not appear to reflect that eschatological outlook.

At the same time, it would be wrong to give the impression that Elim pastors have suddenly been converted wholesale to a- or post-millenialism. I do not believe that this is so. Most Elim pastors are still of a premillenial persuasion and not a few adhere to it in its dispensational form. The reason that premillenialism was removed from the Elim fundamental beliefs was not because Elim had suddenly been converted to some other school of prophetic thought, but rather signalled a desire not to make one school of thought a basis of fellowship; in the past, the statement concerning the Lord's coming proved an insurmountable stumbling block to some who wanted to become pastors.

If Pentecostalism wants to embrace a concept of the kingdom that sees it as already present and at the same time wants to adhere to premillenialism, then the theology of someone like the late G.E. Ladd might prove helpful for a recovery of emphasis on the nearness of Christ's return. Most Pentecostals would agree that as the Spirit continues to move amongst the churches, that emphasis will become more and more prominent.

At the outset of this chapter, I stated that I did not believe that it was necessary to jettison the past in order to progress. That would imply that premillenialism in its dispensationalist and classical forms has a place in the Pentecostal theology of the future, and it is intended to imply that. It may well be that the weakness of Pentecostal eschatology lay in its power to control and influence almost every aspect of Pentecostal faith and life. When eschatology is given its proper place within the theology and practice of the Pentecostal community as an encouragement to holiness and a ground of hope for the future, then whatever millenialist shape it takes will matter less. This might mean that the incarnation, crucifixion and resurrection of Christ and the coming of the Holy Spirit would have as formative a role in shaping the Pentecostal worldview as the parousia. This would allow Pentecostals to interpret and understand their role in society from a wider theological perspective without sacrificing their distinctive contributions to eschatology.

Whatever shape Pentecostal eschatology takes in the future, it is vital that it does not become alienated from the contexts in which it spent its formative years, namely the local church and evangelistic outreach. Perhaps it is more crucial than ever to find a positive place for eschatology in evangelistic preaching. We live in a world, especially in the West, which has lost hope. The political and economic visions that promised so much have proved to be the fantasies of a narcotic worldview which presupposed that man was the measure of all things. The task of the Pentecostal preacher and theologian is to articulate Pentecostal eschatology in such a way that it addresses both the great issues that concern the people of our time and the great purposes of the God of eternity. In so doing, our world will hear a message of clear and present danger, but also one of sure and certain hope. And that hope is bound up in the true centre of all eschatology, Jesus Christ.

Chapter Seven

# Healing and Exorcism:
# The Path to Wholeness

Keith Warrington

## Introduction

Classical Pentecostalism has, since its inception, believed in the possibility of divine healing and exorcism as legitimate expressions of the ministry of the church as entrusted to it by Christ and mediated through the power of the Holy Spirit.[1] This belief has rested on Old Testament[2] and New Testament texts[3] and has been reinforced by occurrences of healings and exorcisms throughout the history of Pentecostalism.[4]

The prime motivational force has, however, been the fact that Jesus healed, and the record of the Gospels that he healed all who came to him.[5] Jesus is seen to be the paradigm for the contemporary Christian.

---

[1]  See the Fundamental Beliefs of the Assemblies of God (AOG); the Elim Pentecostal Church (Elim); the Church of God of Prophecy; the New Testament Church of God (NTCG) and The Apostolic Church.

[2]  Exod. 15:26; Ps. 103:2f.; Isa. 53:4f.; Mal. 3:6; W.J. Maybin, 'Divine healing as taught in the Bible', *Elim Evangel* (22 June 1963), 389.

[3]  Matt. 4:23, 8:16f, 10:8; Mark 16:15ff.; Luke 9:1f.; Acts 10:38; Heb. 13:8; James 5:14f.; 1 Peter 2:24.

[4]  E.C.W. Boulton, *George Jeffreys: A Ministry of the Miraculous* (London: Elim, 1928), 180; G. Canty, *The Practice of Pentecost* (Basingstoke: Marshall Pickering, 1987), 2ff.

[5]  G. Canty, *In My Father's House* (London: Marshall, Morgan & Scott, 1969), 83.

This, however, has often been at the expense of other aspects of teaching that Jesus was concerned to present via his healings and exorcisms. Besides recognising the fact that Jesus healed and delivered people from Satanic bondage, it is important to know *why* Jesus healed and *why* the synoptists recorded the accounts.

Various reasons have been offered for the healing and exorcism in the ministry of Jesus. A popular, though inadequate belief as far as the Gospels are concerned, is that Jesus healed people fundamentally because of his compassion for the sick; at the same time, it is assumed that his healing ministry confirmed his deity and Messiahship.[6] The supernatural ministry of Jesus is also assumed to be of evangelistic importance in drawing people to Christ[7] while the concept of a cosmic battle between Jesus and Satan is also rooted, though not exclusively, in the healing and exorcistic ministries of Jesus.[8] At the same time, the supernatural exploits of Jesus are seen to attribute glory to God. However, for many Pentecostals, the most significant aspect of the healing and exorcistic ministry of Jesus is that he is viewed as operating with the same potential through Christians today. As a result of these elements, there has always been a belief that such supernatural phenomena have continued throughout the Christian era to the present.[9]

Consequently, it has generally been understood that divine healing should be part of the ongoing ministry of the church. Jeffreys,[10] the founder of the Elim Pentecostal Church, offered four reasons:

1. Because our Lord who healed in the days of His flesh is declared to be the unchanging one: Heb. 13:8 . . .
2. Because the commission to go and preach and to expect the signs, including healing, to follow, has never been withdrawn: Mark 16:15–18 . . .

---

[6] W. Allen, 'Divine Healing: part 1', *Elim Evangel* (30 July 1966), 488.
[7] H.P. Jeter 'Power: Present to Heal', *Paraclete*, 8.1 (1974), 5.
[8] M. Banks, *Healing Secrets* (Basingstoke: Marshall Pickering, 1986), 38.
[9] J. Richards, 'The Church's Healing Ministry and Charismatic Renewal' in D. Martin and P. Mullen (eds.), *Strange Gifts* (Oxford: Blackwell, 1984), 151ff.
[10] G. Jeffreys, *The Miraculous Foursquare Gospel – Doctrinal* (London: Elim, 1929), 36ff.

3. Because the gift of healing with the other miraculous gifts of the Spirit were set in the church which is still on the earth: 1 Cor. 12:7–11.
4. Because we are instructed how to act in case of sickness: James. 5:14 f.

Carter[11] notes ten aspects of divine healing upon which we [Pentecostals] can all agree:

(a)   That sickness and disease are the outcome of the Fall.
(b)   That sickness and disease in themselves are evil.
(c)   That sickness sometimes comes as a judicial infliction.
(d)   That sickness is not always the result of personal sin.
(e)   That healing was included in God's covenant.
(f)   That healing formed a major part of Christ's ministry.
(g)   That healing was one of the confirmatory signs.
(h)   That gifts of healing were placed within the church.
(i)   That salvation includes healing for the body.
(j)   That healing and faith are closely associated.

Though over thirty-five years have passed since the formulation of the above list, it would still be acceptable to most Pentecostals, though increasingly many would prefer to allow for the *possibility* of healing rather than hold to an unconditionally promised gift of healing for all believers.

There might also be disagreement on some other issues relating to divine healing, such as the general acceptance of the validity of gradual rather than immediate healing.[12] Greenway[13] states that healings 'should always be immediate' and Petts[14] notes 'that there is very little biblical evidence for partial delayed healings . . . and [these] should hardly be considered to be normal'.

---

[11]   J. Carter, 'The Doctrine and Practice of Divine Healing and Deliverance: paper I', a paper presented to the British Pentecostal Fellowship, London, 1960, 1.
[12]   P.S. Brewster, *The Approach to Divine Healing* (London: Elim, n.d.), 8f.; W.G. Hathaway, *The Gifts of the Spirit in the Church* London: Benhill Church Press, 1933), 47.
[13]   H.W. Greenway, *The Person and Work of the Holy Spirit* (London: Elim, n.d.), 10.
[14]   D. Petts 'Mattersey Hotline', *Redemption* (March 1991), 38.

**Healing and Evangelism**

Following the pattern of North American healing movements,[15] Pentecostalism, for many years, experienced healings in the context of large and often evangelistic settings[16] when an individual with a particular gift of healing would minister to those in need of restoration. This relationship between healing and evangelism has always been prominent in Pentecostalism,[17] Gee noting that healings 'have their true sphere in evangelism rather than among the saints',[18] and Petts citing Mark 6:16–20 as evidence for 'divine healing in the context of evangelism'.[19] Wright[20], however claims, 'God sometimes heals the non-Christian, but the promises of healing are to His people'.

Problems were created by these campaigns in that often few lasting conversions were recorded[21] and the costs were high.[22] Consequently, they lessened through the 70s and 80s until they were a rare occurrence in the normal life of British Pentecostal churches, the ministries of Alex Tee and George Canty (Elim) and Melvin Banks (AOG) being notable exceptions.

---

[15] P.G. Chappell, 'Healing Movements', in S.M. Burgess, G.B. McGee and P.H. Alexander (eds.), *The Dictionary of Pentecostal and Charismatic Movements* (Grand Rapids: Zondervan, 1988), 353–374.
[16] P.S. Brewster, *The Spreading Flame of Pentecost* (London: Elim, 1970), 46.
[17] Banks, *Healing Secrets*, 39; J. Partington, 'Miracles Should be the Norm', *Redemption* (April 1991), 5–7.
[18] D. Gee, *Trophimus I Left Sick* (London: Elim, 1952), 9f.; C. Dewet, 'The Missing Element', *Redemption Tidings* (October 1988), 14.
[19] D. Petts, 'You'd Better Believe It', *Redemption* (April 1991), 37; A. Linford, *A Course of Study on Spiritual Gifts* (London: Assemblies of God Publishing House, n.d.), 48.
[20] G. Wright, *Our Quest for Healing* (Cheltenham: Grenehurst Press, 1981), 145.
[21] W.K. Kay, *Inside Story* (Mattersey Hall: Mattersey Hall Publishing, 1990), 341; D. Gee, 'Deliverance is Not Enough', *Elim Evangel* (15 April 1961), 230f.
[22] Circumspectus, 'Looking Around', *Study Hour* (5 December 1949), 224f.

The role of the healing evangelist has largely been replaced by a local church-based practice of prayer by the leadership in the context of corporate prayer for those suffering. Latterly, the charismatic renewal and John Wimber, in particular, have been influential in establishing the context of divine healing as the corporate gathering of Christians where prayer for one another or by a wider group is undertaken, somewhat akin to the pattern of James 5:13–16, though exegesis of this formal healing scenario has been limited.

## Reasons Offered for the Lack of Healing

Pentecostals have always assumed that all sickness is a direct result of sin entering the world, Jeffreys[23] affirming: 'the author of it . . . is Satan'. Coupled with New Testament evidence,[24] this belief leads many Pentecostals to conclude that sickness may be caused by demonic influence, though Barrie cautions: 'it is a great danger to attribute every ailment to the work or possession by evil spirits'.[25]

There is also biblical support for the idea that sickness may be for the purpose of chastisement.[26] Consequently, personal sin has been understood to be a possible reason for a healing not occurring.[27] Nevertheless, Richards[28] cautions against the conclusion 'that if a person is sick he must have sinned'. Similarly Gee,[29] commenting on Trophimus, notes that there is nothing to suggest that he was spiritually or morally in error; thus he advises: 'If no apparent reasons for failure to receive supernatural healing are made clear to the conscience . . .

---

[23] Jeffreys, *Foursquare Gospel*, 31.

[24] Allen, 'Divine Healing: part 2', *Elim Evangel* (27 August 1966), 554; pace G. Canty, 'Do Demons Cause Sickness?' *Elim Evangel* (2 February 1968), 67.

[25] R. Barrie, 'The Discerning of Spirits', *Study Hour* (15 January 1948), 35.

[26] I Cor. 11:30ff.

[27] P.G. Parker (ed.), *First Bible Course* (Elim Bible College Correspondence School, n. d.), 12. 4; E. Maddison, 'Preventative Medicine', *Redemption Tidings* (24 November 1983), 4f.

[28] W.T.H. Richards, *Divine Healing* (Slough: Advance Press, 1968), 22f.

[29] Gee, *Trophimus*, 12f.

we . . . leave the case in the hands of our Heavenly Father . . . without condemnation of ourselves or others'.

Lack of faith on the part of the recipient has also been offered as a valid reason why healing may not occur.[30] This view, however, has increasingly been qualified from pastoral and biblical perspectives.[31] Smith, reflecting on the fact that not all who are prayed for are healed, writes 'some tragic suggestions have been made to explain this situation, the most disgusting of which is that the individual did not have enough faith. Such comment leaves behind it . . . despair'.[32]

The ambiguity, difference of opinion and lack of clarity concerning the faith demanded in order to receive healing have been, and to an extent, still are a major problem in Pentecostal thought and praxis. Emphasis needs to be placed on the fact that at times faith was non-existent prior to the healings by Jesus; sometimes faith was created or given the opportunity to be identified *after* the miracle. Even the identification of the faith commended by Jesus when it was expressed prior to a healing was little more than a readiness on the part of individuals to come to Jesus because they had a need. There is no suggestion that such people knew he would heal or demanded healing. They expressed their faith simply by coming to Jesus; the response was up to him. Whatever his response, they had shown the existence of their faith by coming to him. In so doing, they were making a statement concerning their perception of him. It is important to note that Jesus never encouraged anyone to increase their faith in him; their coming to him in the first place brought forth his commendation.

Other reasons for a lack of healing have been offered. It may result from a prayer for healing not being offered,[33] a fault in the prayer[34] or

[30] J.N. Parr, *Divine Healing* (Stockport: AOG, 1930), 33; A. Murray, 'I am the Lord that Health Thee', *Elim Evangel* (1 October 1966), 627f.; R. Croucher, 'Hard Questions on Healing', *Elim Evangel* (8 March 1986), 5.

[31] R. Barrie, notes that 'the callous method of segregating the unhealed into the unbelieving . . . classes is surely an indication of spiritual pride' ('The Gifts of Healing', *Study Hour* [15 October 1948], 188).

[32] P. Smith, 'A Question of Balance', *Elim Evangel* (23 May 1987), 4.

[33] Wright, *Our Quest*, 158.

[34] G. Cove, *Why Some Are Healed by Christ and Some Are Not* (Coulton: Nelson, n.d.), 89.

the attitude in which the prayer was offered.[35] Persistency[36] has at times been stressed, though this should not be equated with insistence.

The famous example of Paul's thorn in the flesh has been appropriated by differing camps within Pentecostalism who hold to widely differing views of healing. Some link it to physical illness,[37] demons[38] or persecution[39] while an interesting, though older, view assumed that it could not be a paradigm relevant to other believers for Paul's experience with God was on a different level to that of most other Christians.[40]

## Healing and the Will of God

Views on the conditional nature of divine healing have changed within popular Pentecostalism. Many now believe that although God has the power to heal, he does not always choose to do so, and in the case of the latter, it is due to his sovereign will. Similarly, though it is believed that God can heal, the timing is uncertain. These views have also been expressed throughout the history of Pentecostalism.[41] The official Statements of Faith of the Classical Pentecostal denominations

[35] P. Parker, *Divine Healing* (London: Victory Press / Christian Workers' Bible Correspondence School, 1931), 47; A.L. Hoy, 'Healing by the Spirit', *Paraclete* 20.4 (1986), 17.
[36] *ibid.*, 7f.
[37] A. Orfila describes it as an illness ('A Thorn in the Flesh' *Paraclete* 18.1 [1984], 30); P. Parker believes it was a description of an eye disorder, not opposition (*Divine Healing*, 67–72); however, J.N. Parr and K. Gerver reject the possibility that it was a sickness (Parr, *Divine Healing*, 47; Gerver 'Gifts of Healing', *Redemption Tidings*[1 February 1973], 14).
[38] P.R. Angold, 'Paul's Thorn in the Flesh', *Elim Evangel* (9 October 1965), 642.
[39] G. Canty argues that it was a reference to people ('Positively Negative', *Elim Evangel* [27 January, 1962], 52).
[40] Parr, *Divine Healing*, 47; Gerver, 'Gifts of Healing', 14: Angold, 'Paul's thorn', 643.
[41] W.J. Hollenweger, *The Pentecostals* (London: SCM, 1972), 357; D. Gee, *The Pentecostal Movement* (London: Victory Press, 1941), 164; H. Horton, 'More about "Gifts"', *Study Hour* (15 March 1950), 46.

offer the hope and potential of divine healing but refrain from any guarantee of healing.[42]

Hathaway,[43] in the editorial of an issue of the *Elim Evangel* that was dedicated to the topic of divine healing, whilst accepting 'most wholeheartedly that all believers should seek and claim divine healing' concludes: 'it is obvious, both from Scripture and from present day experience, that God does not choose in this dispensation to deliver every child of his from sickness'.

Tee[44] states, 'In the matter of divine healing we must always remember that God is sovereign and can do exactly as he wants.' Similarly, Gee, the foremost writer of the Assemblies of God, notes: 'we have erred by refusing any place in our doctrine or at least a very insufficient place for the sovereign will of God'. He also remarks that 'to ask for Divine healing without any accompanying "nevertheless, not my will but Thine be done" seems to pose an attitude out of keeping with every other right attitude we take in prayer'.[45] Allied to this view is the potential that God may use illness for the benefit of the sufferer. Thus, Orfila[46] asks 'can any of us question God's sovereign right to use an illness, perhaps temporarily, for a higher purpose?'.

An assessment of Pentecostalism would suggest an increasing alliance with the above views.[47] This is the result of a major paradigm shift in theological understanding and a recognition that although the Kingdom has been established by Christ, not all its benefits may be experienced in this life. Experience and a re-examination of biblical principles concerning healing and exorcism have been the major causes of this development. This is a welcome change and shows a marked increase in sensitivity to the issues involved, a

---

[42]   See the revision of the fundamental beliefs of Elim (from 1993 on).

[43]   A. Hathaway, 'The Matter of Healing', *Elim Evangel* (30 March 1963), 194.

[44]   A. Tee 'The Doctrine of Divine Healing' in P.S. Brewster (ed.), *Pentecostal Doctrine* (Cheltenham: Elim/Grenehurst Press, 1976), 198.

[45]   Gee, *Trophimus*, 27f.; Brewster comments 'the Bible has never pronounced healing for all, independent of conditions', noting that some are not healed because 'it is not God's will and plan' (*The Approach*, 19).

[46]   Orfila, 'A Thorn', 32.

[47]   Hollenweger traces this move within the AOG, although he notes that some still cling to the older view (*The Pentecostals*, 358).

reflective humility in the expression of one's beliefs as well as a readiness to acknowledge failures and a maturity in reading and reacting to the biblical text, allowing it to set our agenda of practice and belief and not vice versa.

However, throughout Pentecostalism, there have always been those who state that it is always God's will to heal.[48] Thus, at times, the ministry of healing takes place in a context of claiming or commanding healing; instead of healing being requested, the illness is often addressed and forcibly commanded to go.[49] However, increasingly, there has in Pentecostalism been a move away from an assumption that the will of God is always to heal sickness. More importantly, the determining of God's will in all situations, including sickness, is attracting greater recognition by Pentecostals. While accepting that God does heal today, it is being recognised that he chooses at times not to and that this need not be due to sin or lack of faith on the part of those praying or those needing restoration.

There has been increasing honesty and willingness to express ignorance concerning the reasons why some Christians remain ill after prayer for restoration. Jones[50] comments: 'we have to accept that pain is God's mystery and there are some questions that we cannot give an answer to'. Kingston[51] acknowledges that 'Christ left many unhealed'. Gee[52] reminds his readers that ultimately 'the mystery of sickness is an inevitable part of the life of the Christian'.

The claim of Pentecostals, and others, that God exercises the right to heal through the ministry of the church has often been clouded by those who, on the basis of presumption, faulty teaching or ignorance, claim more than the Bible warrants when they state that God's will is always to heal the sick. Such insistence often leads to confusion, guilt,

---

[48] R. Hicklin, 'Divine Healing', *Redemption Tidings* (18 March 1982), 5; K. Chant, 'Who Said Divine Healing is not for Today?', *Elim Evangel* (1 March 1969), 145; G. Canty, 'Belief or Believing', *Redemption Tidings* (21 July 1983), 10.

[49] M. Banks, *Healing Revolution* (Basingstoke: Marshalls, 1985), 54, 85, 138, 148.

[50] D. Jones, 'A God of Love: A World of Pain', *Redemption* (April 1989), 7; Richards, *Divine Healing*, 22.

[51] C.J.E. Kingston, *Fulness of Power* (Victory Press: Clapham, 1939), 45; Linford, *A Course*, 49.

[52] *Trophimus*, 29f.

despair and, worst of all, an imperfect perception of God who appears arbitrary and unfeeling in his dealings with his people, especially when healing does not occur.[53] However, reluctance to abandon the belief that it is God's will to heal the sick still causes some tensions in Pentecostal belief and practice. Many would therefore still follow the suggestion of Hacking[54] that 'unless and until the Lord makes it very plain to you that healing is not for you, lay claim tenaciously to the word of promise'.

Similarly, death has been infrequently viewed positively as an entrance into the presence of God. Although this perspective has seen change,[55] the crucial need for an articulated Pentecostal theology of suffering is still awaited.[56] Within Pentecostalism, the developing role of the gift of teaching and the increasing recognition of its importance to the stability and edification of the church is helping to inform and instruct believers in a more biblical perspective. The more Pentecostalism concentrates its focus on God and his will, the more fruitful will be its ability to minister to those in need of restoration, though that ministry may and should take the form of support in, as well as salvation from, the situation.

## Divine Healing and Medicine

Mainstream Pentecostalism tends not to contrast medical healing and divine healing, nor is the former viewed suspiciously or negatively.[57] Instead, it has generally been assumed that divine healing and medicine should not be confused[58] and that divine healing is not 'a substitute

---

[53]   Canty, G. *In My Father's House* (London: Marshall, Morgan & Scott, 1969), 86f.

[54]   W. Hacking, 'Questions on Divine Healing', *Redemption Tidings* (14 May 1981), 10.

[55]   Tee, 'Divine Healing', 207; Cove, *Why Some Are Healed*, 106ff.

[56]   P. Smith, 'Suffering: God's Teacher', *Elim Evangel* (November 1986), 7; K. Munday, 'A Ministry to the Unhealed', *Redemption Tidings* (March 1988), 5f.

[57]   Brewster, *The Approach*, 10; G.W. Gilpin, 'The Place of the Pentecostal Movements Today', in P.S. Brewster (ed.), *Pentecostal Doctrine*, 116.

[58]   H.W. Greenway, *The Person*, 10; H. Carter, *The Gifts of the Spirit* (London: Defoe, 1946), 92.

for obedience to the rules of physical and mental health' or 'a means of avoiding the effects of old age'.[59] There has been a tradition that would advocate an anti-medical stance,[60] though this view has receded in recent decades. Instead, it has been recognised that medical healing may be understood as having a divine orientation, and that all healings have divine origin, and therefore recourse to medication is appropriate for the Christian.[61] Dialogue and integration with medical practices have not yet been adequately developed within Pentecostalism, though there have been limited moves in this direction.

## New Testament Issues in Healing

Methodologies and practices involved in healing and exorcism vary within Pentecostalism.[62] A survey of the key aspects of the advice offered by James 5:14–16 may serve as a useful starting point for comment on Pentecostal healing praxis, after which other issues not referred to by James will be addressed.

The healing anticipated by James probably refers more to forms of weakness than to sickness or disease. Indeed, the Greek terms used to identify the weakness concerned and the anticipated restoration may be translated in a way that encompasses many conditions of weakness, including physical illness but also other problems that need to be resolved.[63]

### The Role of the Elders

Although Pentecostals recognise the significance of the role of the elders (and other leaders) in ministering to those desiring prayer for illness,[64] such ministry has developed within the body of the local church over the past two decades. Nevertheless, it has been understood that it is the responsibility of the one suffering to call for the

---

59   AOG, 'Our Position on Divine Healing', *Paraclete* 9.2 (1975), 10.
60   Parr, *Divine Healing*, 38ff.; H. Carter, 'The Supernatural Aspect of All the Gifts', *Study Hour* (13 September 1941), 2.
61   R. Baldwin, 'Health and Healing', *Redemption* (August 1990), 37.
62   Gee, *The Pentecostal Movement*, 163; Tee 'Divine Healing', 202.
63   K. Warrington, 'James 5:13–18', *EPTA Bulletin* 8.4 (1989), 160–177.
64   Parker, *Divine Healing*, 6.

elders.[65] The significance of the elders to James is probably twofold. Firstly, as the leaders, they represented the fellowship whenever they visited any of the believers who were absent due to weakness or sickness. As leaders, they were also the most appropriate people, though not the only ones, to pray for those who were suffering. Their position of leadership presupposes that they were people who would more likely know the mind of God in a given situation and pray accordingly.

### Anointing with Oil

Based on Mark 6:13 and James 5:14, anointing with oil has retained its place in the context of prayer for the sick in Pentecostal practice,[66] though in recent years it has increasingly been omitted, probably because of an ignorance of the symbolism of oil in a first century culture and in a Jewish context.

Oil is understood by most Pentecostals as symbolising only the Holy Spirit,[67] and since his presence is evidenced by the action of prayer for the sick, the symbol to remind people of this is deemed unnecessary. Parker[68] thus notes that the oil is not essential for it is 'to show that the healing is of the Holy Spirit'. Pentecostals have traditionally used oil, generally sparingly applied to the forehead[69] but (along with many other evangelical Christians) have failed to appreciate its Jewish cultural and biblical significance.

Oil was used medicinally in the Greco-Roman world[70] and we also find mention of such use in the Old Testament[71] and in Rabbinic literature.[72] However in James 5:14, the use of oil is not linked to any

---

65   Parker (ed.), *Bible Course*, 12.4.
66   R.E. Darragh, *In Defence of His Word* (London: Elim, 1932).
67   Brewster, *The Approach*, 16; Tee 'Divine Healing', 202.
68   Parker (ed.), *Bible Course*, 5; similarly, M. Banks, *Divine Health is for You* (private publication, n.d.), 12.
69   Banks, *Healing Secrets*, 87.
70   Hippocrates recommends the use of oil for wounds in 'On Joints' (63) and 'On Fractures' (24) (see H. Kuhlewein [ed.] *Hippocrates Opera* [Leipzig, 1894–1902], 2.63, 81). Its use is also referred to by Josephus, Philo and Pliny.
71   2 Chron. 28:15; Isa. 1:6; Jer. 8:22.
72   To anoint a sore (b. *Shab.* 53b, *Yoma* 77b); to heal toothache (b. *Gittin* 69a); to heal skin diseases (Mid. *Gen.* 85.1).

specific ailments. Moreover, the term 'astheneo' is more appropriately and accurately translated as 'weakness',[73] rather than sickness. This suggests that James does not regard this anointing as medicinal.

In fact to Jews, oil symbolised a number of characteristics that may have influenced and encouraged the one who was to be anointed.[74] This is particularly important given the fact that the addressees of the letter from James were, in the main, Jewish Christians. Oil indicated the presence of the Spirit and was also used to signify an infusion of the deity in whose name the person was anointed.[75] This sometimes involved participation in the strength[76] or wisdom[77] of God, and would have formed a clear reminder to the Christian sufferer of his/her privileged position in the church.

Anointing was also linked with restoration and strength.[78] It occurred when a person had been healed of leprosy, confirming the purification[79] on the basis of which they were welcomed back into society again. On other occasions, oil was used to demonstrate that a new situation had come into being. Examples of this include the completion of a marriage or a business contract and the confirmation that a slave had been legitimately emancipated.[80] This aspect would have been most encouraging to a sufferer about to be anointed, for it would articulate a hope that the suffering would soon be over. Anointing was also linked with joy,[81] while abstention from oil

---

[73]   K. Warrington, 'An Exegesis of James 5:13–18' (unpubl. MPhil, London Bible College, 1991), 38–45.

[74]   M. Meinertz, 'Die Krankensalbung Jak. 5:14f,' *Biblische Zeitschrift* 20 (1937), 24.

[75]   1 Sam. 10:1, 6; 16:13; Isa. 61:1; Acts 10:38; 2 Cor. 1:21f.; So Z. Weisman, 'Anointing as a Motif in the Making of the Charismatic Kings', *Biblica*, 57 (1976), 387–398, esp. 395ff.; M. Alberton, 'Un Sacrement pour les Malades dans le Contexte Actuel de la Santé', *Etudes Théologiques et Réligieuses*, 54 (1979), 107.

[76]   Ps. 88 (89):21–25.

[77]   Isa. 11:1–4; 1 John. 2:20, 27.

[78]   G.R. Carlson, 'Anointing with Oil', *Paraclete* 3.2 (1969), 16.

[79]   Lev. 14:12, 16.

[80]   T.N.D. Mettinger, *King and Messiah* (Lund: Liberlaromedal, 1976), 216–222.

[81]   Ps. 44(45):7; Eccles. 9:7f.; Isa. 61:3; Heb. 1:9; *mashach* (mentioned 39 times in the O.T.) means 'anointed with oil' and because of its association with the 'Messiah' was linked with great joy.

signified a time of mourning.[82] James thus includes a symbol of joy in a prayer for one who is suffering. Although this appears initially to be incongruous, it is clarified by the expectation of restoration that he offers.

Anointing with oil was linked with the granting of eternal life,[83] with prosperity,[84] with friendship and love,[85] with goodness and purity[86] and was understood to be a gift of God.[87] Clearly, such features may have aroused hope within the person receiving prayer.

Anointing with oil was also associated with the bestowal of honour.[88] Oil was regarded as precious and therefore the one who was anointed was often regarded as superior to others.[89]

Oil was also used as part of religious formulae by the Jews and by pagan cults,[90] anointing with oil marking a separation by God of kings and prophets,[91] priests,[92] and objects[93] for his service.[94] Not only does this imply the importance to God of that which has been anointed, but it also suggests the idea that God will care for them.[95] Such a thought would be highly encouraging to a sufferer.[96]

If the anointing procedure and the use of oil communicated even only some of these implications to the sufferer, it is clear why James

---

82   1 Sam. 12:20; 14:2; Isa. 61:3; Dan. 10:2f.

83   2 Enoch 22:8ff. See also B. Reicke, 'L'Onction de Malades d'après Saint Jacques' *La Maison Dieu*, 113 (1973), 54f.

84   Deut. 33:24.

85   Ps. 22(23):5; 132 (133):1f.; Luke 7:46; John 11:2.

86   Philo, *Gen.* 2.42; 4.1; *Exod.* 2.33, 103.

87   Jer. 31:12; Joel 2:18; 3 Bar. 15:1.

88   Matt. 26:7; Luke 7:46; John 11:2; 12:3.

89   Mid. *Ex.* 48:1; *Lev.* 3:6, 26:9; *Num.* 6:1, 18:9.

90   W.A. Jayne, *The Healing Gods of Ancient Civilisations* (New York: University Books, 1962), 230f., 240ff.

91   Judg. 9:15; 1 Sam. 10:1; 16:1; 1 Kgs. 19:16.

92   Exod. 28:41; 30:30; Lev. 8:12.

93   *Wars* 5. 565; b. *Shebu* 15a, 16b.

94   1 Sam. 10:1; 16:13; 2 Sam. 12:7.

95   1 Sam. 24:8ff.; 2 Sam. 12:7; Ps. 83 (84):9; 104 (105):15; Mettinger (*King*, 222).

96   See F. Vouga, 'Jc. 5:13–18: Prière et Onction des Malades' *Bulletin du Centre Protestant d'Etudes*, 30 (1978), 44.

sought to include it in his advice to the early Christian community.[97] The significance of anointing with oil is therefore primarily symbolic,[98] reminding sufferers that they can feel secure in the presence of friends who care and a God who restores.

## The Laying on of Hands

The laying on of hands is a significant feature of Pentecostal praxis,[99] Dinsdale[100] describing it as a 'central doctrine'. In healing situations it has generally involved a desire to lay hands on the head of, or towards, the one for whom prayer is offered.[101] Although traditionally the practice has been carried out only by the minister, it has now been recognised as the privilege of others also in the congregation.

Sacramental tendencies have been generally deemed to be inappropriate in this context.[102] It is recognised that the act itself has no supernatural value unless it is combined with faith.[103] Rather, it has been regarded more as 'an act of sympathy and compassion rather than a formal rite',[104] a symbolic act,[105] and the opportunity for God's power to be manifested.[106]

Some of those who have laid hands on the sick have claimed to have felt physical manifestations (shaking, tingling, heat). It has been suggested that these manifestations are proof of divine activity, though this, of course, does not always follow.

---

[97]   W.J. Sneck, *Charismatic Spiritual Gifts: A Phenomenological Analysis* (Washington: University Press of America, 1981), 55f.
[98]   G. Shogren, 'Will God heal us?', *Evangelical Quarterly*, 61:2 (1989), 105f.
[99]   P.S. Brewster, 'The Stigma of the Supernatural', *Elim Evangel* (24 February 1962), 116.
[100]   E. Dinsdale, 'Ointment', *Study Hour*, (15 March 1949), 59f.
[101]   Darragh, *In Defence*, 18ff.
[102]   Allen, 'Divine Healing', (30 July 1966), 489.
[103]   Dinsdale, 'Ointment', 62; Banks, *Healing Secrets*, 70.
[104]   C.E. Kingston, 'Laying on of hands,' *Elim Evangel*, (23 July 1966), 473.
[105]   Tee, 'Divine Healing', 202.
[106]   Brewster, *The Approach*, 15.

### The Role of Faith

Whether faith is to be exerted by the sufferer, the one who is praying or by both of them is a vexed issue. Kingston[107] believed that 'the emphasis on faith bears rather on the one who lays hands on than on the sick person'. However, Evans[108] states that 'usually, this is the faith of the person healed'. Banks[109] argues that 'healing can be helped by the faith of those around us'. This difference of opinion mirrors the varied perspectives among Pentecostals.

Some have assumed that before God can heal them, they have to believe that he *will* heal them. Anything less than this total confidence is deemed to result in rejection by God as far as receiving healing is concerned.[110] The official view of the AOG is against this perception and the vast majority of Pentecostals would concur.[111] However, this aspect needs careful attention as the issue of faith has been and still is a confusing issue to many, not least because of the variety of opinions reflected above.

Those who have not been healed are deemed, by some, not to have enough faith and those who are healed are assumed to have passed the faith threshold, whether they be believers or not.[112] Although such views, in which the role of faith is of paramount importance in receiving restoration, are still held by some Pentecostals, other views have increasingly been presented which stress the importance of faith being located in the context of a relationship with God,[113] that is, exercised as an expression of obedience to God.[114]

---

[107] Kingston, 'Laying', 473.
[108] F.G. Evans, 'Divine Healing', *Elim Evangel* (3 February 1968), 69.
[109] Banks, *Healing Secrets*, 118.
[110] *ibid.*, 3, 6ff.; Banks (*Healing Secrets*, 66) states that faith is 'a total and deep seated surrender to God in the trust that his will is for your healing and restoration'.
[111] AOG, 'Our position', 11.
[112] Tee, however, argues that 'it is not more faith we need, but correct faith', identifying the latter as being a gift of faith from God that God will heal. ('Why are?' 200f.).
[113] D. Cartledge, 'Faith Confusion', *Redemption Tidings* (26 January 1984) 4.
[114] M. Banks, '5 Keys to a Miracle Ministry', *Redemption Tidings* (28 March 1985), 5.

It is true that faith sometimes figures in the healing ministry of Christ. However, it is significant to note the occasions when people were healed in the New Testament when no mention of faith on the part of the sufferer was sought or even mentioned.[115] No one *claimed* their healing from him; they asked for healing on the basis of a belief that he was empowered to heal.

Mark 6:5ff. is a key text in the debate over the significance of belief in the context of healing. Hathaway,[116] commenting on it, mistakenly believes 'if lack of faith could bind the hands of the Master himself, then no small wonder if it binds the hands of His servants', concluding that 'gifts of healing . . . still depend largely on personal faith'. However, rather than the passage being understood as showing that unbelief a blocks the activities of the omnipotent Son of God, it is better interpreted as a sovereign decision on his part not to so minister to them because they rejected his person, message and mission.

The absence of faith in Jesus is to be understood in the context of their desire to destroy him. This was not an uncertainty as to whether he would heal or some doubt as to whether he could heal. This was blatant rejection of him in his entirety; it is not to be used as a proof-text for the need of faith in contemporary healing scenarios. Their lack of willingness to believe in Jesus proved that they were not ready for entrance into the Kingdom of God; to perform miracles there would thus place the people of Nazareth in a state of greater condemnation for it would accentuate their guilt in rejecting Jesus. Such was the lot of Chorazin, Bethsaida and Capernaum.[117]

The statement that a mustard seed of faith is all that is necessary to move a mountain is another major impediment to any attempt, however sincere, to harness more and more 'faith' until God has little alternative but to grant healing. Jesus never rebuked those who came to him, though at times the disciples did, for in coming they were already expressing faith in him. The account of the man with the demonised son[118] records the man as having faith in Jesus. His request

---

[115] Matt. 8:14, 28ff; Luke 7:1 1ff.; 9:37ff.; 22:50f.; Jn. 11:2ff. On occasions, the faith on the part of the sufferer was no more than a belief that Jesus could help them, rather than a certainty that he would do so (Matt. 8:5ff.; 9:27ff.; Mark 1:40ff.; 10:46ff.).

[116] Hathaway, *The Gifts*, 47.

[117] Matt. 11:20–24; Luke 10:13–15.

[118] Matt. 17:14–18; Luke 9:37–43; Mark 9:17–27.

to Jesus, 'help my unbelief', may be an honest assumption that his
faith is inadequate, but given that Jesus does not accede to his request
either by giving him a homily on faith or commending his confession,
it may reflect a misunderstanding on the man's part. His question is a
contradiction in terms: he expresses belief and then requests that Jesus
help his unbelief. These are the words of a desperate man whose sense
of logic has deserted him. In reality, the standard of faith he anticipates
that Jesus demands has already been achieved in his coming to Jesus
in the first place. The proof of this is that the exorcism is achieved.

## Prayer

Prayer has always been recognised as having a fundamental role in
ministry to those who are suffering.[119] Fasting has also been advocated
by some.[120] Prayer is best understood as an opportunity to identify
God's will rather than to persuade God to carry out our will.

The term 'prayer of faith' is only used once in the New Testament
(James 5:15) though the connection between faith and prayer is
referred to elsewhere. This aspect of divine healing has probably been,
and still is, the cause of greatest confusion amongst Pentecostals today
and clarification is often lacking in popular preaching and writing.[121]

James 5:15 clearly expects the prayer of faith to succeed and regards
the faith referred to as integral to the request being granted, as a result
of which it may be stated that 'it is the prayer of faith . . . which
guarantees healing'.[122] The faith that has already been mentioned in
James 1:6 and 2:23 is trust in God's promise, on the basis of which
one can pray expecting a positive response. It is in this way that faith
in chapter 5:15 is most appropriately interpreted. Cooper defines it as
'asking for that which God has already told me that He *will* give me
. . . Faith isn't blind . . . It is . . . listening for a promise . . . and then
waiting for its fulfilment'.[123]

Parker[124] acknowledges that 'such faith is only possible . . . by the
direct gift of God . . . Divine healing is all a matter of specific leading

---

[119]　Banks, *Divine Healing*, 9.

[120]　*ibid.*, 10; J. Smith, 'Divine Healing', *Elim Evangel* (24 November 1962),
746.

[121]　Carter, *The Gifts*, 74.

[122]　Parker (ed.), *Bible Course*, 12.4.

[123]　Cooper, 'The Nature', 9.

[124]　Parker (ed.), *Bible Course*, 5.

in specific cases'. This is a stronger view than that of Petts who deduces that the prayer of faith is 'a prayer that commits the sick one to God knowing that His will is best and that He can be trusted to "raise up" the sick whether it be immediately by a miracle of healing or ultimately at the Parousia'.[125] Cognisance of the necessity of knowing the will of God in prayer may therefore be presupposed by James in the context of 5:15.[126] Of course, there is a difference of opinion within Pentecostalism as to whether divine healing is an unconditional promise or not, as will be illustrated later. However, the normative understanding is that as a result of Christ's mission, healing may be available for the believer, though in each case this is to be in the context of the overarching will of God.

The prayer of faith is not to be understood as a presumptuous assertion that God always responds by granting the request. Nor is it only a statement of belief that God can provide restoration, or merely to be equated with a desire to be restored on the part of the sufferer or those involved in offering support. Rather, because of its complete and guaranteed success rate, it is to be understood as a dynamic belief derived from God.[127] The faith required is itself given as a gift by God.[128] The trust is best experienced and the obedience most clearly practised if the will of God in the particular situation is determined.

A number of principles and implications may be drawn from James' concept of faith in relationship to prayer:

1. Only the prayer that is offered in the will of God may be appropriately termed 'the prayer of faith'.
2. Consequently, before the prayer is offered, an attempt should be made to ascertain the will of God in order to pray most appropriately (1:6).
3. The elders (v.14) and/or righteous believers may be best able to offer such a prayer because of their experience, wisdom and righteous lifestyles. Here, righteousness is not being thought of in Pauline terms, but rather as James (and Jews) would interpret it. James' understanding of righteousness stresses the relational aspects of life and the conduct of the individual in the community and before God. Those who

---

[125]   D. Petts, *Healing and the Atonement* (unpubl. PhD thesis, University of Nottingham, 1993), 185.
[126]   Woodford, *The Doctrine*, 6.
[127]   P. Newberry, 'Faith', *Redemption Tidings* (21 July 1983), 4.
[128]   Carter, *The Gifts*, 76f.; Tee interprets Mark 11:22 as 'have the faith which God gives'. ('Divine Healing', 206).

exhibit a godly lifestyle may be deemed righteous. Such believers are the most appropriate ones to pray for those who are suffering as they are more likely to be aware of the mind of God in particular situations.

4. Thus, the prayer of faith may be identified as a prayer that engages the members of the church in a process that seeks to identify and effect the will of God in the life of the suffering member. Such a prayer is able to be offered by one who has taken time to tap God's resource of wisdom and appropriate it to a particular situation. Only this prayer can provide the comprehensive guarantee of restoration promised by James.

## The Gift of Faith

The Pauline gift of faith, which is different to the faith involved in trusting Christ for salvation,[129] and to the fruit of the Spirit,[130] is to be understood as a supernatural gift of the Spirit which allows a person to be confident that a prayer offered or an act discharged is in keeping with God's will and will therefore be successful.[131] It is strongly related to the prayer of faith. With regard to praying for the sick, it is sometimes the case that in the absence of an unconditional guarantee of healing for a believer, those praying may feel confident that a prayer for healing will result in restoration. This supernatural burst of confidence or faith is to be identified as a gift of faith, the restoration confirming this analysis. However, this is very different to presumption or to any attempted manipulation of God.[132] One may not exercise this gift indiscriminately or mechanically for it is sovereignly initiated by the Spirit; thus, it cannot be manufactured or stimulated or encouraged.[133]

---

[129] R.M. Pruitt, *Fundamentals of the Faith* (Cleveland: White Wing, 1981), 317; Kingston, *Fulness*, 33ff.
[130] Kingston, *Fulness*, 36.
[131] Linford, *A Course*, 55.
[132] Greenway notes that when given 'to the believer he has a perception of God's purposes that brings complete certitude – he knows . . . becoming conscious of what God was going to do' (*The Person*, 118).
[133] Hathaway, *The Gifts*, 33, 35; Tee, 'Divine Healing', 208; Canty, *The Practice*, 172.

### The Use of the Name of the Lord

One of the clearest emphases in Pentecostal prayer is the use of the name of the Lord. The incorporation of the name in prayer is part of Pentecostal practice,[134] though the reason for this on the part of many may be more received practice than an understanding of its biblical basis.[135] Jeffreys[136] states: 'The servant may lay hands upon the suffering, but it can only be efficacious when done in the name of the Lord' though he does not clarify or explain this comment. The clearest derivation of the practice is from the apostolic use of the name of Jesus in prayer as recorded in the Acts of Apostles.[137] Promises by Jesus to his disciples concerning the efficacy of his name[138] also form a fertile environment for a belief in the importance of the regular articulation of his name. James 5:14 specifically comments on the fact that prayer should be offered 'in the name of the Lord' for someone in need of restoration.

However, it is not the incorporation of the phrase that is most important but the reason for its inclusion. To pray in his name means to pray in accordance with his will. The name of the Lord is therefore appropriately used when the prayer incorporating it is sanctioned or commissioned by God,[139] for then it will effect a change. Claiming healing 'in the name of the Lord' is to be equated with presumption unless God has specifically assured the one concerned that such a claim is valid and in accordance with his will, as a result of which, he can sanction the use of his name in the proposal.

In the context of prayer, the activation of that authority is based on adherence to the will of God.[140] The use of the name in Jesus' guidance concerning prayer[141] is to be understood as revealing the

---

134  Darragh, *In Defence*, 38, 70; Banks, *Healing Revolution*, 54ff.
135  Willis, 'Faith in His Name', *Elim Evangel* (4 July 1964), 429f.
136  Jeffreys, *Foursquare Gospel*, 8.
137  Acts 3:6, 16; 4:10; 9:34.
138  John 14:13f.; 16:24.
139  Exod. 5:22f.; Deut. 18:18f.
140  Tee, 'Divine Healing', 203; K. Warrington, 'The Use of the Name [of Jesus], in Healing and Exorcism', SPS/EPCRA Conference Papers, Mattersey (1995).
141  John 14:13f.; 15:16; 16:24, 26.

importance of the will of God in prayer.[142] 'His name is the revelation of his character and nature. We have that in us only if we abide in Christ and his words abide in us . . . then our will lines up with his, and we can ask what we will and it shall be done.'[143]

That is not to suggest that the name of the Lord may only be appropriately used in a prayer for restoration when the outcome of that prayer is known beforehand. The name of the Lord may be incorporated in a prayer for restoration when it is recognised that it is the Lord and he alone who has the final authority to answer the prayer in the way that he wishes. The use of the name by the petitioner is a helpful reminder of that fact.

### The Relationship of Sin to Suffering

Sickness, via sin, has always been traced back to Satan[144] and various texts have been provided to substantiate this view.[145] Although, on occasions the link between sin and illness/weakness is clear,[146] and sometimes possible,[147] it is untrue to suggest that any particular illness is always linked to individual sin.[148] Such logic would imply that some congenital illnesses are a result of sin in the womb, while healthy people could be deemed to be higher on the scale of perfection.

James does not necessarily associate the sins that need forgiveness (5:15b) with the suffering (5:15a), in the sense that the former have caused the latter. There may be a relationship but it is by no means certain or essential.

Such sins are to be confessed within the context of the community, as a result of which, prayer is offered and restoration (either physical healing or reconciliation) is effected.

---

142   1 John 5:14f.
143   AOG, 'Our Position.'
144   Jeffreys, *Healing Rays* (London: Elim, 1932), 38–42; Jeffreys, *Foursquare Gospel*, 28–34.
145   Job 2:7; Luke 11:20ff., 13:11ff.; Acts 10:38.
146   Jeffreys, *Foursquare Gospel*, 96; Tee, 'Divine Healing', 203.
147   Matt. 9:1ff.; Luke 11:20ff.; 13:11ff.; Acts 10:38.
148   Pruitt, *Fundamentals*, 317; Jeffreys, *Healing Rays*, 150ff.

## The Atonement of Christ

The atonement is recognised as a crucial element in divine healing by many Pentecostals, though this too is being re-analysed.[149] A major debate relates to the substitutionary element of the atonement. Carter[150] argued that on the cross, Jesus 'bore our sicknesses substitutionarily . . . it is not sympathy but substitution'. However, more recently, Petts[151] has concluded that no texts 'when correctly exegeted, support the doctrine . . . of Christ's bearing our sicknesses substitutionarily'. The latter more accurately reflects contemporary Pentecostal thought.

However, others have preferred to teach that bodily healing has been included in the atonement. Matthew 8:17 is a key text in the discussion of healing and its place in the atonement, although few Pentecostals have interacted with the text in a lucid way. Petts understands the verse to be part of 'Matthew's overall emphasis on Jesus as the fulfilment of Old Testament hopes and ideals . . . manifested . . . in the healing of all who are sick'.[152]

One of the other main texts used to support the link between healing and the atonement is 1 Peter 2:24. Of this, Petts notes that 'when correctly exegeted, it cannot reasonably be understood to teach the doctrine that healing is in the Atonement',[153] stating: 'It was because of man's *sin* that atonement . . . was necessary. No atonement was needed for sickness. Sickness is not a misdemeanour which attracts a penalty.'[154] One may argue against a doctrine of unconditional healing in the atonement on the basis of 2 Corinthians 12:7, Galatians

---

149   Fundamental Beliefs of the AOG and the NTCG.

150   Carter, *The Doctrine*, 3.

151   D. Petts, 'Healing and the Atonement' (unpubl. PhD thesis, University of Nottingham, 1993), 288.

152   *ibid.*, 128; see also pages 31–70 for a survey of developments within Pentecostalism concerning the relationship between healing and the atonement of Christ.

153   *ibid.*, 192.

154   *ibid.*, 282; similarly, L.F.W. Woodford believes: 'Sickness and disease did not require atonement . . . they required removal . . . He did not atone for sickness and disease: He conquered them as elements present in a world of corruption' (*Divine Healing and the Atonement: A Restatement* [London: Victoria Institute, 1956], 53).

4:13 and especially Philippians 2:17, 1 Timothy 5:23 and 2 Timothy 4:20.

Although some claim that Christ's death guarantees restoration to physical and mental wholeness before the final resurrection, the standard Pentecostal belief is that although we can claim deliverance from *some* of the impact of sin in our lives, 'we have to wait until some future time before the full benefits of the atoning and redeeming work of Christ on the cross can be realised'.[155] Thus, for most Pentecostals, healing is understood as being an indirect result of the atonement though not necessarily realised in this life.[156]

## Gifts of Healings

These are mentioned in 1 Corinthians 12:9, 28, 30 as an example of the manifestations of the Spirit in the church. Martin[157] defines this as 'a specific gift, possessed by some . . . which provides for healing both within and outside of the community'. The plural form, 'gifts of healings' is generally taken to indicate the potential for healing varied forms of sickness[158] though it may be preferable to understand the term to refer to 'every individual manifestation of healing' as being 'a grace gift'.[159]

The gifts of healing are most appropriately offered in conjunction with the gift of faith, the former depending on the latter for success.

---

[155]   Jeffreys, *Healing Rays*, 37f.; Petts, 'Healing', 293–309.
[156]   Parker, *Divine Healing*, 31; Wright, *Our Quest*, 62f.; Petts provides a careful treatment of the topic, concluding that healing is 'ultimately and indirectly in the atonement'. However, he disallows mechanical healing resulting automatically as a consequence of the atonement, whilst still accepting that healing is ultimately available at the parousia, though it is also possible 'through the work of the Spirit who is given on the basis of Christ's atoning work and who in turn bestows gifts of healing'. ('Healing', 357f.).
[157]   R.F. Martin, 'Gifts of Healing' in Burgess, et al. (eds.), *Dictionary*, 352.
[158]   Pruitt, *Fundamentals*, 317.
[159]   L.F.W. Woodford, 'The Doctrine and Practice of Divine Healing and Deliverance: paper 2', a paper presented to the British Pentecostal Fellowship, London, 1960, 6; Canty, *The Practice*, 180; Kingston combines both options, noting 'The double use of the plural nouns seems to point to the different classes of sicknesses to be healed and the fact that each healing is a particular gift from God' (*Fulness*, 43).

Woodford[160] noted that 'each manifestation of healing through this ministry is conditioned by the will of God'. Those who minister as a result of a gift of healing do not 'carry healing power with them wherever they go providing healings "on tap" '.[161]

## Exorcism

Pentecostalism accepts the existence of a personal devil and influential demons though neither this nor the practice of exorcism is mentioned in the various statements of fundamental beliefs. Similarly, writings concerning the impact of Satan on the world are not readily available from recent Pentecostal authors. Pentecostal beliefs on demonology have largely been generated by popular preaching and a historical context in which the belief in demons has developed through people who have ministered in, or been delivered from, demonised situations. Fundamentally, however, there is a belief that casting out demons is part of the gospel commission,[162] which gives this authority to Christians.[163]

In general, the impact of Satan upon Christians and non-Christians has been assumed to take the form of demonic activity, popularly subsumed under two categories, possession and oppression.[164] These terms have, at times, been unhelpful and do not reflect biblical terminology, which prefers the broader concept of demonisation.

For many Pentecostals, and other evangelical believers, their view of demons owes as much to medieval art and popular fiction[165] as it

---

160  L.F.W. Woodford, 'The Doctrine', 6.
161  Tee, 'Divine Healing', 207; similarly, D. Gee, *Concerning Spiritual Gifts* (Springfield: Gospel Publishing House, 1938), 37; Greenway states 'there are no indications that . . . members of the early churches . . . went around healing everybody . . . or . . . all that were sick within the Church. Then, as now, there were *some* healings' (*The Person*, 181).
162  Matt. 10:8; Mark 16:15–20; Luke 9:1, 2; 10:1, 17; Acts 10:38.
163  P. Stormont, 'Authority', *Elim Evangel* (18 November 1961), 723.
164  L.G. McClung, Jr., 'Exorcism,' in Burgess, et al. (eds.), *Dictionary*, 292; V. Cunningham, 'Can a Christian have a Demon?', *Redemption Tidings* (15 November 1973), 3; Elim Committee on Demon Possession Report (1976), 2.
165  F. Peretti, *This Present Darkness* (Eastbourne: Minstrel, 1989).

does to the New Testament. Visual experiences and phenomena[166] attending exorcisms or demonised activity have often been the catalyst for beliefs concerning demons, rather than the veiled descriptions of the New Testament.

Nevertheless, Barrie confirms that 'there is a definite doctrine of demonology taught in Scripture'[167] and Richards[168] defines demons, with New Testament evidence as being 'real', 'unclean', 'hostile' and 'powerful'. Cunningham[169] writes that the New Testament never ascribes the causes of sin in Christians to demons nor is the remedy for sin in the Christian's life the casting out of a demon.

The lack of biblical parameters for much that is written makes the exercise subjective and, at times, suspect, leaving a trail of speculation and confusion for the readers. Gilpin[170] notes the rarity of exorcisms in the New Testament and suggests they may have been particularly 'associated with the earthly ministry of our Lord and interpreted as an outburst of demoniacal opposition to the work of Jesus'. The purposes of exorcisms are varied, though Richards cautions, Jesus 'did not seek to cast the devils out of everyone who was controlled by them . . . but when He was confronted with demon power then Jesus dealt with it'.[171] This feature is also reflected in the reluctance of Paul to deal with a demon, recorded in Acts 16:17.

Hollenweger describes the issue of demonology as 'an unsolved problem in Pentecostal belief and practice'.[172] There has been a maturing process taking place over the past decade and although there is some variation in belief within Pentecostalism, a number of constants remain:

---

[166]    J. Edwards, 'Delivered from Evil', *Redemption Tidings* (February 1990), 13f.

[167]    Barrie, 'The Discerning of Spirits', 14.

[168]    W.T.H. Richards, 'Demon Possession', *Redemption Tidings* (11 October 1973), 11ff.

[169]    V. Cunningham, 'Demons or the Old Nature?' *Redemption Tidings* (22 November 1973), 3; Richards writes: 'Many are ascribing every fault, mistake, sickness etc. to the work of demons . . . they fail to see the difference between "works of the flesh" and "evil spirits" ' ('Demon possession', 10).

[170]    G.W. Gilpin, 'Demon Possession' (1975), 1f.

[171]    Richards, 'Demon Possession', 13.

[172]    Hollenweger, *The Pentecostals*, 379.

1. The devil and his demons are antagonistic foes of the church.
2. They have been eternally overcome by Christ.
3. They still affect individuals malevolently.
4. They can be resisted and overcome by and through Christ.

Various reasons for demonisation have been suggested,[173] though most do not enjoy biblical support. Pentecostals do not distinguish between leaders/clergy or laity who function in exorcism. However, Richards[174] writes 'there is no place here for the novice or for any Christian believer to act presumptuously'. Few would claim to have a gift of exorcism and the role of exorcist has not been adopted within Classical Pentecostalism. Indeed, exorcism has been generally been uncommon in Pentecostal experience for most of its history in Britain.[175]

Although Satan, always under the authority and in the context of the sovereignty of God, is the cause of all suffering, many would seek to separate sickness from demonic elements, though sickness or suffering may be caused by the presence of demons that need to be exorcised, as a result of which the suffering should cease.

Pentecostals have, in general, refused to accept the possibility of a Christian being 'possessed' by a demon.[176] Kay[177] concludes that in the 1970s, while neo-Pentecostals, in general, affirmed that a Christian could be possessed, 'the classic Pentecostals, after some debate said a

---

[173]   Gilpin, 'Report', 1; hereditary links (K. Gerver, *Spiritual Warfare*, [London: Peniel, n.d.], 18; occult activity (J. Barr, 'The Christian and the Occult', *Elim Evangel* [31 October 1987], 3, and R. Parker, 'The Occult', *Redemption* [Oct. 1991], 36f.); lust (R.T. Hughes, 'Demon Possession', *Study Hour* [15 June 1948], 111); shock (Gerver, *Spiritual Warfare*, 26), and Hughes ('Demon Possession', 97); drugs (Gerver, *Spiritual Warfare*, 28); rebellion (Gerver, *Spiritual Warfare*, 27); physical weakness (Hughes, 'Demon Possession', 110).

[174]   Richards, 'Demon Possession', 11.

[175]   Gilpin, 'Report', 3.

[176]   Parker (ed.), *Bible Course*, 11.3; D. Orloff ('The Christian and Evil Spirits,' *Elim Evangel* [31 October 1987], 12); the official position of the AOG (USA and Canada), rejects the view that a Christian may be demon possessed *(The Pentecostal Testimony* [June 1975], 16–18); as also does the report of the Elim Committee on Demon Possession (Gilpin, 3).

[177]   *Inside Story*, 337.

firm no'. Wright,[178] notes 'A demon-possessed Christian is an impossibility – biblically, theologically and practically'. Some, however, have contradicted this view.[179]

It may be helpful to think of demonic activity directed towards the Christian as on a sliding scale of intensity from temptation, through persistent oppression of the mind, to total control of a specific area of one's life by a demonic force.[180] However, the latter must be differentiated from the dominating influence a demon may have over a non-Christian in that the influence of a demon on a Christian is largely determined by the Christian.[181]

As to the identification of demons, the Bible has little to say;[182] however, some have attempted to discern the names and activities of demons.[183] Although the forms of exorcism are not constant,[184] a number of features would be recognised as being important to both Pentecostals and charismatics involved in exorcistic ministry:

1. Preparation, including prayer (and possibly fasting) and the recognition of the importance of the gift of discernment.[185]
2. The use of the name of Jesus.[186]

---

[178] R.E. Wright, 'Demon-Possessed Christians; A Contradiction of terms', *Paraclete*, 7.3, (1973), 24. Similarly A. Linford argues that 'such an invasion . . . is anti-God'. While he accepts that Satan 'may oppress us, even obsess us, he can never possess us', adding 'It is impossible that the Spirit of God and demons can occupy the same body' ('No Entry', *Redemption* [February 1990], 16). M. Livesey writes 'there is no Scripture . . . for the possessed believer teaching . . . The idea must be rejected . . . it makes nonsense of almost the entire theology of the Church on the subject' ('The Ministry of Casting Out Demons', *Redemption Tidings* [24 January 1980], 8f.)

[179] Edwards, 'Delivered', 13–15; Hughes, 'Demon Possession', 95.

[180] Hughes, 'Demon Possession', 96.

[181] J. Barr, 'The War is On', *Direction* (February 1991), 24.

[182] Luke 8:30; 13:11; Acts 16:16.

[183] Livesey, 'The Ministry', 8; Gerver believes that the different descriptions of demonic spirits or powers represent different demons (*Spiritual Warfare*, 12ff.); Canty rejects the view that 'a particular demon can hold sway over certain geographical areas' (*The Practice*, 1993f.).

[184] Parker (ed.), *Bible Course*, 9.

[185] Canty, *The Practice*, 194–197; Gilpin, 'Report', 2.

[186] Mark 16:17; Acts 16:18.

3. A command that the demon leave its victim.[187]
4. A recognition of the authority of Christ that is vested in the Christian.[188]
5. Permanent relief 'is obtained only by and in the power of Christ'.[189]

Other elements that have little biblical precedent vary depending on the religious, social and cultural context of the people concerned and have received limited comment by Pentecostal writers. Such issues include inviting people to receive exorcism,[190] the laying on of hands,[191] physical manifestations of the sufferer,[192] conversation[193] with and identification of the demon,[194] forms of actual expulsion,[195] longevity of the exorcism[196] and post-exorcistic care of the sufferer.[197]

## Conclusion

As far as divine healing is concerned, a number of constants may be identified within Pentecostalism, foremost of which is that the ministry of the Holy Spirit through the church means that healing is available whenever it is in keeping with the will of God. It is to be hoped that the Pentecostal theology of healing, based on a more incisive and exegetical investigation of the New Testament's teaching on healing and its role in the ministry of Jesus, will be balanced with a positive and constructive Pentecostal theology of suffering. As in other parts of the church, greater co-operation with medicine and other health bodies may prove a useful development.

---

187 Livesey, 'The Ministry'.
188 Richards, 'Demon Possession', 13.
189 Parker (ed.), *Bible Course*, 9; Gilpin, 'Report', 2.
190 Richards, 'Demon Possession', 11.
191 Gerver, *Spiritual Warfare*, 31.
192 Linford, 'No Entry', 17; V. Cunningham, 'The Claims of Exorcists', *Redemption Tidings* (6 December 1973), 3.
193 Livesey, 'The Ministry', 4; Cunningham, 'Can a Christian', 25.
194 Cunningham, 'The Claims', 7.
195 Gerver, *Spiritual Warfare*, 31.
196 Livesey, 'The Ministry', 4.
197 Gerver, *Spiritual Warfare*, 33ff.

Though confined mainly to the ministry of a few, exorcism has also occupied a platform within Pentecostal theology and praxis. The Pentecostal awareness of the role of the demonic within the human psyche needs to be supplemented with greater awareness of the power of the mind, psychiatry, psychology and psychosomatic issues in order to create a sound basis for methodology.

Chapter Eight

# Worship: Singing a New Song in a Strange Land

## D. Neil Hudson

My first encounter with Pentecostalism came during the late 1970s. For many of us coming into Pentecostal churches from other Christian traditions during that time, it was the vibrancy and immediacy of the worship which attracted us and subsequently fashioned our view and understanding of God. Worship was no longer simply a rational, cognitive assent to certain articles of the credal statements of the church. It was a time when we were encouraged to experience the presence of God in our midst. We no longer had to merely sing about and commemorate the experiences of believers who had met with the living God in days gone by; this was now open to us all, male or female, young or old, rich or poor. The liberation found was not to be analysed but simply enjoyed. The freedom of knowing that God loved us, not because we had been told this, but because we felt his touch in our lives, was exhilarating.

Worship can have a variety of meanings ranging from indicating solely the corporate singing that happens in a service through to the way a person conducts his/her whole life. In this chapter, worship is understood as referring to the corporate expression of worship in singing, praise, intercessory prayers, preaching, communion and ministry offered to the sick.

Inevitably, many elements have changed in worship over the past nine decades of Pentecostal history and this chapter reflects some of these developments. The current practice of worship in both white and black classical Pentecostal churches will be examined, some of the challenges facing Pentecostals in their worship will be presented and some tentative solutions offered.

## The Historical Development of Pentecostal Worship

### *Pentecostal Pioneers*

The dawn of the twentieth century was marked amongst evangelicals in Britain by a mounting belief that God was about to do a work in the nation that would be significant, visible and possibly the final act before the return of Jesus to earth.

It is against this background that the Welsh revival broke out in 1904. This revival was to become a powerful influence on the Pentecostal movement. This movement of God, bringing changes to the social activities of whole communities, became a marker of what true revival was like. However, it was the particular style of spirituality that was the thread carried on into nascent Pentecostalism. Orr writes 'Both stressed an unplanned ministry of the Holy Spirit; both were emotionally demonstrative, and both also suffered from a tendency to occasional emotionalism, the exploitation of the emotions to achieve certain feelings.'[1] Hollenweger echoes eyewitness accounts of the revival, writing 'The characteristics of the services of the Welsh revival were the hours-long singing of Welsh hymns in harmony, the decline of the sermon, prayer in concert by the congregation, interruptions from the congregations, an emphasis on the experience of the baptism of the Spirit and the guidance of the Spirit.'[2]

This style of worship continued after the initial social impact of the revival had waned. Those who had come to Christ during the revival became known as 'Children of the Revival' and met to worship in homes after, in some cases, being ostracised from their churches and chapels. Their meetings were flexible, free of ritual and organisation, and the believers were expectant, fervent and desirous of more of God's blessing in their lives. They were hungry for the Holy Spirit and many entered into the new Pentecostal blessings. Their experience in worship

---

[1]  J.E. Orr, *Evangelical Awakenings 1900–1975* (Chicago: Moody Press, 1975), 184.

[2]  W.J. Hollenweger, *The Pentecostals* (Peabody: Hendrickson, 1988), 177.

and prayer became one of constantly sensing the presence of God. They were edified as they used their gifts of tongues and prophecy; on occasions, the power of God would cause them to fall down whilst at other times they would weep, laugh, shout or sing. Gee outlines the situation well, writing 'It was not to be surprised at, that among these "Children of the Revival", temperamentally disposed to emotionalism, and left by the ministers like sheep without a shepherd, there should arise those who knew not how to control the deep surges of pure emotion occasioned by the new blessing'.[3]

The brakes that stopped the newly fledged Pentecostal movement from careering out of control were the policies regarding worship formulated by the Sunderland Convention.[4] If the Welsh Revival and its aftermath would mark future Pentecostalism in its tendency to emotionalism, the Sunderland Conventions would bring an order and sense of purpose to Pentecostalism that the denominations would bear right up to the present day.

Although the Pentecostal movement was in its earliest infancy, it was already apparent that the freedom and liberty discovered in worship could bring its own real problems. Boddy realised that if the conventions were going to produce healthy growth and development there needed to be some order that would be accepted by all. Accordingly, only those willing to sign the following declaration were eligible to receive a ticket to the convention.

> I declare that I am in full sympathy with those who are seeking 'Pentecost' with the sign of tongues. I also undertake to accept the ruling of the chairman . . .
>
> 1. Prayer and Praise should occupy at least one third of our meetings for Conference.
> 2. As to choruses it is suggested that, as far as possible, they shall be left to the leader to commence or control, and friends are asked to pray (silently) that he may be led aright. Confusion is not always edifying, though sometimes the Holy Spirit works so mightily that there is a Divine flood which rises above barriers.

---

[3] D. Gee, *The Pentecostal Movement* (London: Victory Press, 1941), 40.
[4] An annual Whitsuntide Pentecostal Convention, hosted by A.A. Boddy in Sunderland from 1908–14, became an early focal point for the nascent Pentecostal churches, with representatives attending from both British and European churches.

3. The Chairman's ruling should be promptly and willingly obeyed in cases of difficulty. There should at those moments, if they occur, be much earnest prayer (in silence) that God may guide aright and get glory through all.[5]

This wise guidance had no quenching effect on the gifts of the Spirit; on the contrary, the early conventions in Sunderland demonstrated that it was possible to have a sense of order and yet still be open to the Spirit in all its fullness.

However, if the Welsh revival spawned the desire for further moves of God and in some ways made emotionalism acceptable in worship, and the Sunderland Conventions gave the new movement some order, it was the evangelistic thrust of the early Elim movement which contributed the final component of worship in Pentecostalism.

While there seemed to be little impetus for home mission, there was a growing awareness among Pentecostal leaders that this was needed to stop the new movement petering out into merely a pleasant pastime for the committed. Boddy records 'Brother Stephen and Brother George and I had a long heart to heart talk. They feel that the Lord needs evangelists in Pentecostal work today. There are many teachers and would-be teachers, but few evangelists. The Lord is giving an answer to the criticism that the Pentecostal people are not interested in evangelistic work, and only seek to have good times. (May the Lord shake this out of his people. Amen).'[6]

The move from small house meetings, where only a few would gather, to the mass evangelistic meetings of the late 1920s took over ten years to accomplish, but the emphasis on evangelism meant that some of the self-indulgent activities of many Pentecostal groups had to stop. Emotional excesses had to be curbed so as to reassure onlookers of the sanity of Pentecostal believers. Preaching changed from merely encouraging believers to enjoy their new-found spiritual adventures to calling nonbelievers to conversion. The songs and choruses changed accordingly. They were used to attract people's attention, to convey the Christian's testimony and to keep a service as attractive as possible.[7]

---

[5]   Gee, *Pentecostal Movement*, 1–42.
[6]   A.A. Boddy, *Confidence* (March 1913), 48.
[7]   Early Pentecostals would often speak about the need to keep a service 'light'. This presumably was in contrast to the quietness and solemnity of the more traditional denominational churches.

Prior to the Second World War, Pentecostals saw thousands attending their massed rallies and many large churches were founded. Unfortunately, the disruption caused by the war brought this period of Pentecostal history to a close. The ending of the war brought a change to the whole religious outlook of people in Britain and the Pentecostals suffered from the changed expectations. It was a difficult phase of their history as they struggled to be accepted by other churches, while still retaining their own distinctive doctrines. This desire was epitomised by the phrase 'Pentecost with dignity'.

### Stagnation: 1950s–1960s

One recurring feature of Pentecostalism has been the need it has felt to regularly reassess itself. It is almost intrinsic to Pentecostalism that it promises more than it can deliver on an ongoing basis. If, for the individual Pentecostal Christian, the expected Christian life is one of ongoing victory and spiritual growth, then for the local church it is one of increasing openness to the work of the Spirit alongside ongoing revivalism.

Just eight years after the initial outpouring of the Spirit in Sunderland, Jack Tetchner spoke forcefully to the London Conference,[8] 'a lot of God's dear children who were flames of fire just a few years back are today dried up, withered up, and they scarcely know where they are, and what they believe, and what is true and what is false . . . with (their) unforgiving spirits and hardness and indifference to the claims of God'.[9] Accepting the possibility of hyperbole for preaching effect, it is true that Pentecostalism has been as prone as any other religious movement to dull formalism and lifeless ritualism.

Certainly by the 1960s, there were many in the Pentecostal movement concerned at what was happening to the worship in the churches. The temptation for the churches to flounder, showing all the outward forms of past revival, and yet none of the associated power, was all too evident to John Lancaster. A senior Elim pastor, for the past forty years he has been an incisive commentator on Pentecostalism. In 1962 he wrote, 'The truth is, for all our enthusiasm,

---

[8] An annual Pentecostal convention, hosted by Cecil Polhill, similar in intention to the Sunderland Conventions but with less overall significance.
[9] *Confidence* (August 1916), 132.

our freedom, our bright, happy choruses, our breathless round of meetings, our sermon-tasting at conventions, we can be as devoid of true Pentecostal life as those we sometimes criticise. Even a chicken with its neck wrung will continue to kick for a while, and some of the manifestations of modern life seem little more than the pathetic reflexes of spiritual strangulation.'[10]

In the same year in *Pentecost*, Donald Gee criticised the abuse of tongues and interpretation, claiming that erroneous traditions surrounding the use of these gifts brought the gifts into disrepute and eventually sidetracked the churches who used them.[11]

The crusades and the rallies continued, reminders of the successful mass meetings of pre-war days. Often occurring on the weekends of the major Christian festivals, the worship was geared to preparing the people to receive the guest preacher. Pentecostals were still viewed with suspicion among the other denominations and it was during these times that the 'family' could come together and feel a certain degree of excitement and significance. The meetings were well attended, eagerly anticipated and important in giving people a sense of belonging, while the worship fostered a sense of community that was so needed at a time when Pentecostals were being looked at askance.

### Renewal and Restoration: 1960s–1980s

William Kay's comment regarding the reaction of the Assemblies of God to the renewal that occurred in the mainstream denominations in the early 1960s would be equally pertinent to others in the classical Pentecostal Church: 'A fat person sees those of average weight as being skinny. The Assemblies of God saw the Charismatic movement as odd. At least that was the first reaction. Gradually, as acquaintance improved, judgement became more discriminating and accurate. The Assemblies of God itself was not entirely healthy in the 1960s and so its initial reaction may have been jaundiced.'[12]

Within Elim, 1963 was the first year that the renewal of churches in the historic denominations was noticed and commented upon in

---

10   *Elim Evangel* (10 November 1962), 714.
11   *Pentecost* (June–August 1962), 17.
12   Kay, W. *Inside Story* (Mattersey: Mattersey Hall, 1990), 285.

the *Evangel*. Jack Hywel Davies, the National Youth Director, wrote a series of articles outlining the new move of the Spirit ending with a provocative challenge to Pentecostals. It was all too obvious that the 'new' Pentecostals had a freshness about their spirituality that was lacking in classical Pentecostalism. The Renewal movement seemed to highlight to the leaders of the Pentecostal churches all that they were already aware of, namely that they had stagnated and were now in danger of being marginalised due to the fact that they no longer had anything to offer.[13]

The central focus of change in the renewal churches was the style of, and the central place given to, worship. The hymns used until then had been based heavily on the Methodist tradition, and the choruses of the 1930s–1950s had reflected the style and rhythm of the old time music hall. The new style of worship moved away from the use of the traditional hymns and introduced new songs drawing on contemporary musical styles, primarily the folk ballad. The older Pentecostals resisted the changes, charging the new charismatic groups of jettisoning doctrine in favour of experience, of being elitist by separating themselves from other members of the church, of compromising their experience if they remained within their denominations, and of theological naivety. These allegations, so reminiscent of many of the accusations levelled at an earlier generation of Pentecostals, were gradually dropped as the classical Pentecostal churches themselves became more influenced by the new charismatic groups.

Often, the changes were not introduced without real pain in the local assemblies. On occasions, pastors were so eager to introduce the new styles of worship marked by flexibility, spontaneity and the use of new songs that they could be singularly insensitive to the needs and

---

13   He writes, 'Are we in danger of relying on past experiences which seem only to be remembered by some as a reason for our doctrine? How do our churches compare with our teaching? What gifts of the Spirit are regularly manifested in our midst? And here it is necessary to observe that we should not be simply content with the lesser, and neither must we allow the spurious, because there is an absence of the real . . . Other than a fresh infilling of the Holy Spirit for most members of Pentecostal churches I can see no way in which the Pentecostal movement can participate in this new Pentecost. Indeed there is every danger of being by-passed' (*Elim Evangel* [18 December 1963], 792).

feelings of older established members. These members, in turn, could be resolutely determined not to lose any of their own traditions.

However, change did come. By 1981, many truths which their younger counterparts had been proclaiming for the previous twenty years were acknowledged by the older Pentecostal groups. The newer songs did not just express truths about God, or testimonies of what God had done, but provided vehicles for people to communicate directly with God. There was much talk of the need for relationships to be right, for worship to 'flow' and for the need for varied expressions of worship to be accepted, including dance.

The concept of worship changed from the idea that praise and worship simply expressed the truth of what God had done, to an understanding that praise and worship could express the believer's relationship to the Father in terms that were distinctly personal and intimate. Along with this change in understanding came the reintro-duction of the use of the various gifts of the Spirit. The gifts of tongues and interpretation had often been the sole gifts used in Pentecostal churches for many years. Now, taking a cue from the newer churches, emphasis was placed on prophecy and words of knowledge and wisdom. There was a new emphasis on healing. There had always been healers who claimed to have the gift of healing, but the emphasis changed, for now it was accepted that all committed Christians could pray in faith for healing to occur in another person's life. The gift of healing no longer necessarily set the healer apart from the rest of the congregation, but could be exercised as part of the corporate life of the church.

In 1984, John Smyth, reviewing the year in which he held the presidency of Elim, noted, 'The openness in the churches for the prophetic ministry is quite startling. A new emphasis and acknow-ledgment of the importance and relevance of the vocal gifts of the Spirit, tested and approved by the word of God, has created a new sense of the "immediacy" of God in our midst'.[14] In terms of worship style, many Pentecostal churches became indistinguishable from their charismatic counterparts; they shared the same songs, followed the same 'unwritten' liturgies, and struggled with the ongoing problem of transposing yesterday's radical blessing into today's mundane ritual.

---

[14]    Report to Elim's annual conference, 1984.

With the development in restorationism and the renewal move-ment[15] the songs changed from very simple three-chord folk tunes that anyone with a modicum of talent could pick out on a guitar to the sophisticated rhythms and lyrics of musicians such as Graham Kendrick.

## Black Pentecostalism[16]

During the 1950s–1960s, many black Pentecostals emigrated from the Caribbean and Africa, drawn to Britain by the prospect of jobs and a new life. On arrival, they found that the mainstream churches either rejected them outright, or held services that were so very different in style to the ones to which they were accustomed that they felt alienated. On the whole, therefore, excluded from mainstream white classical Pentecostalism, they formed their own churches which ex-pressed their worship in a style with which they felt more comfortable.

Within black Pentecostalism, there has always been a greater degree of liberty than that experienced by their white brothers and sisters. Afro-Caribbean culture has radically different roots from Enlightenment-based white European Christianity. Its history of slavery, poverty and prejudice has meant that 'the soul of the people rather than the reasoning of the people has been the dominant feature'.[17] Worship is expressed through the filter of experience much more than through theology, the hymns and songs of the black

---

[15]    The differences between these two movements have been well defined elsewhere (e.g. A. Walker, *Restoring the Kingdom* [London: Hodder & Stoughton, 1985]). Generally speaking, the renewal movement began and continued as a charismatic emphasis within the mainstream denominations. Restorationism was a radical understanding of what it meant to be a charismatic church and involved a complete break with existing denomina-tions, often grouping together under the authority of an apostle.

[16]    For this section, I am indebted to J. Edwards ([ed.] *Let's Praise Him Again* [Eastbourne: Kingsway, 1992]), especially the chapter that Joel Edwards contributed. I am aware of problems in finding a suitable label to indicate what exactly is meant by Black Pentecostalism. In using the term 'Black Pentecostalism', I am following Edwards and mean the major denominations such as the New Testament Church of God, the Church of God of Prophecy, as well as the many smaller groupings.

[17]    Edwards, *Let's praise*, 90.

Pentecostal churches unifying and distinguishing them. Generally, the music is rhythmic, repetitive and participative, encouraging movement, clapping and dancing, the words often simply declaring truth that is easily memorised and so becomes part of the Christian's belief-system.

Black churches are more likely to be active in their support for area and national conventions. Inter-congregational links are kept strong as people meet each other at regular intervals. They provide a forum to meet like-minded people, which reassures them that they belong to something that is significant and relevant.

With their emphases on a theology of separation from sinful society and a strong eschatological hope, the black churches are reminiscent of the earlier days of white classical Pentecostalism. Some similarities in background probably explain the similarities of practice: both were estranged from the traditional denominations, denounced for emotionalism, on the whole economically and socially marginalised, but aware of the radical changes that Christ had brought into their lives.

Edwards outlines some of the current issues facing the black churches with regard to their worship. One of these is the need for the churches to guard the simplicity of some of their older songs. At a time when massed gospel choirs have become popular in the youth culture, there is a danger that the focus of the song becomes the music rather than the message. Many black churches are being attracted by the worship songs of the white new churches, and there is a real possibility that the black churches will lose contact with their own culture completely. With the emergence of a generation of young black Christians who are completely at ease in their environment and with the Western rational mind-set, the culture of black Pentecostal worship may be undergoing the same change that white Pentecostal churches faced fifteen years ago.

Another difference between black and white Pentecostalism may be seen in the priority given to spiritual gifts. Edwards notes that spiritual manifestations are not notable in black churches while Root comments 'overall, the significance of being Pentecostal would seem to lie in, firstly, the emphasis given to divine healing, and secondly in an emphasis on ecstatic worship and on being filled with the Spirit as evidenced by intense emotional experiences'.[18]

---

[18] J. Root, *Encountering West Indian Pentecostalism: Its Ministry and Worship* (Bramcote: Grove Books, 1979), 22.

Over the years, the white Pentecostal churches have become much more open to the emotional side of worship, which has meant that they are much more akin to their black counterparts. As the black churches attempt to relate the gospel to a changing culture, they will find that they have much to offer white Pentecostal Christians. Their vibrancy, their awareness of and struggle with injustice and their solidarity all need to be acknowledged and learnt from by white middle-class Pentecostal and charismatic churches that can easily retreat into an anaesthetised form of worship, comfortably cushioned from the struggles experienced by many in today's society.

## Typical Experiences of Corporate Worship

Pentecostals have always prided themselves on the spontaneity of their services, at times feeling somewhat superior to other church traditions that use a written liturgical format. Spittler's comment is one which all Pentecostals would want to assert vigorously: 'Spontaneity is prized in Pentecostal piety. The Holy Spirit guides worship and leads each believer and he moves unpredictably. All the members expect anyone of the local assembly to follow the Spirit's leading and to do so at once.'[19]

However, Edwards' comment about black Pentecostal churches may be nearer the truth in reference to all Pentecostal churches, black or white when he writes 'Pentecostalism has its own well-formulated liturgy. To the uninitiated, black church worship may appear to be a random collection of spontaneous and apparently unrelated events . . . However the regular visitor has another story to tell. Short of divine intervention, the order of a church service can be very predictable.'[20]

---

[19] Russell P. Spittler, 'Spirituality: Pentecostal and Charismatic' in S.M. Burgess, G.B. McGee and P.H. Alexander (eds.), *The Dictionary of Pentecostal and Charismatic Movements* (Grand Rapids: Zondervan, 1988), 805. G.W. Gilpin writes ' "Good" Pentecostal meetings are characterized by ecstasy, exuberance and an exercise of the gifts of the Spirit' ('The Place of Pentecostal Movements Today', in P.S. Brewster [ed.], *Pentecostal Doctrine* [Cheltenham: Elim/Grenehurst Press, 1976], 117).
[20] Edwards, *Let's praise*, 68.

There is, of course, no reason at all to suppose that liturgy is de facto unhelpful or Spirit-quenching. In fact, it is impossible for any group to worship without some accepted liturgical framework. It is clear to observers that there is a discernible framework within which Pentecostalism does operate, with particular elements that are common to most Pentecostal churches. However, it needs to be noted that specific emphases do differ from church to church.

### Sunday Services

It has already been pointed out that Pentecostal worship has changed over the years and the customs and practice of churches may well be very different from the services of a previous generation. In earlier days, the Pentecostals mirrored the Holiness churches, in that the morning service was for believers who congregated to 'break bread'. It was at this meeting, as well as at the midweek bible study and prayer meetings, that the gifts of the Spirit, in essence the gifts of tongues and interpretation, were encouraged and expected. Traditionally, the Sunday evening service was the gospel service, in many cases resembling any other evangelical church. Latterly, the celebration concept of worship has replaced both previous distinctions. Both morning and evening services have become almost indistinguishable in purpose, both services catering primarily for the believers.

Over the past six years, there has been a change in some of the larger Pentecostal churches. Due to their growth, some of the churches have added extra earlier morning services, including communion, but often in a quieter, more reverential style. This may be followed by a family celebration, again including communion, but offering a much livelier service. The evening service often functions as a celebration-type event including guest singers and speakers, inspirational testimonies and life-application preaching. In general, it is clear that these Pentecostal churches are returning to their roots, with the evening service being the gospel service, albeit renamed, revamped and revived. Services will often end with a rousing hymn or chorus designed to encourage the believers to re-enter the sceptical world with a renewed faith in a God who is at work in their lives.

## The Role of the Worship Leader[21]

In many churches, the pastor is still the worship leader as well as the preacher. The ministry of the worship leader is of increasing importance to Pentecostals for he or she is expected to respond to the impulse of the Spirit and to the perceived needs of the people. Services generally begin with some 'praise songs', modern and older hymns and new, lively choruses expressing truths about God and what he has accomplished for his people, the desired effect being cumulative rather than specific. The congregation will be encouraged to participate by singing, standing, clapping and raising their hands, when appropriate.

## Physical Expressions in Worship

Dancing is one example of the presence of a physical element used by some Pentecostal believers as an expression of their worship. It has a long tradition within Pentecostalism, in earlier days being delineated carefully as 'dancing in the Spirit' – always alone, never in couples; always done for the Lord, never for effect; and if done 'in the Spirit', never viewed as provocative. With the advent of the Renewal movement, dancing came to be seen as a mark of liberty rather than ecstasy.[22] The raising of hands is seen as a symbol of submission and receptivity. As they raise their hands, the worshippers are able to express their need of the Spirit and receive him afresh into their lives.

---

[21] In describing the typical format of a Pentecostal service, it could be mistakenly thought that the pastor is being manipulative. This is not true. The fact that the description will be generally recognisable by all Pentecostals serves to emphasise the earlier comment that Pentecostals do have a very definite liturgical pattern, albeit unwritten.

[22] Dancing would involve hopping from one foot to another, a sort of country jig type dance rather than the more flowing 'dancing in the Spirit' of the earlier days when the individual was apparently caught up in worship and unaware of the rest of the congregation.

## Reflective Worship

'Praise' times may be terminated either by a prayer from the leader, or by a song that will quieten a congregation so that they can enter a period of more reflective and intimate worship. The songs become simpler in lyrical content and more intimate in emotional intensity. The words are easily remembered and many of the songs are sung without the need for books or overhead projectors. It is accepted that during this period, the gifts of tongues or prophecy may be exercised. Often, the prophetic gift will be in terms of an individual's needs and the response required. The word of knowledge may also be seen in action, the accepted understanding of this gift being that someone's needs will be pointed out and that God will minister to them in an appropriate manner.[23]

In the midst of the quieter songs, the congregation may begin to sing using the gift of tongues. The biblical justification for this practice has been the interpretation of Paul's statement in 1 Corinthians 14:15, 'I will sing with my spirit, but I will also sing with my mind'. Although this may happen only infrequently and only last for a short time, in its purest form, the rising cadences of a gathered body of believers singing unlearnt songs in a 'heavenly language' is genuinely moving and impressive. It has been at these times that people have been able to sense God's presence. Smail explains the use of the gift well, writing:

> singing in the Spirit by-passes the rational faculties; it reminds us that alongside the praise of the renewed mind there is the praise of the renewed heart that, when it is being evoked by the Spirit, expresses not simply our superficial feelings, but engages the deep primal emotions at the hidden centre of our being in our self-offering to the living God. Such praise is direct, spontaneous and simple. It escapes from a complicated conceptuality and a second-hand dependence on such liturgical resources as prayer-books and hymn-books, and responds in immediacy and freedom to the contact with the loving Lord that the Spirit makes possible and, in joyous serenity, rejoices in and meditates upon his poured out grace and his revealed glory.[24]

---

[23]  F. Martin, 'Word of Knowledge', in Burgess et al., *Dictionary*, 528.

[24]  T. Smail, A. Walker, N. Wright, *Charismatic Renewal: The Search for a Theology* (London: SPCK, 1993), 110.

During any of these activities, people may be encouraged or invited to offer spontaneous prayer. It is worth noting, however, that where the gifts of the Spirit are most often used, the practice of spontaneous prayer may be less likely to happen. The time of praise and worship may last from thirty to sixty minutes.

### The Lord's Supper

For older classical Pentecostals, the 'breaking of bread' was the central event of the Sunday morning service. In recent years, however, it would be fair to say that, in one sense, the worship time has replaced the act of communion. Traditionally, the act of communion was the locus for an existential encounter with the risen Lord. With the revitalisation of worship, and the heightened expectation that the individual believer will meet with God in personal worship, the emphasis on communion with the Lord at the Table has lessened, for it has been increasingly realised that such communion can take place in other contexts.

The act of the breaking of bread is a memorial, rather than an active agent of the Lord's presence. Lancaster notes that

> the attitude of so-called 'classic' Pentecostals to the sacraments was due at least in part to the particular ethos of the movement. With roots going back into the soil that nurtured early Methodism, the growth of the modern Pentecostal movement was accelerated by a growing disenchantment with the prevailing formalism and spiritual deadness of the institutionalised Church . . . No doubt in some ways they over-reacted, but, in their attitude to the sacraments, they were probably much nearer to the New Testament than most scholars would care to admit.[25]

### Preaching

A major feature of the worship service is the preaching. In earlier days, the preaching would predominantly be typological and inspirational. There would be a heavy dependence on the Old Testament, drawing out lessons and meanings that would lie hidden for ordinary believers. In British Pentecostalism, Bible college training has always been viewed with a certain suspicion, with the result that for many years

---

[25]  J. Lancaster, in Brewster, *Pentecostal Doctrine*, 80–81.

Pentecostal pastors have relied on this inspirational approach to the Scriptures. While holding to the inerrancy and infallibility of the Bible, in practice the preaching has sometimes taken great liberties with the text. Having said that, there is a changing tide and a recognition that the Bible needs to be taught carefully and expositionally.

## Prayer and Ministry

An important element in corporate worship is the provision of spiritual sustenance to individual members of the Fellowship, either by the leadership or by members of the congregation itself. Those requiring ministry may either congregate at the front of the church to have hands laid on them by the pastor or leaders, or stand in the body of the church while the pastor leads them in a single congregational prayer. On other occasions, the pastor may encourage other people nearby to pray with and for them. The element of touch is important in ministry. Even when people are standing at the front of the church, the minister may ask the congregation to extend their hands towards the people being prayed for, in a symbolic laying on of hands. The touching provides people being prayed for with an expectancy that Jesus will minister to them and that the Holy Spirit will impact them.

From the earliest days, some believers have on occasion fallen to the floor in a virtual faint while being prayed for. Terminology has varied from being 'slain in the Spirit,' which some felt to have too many militaristic overtones, to 'resting in the Spirit', to 'falling under the power'. In the mid–century years, this phenomenon tended to be associated with well-known American healers. However, in recent years, with encouragement from the newer churches, it has emerged as an example of God's power at work in the local church.

For the individual concerned, it can best be described as a relaxing of all the muscles, the person being prayed for simply feeling it easier to fall than to stay standing. While on the floor, the individual concerned may be conscious of what is happening around them, but they may also be receiving a sense of God ministering to them, imparting a sense of peace or power. In certain cases, this may be accompanied by shaking, laughter or crying. In each case, it is assumed that the Holy Spirit is doing a specific work of release in the believer's life.

In 1994 and 1995, these reactions became a much more common feature of church life and ministry in many Pentecostal churches in the wake of the so-called 'Toronto Blessing'.[26] Many of the phenomena that had previously been consigned to the domain of interested church historians became accepted practices again in many Pentecostal churches. The most notable phenomena were laughter, crying, shaking, and lying on the floor for protracted periods of time. These reactions occurred in individuals either when they were being prayed for individually, or as they were worshipping as part of the congregation. Explained as part of the Spirit's wider work of refreshing and preparing the church for an imminent revival, these phenomena were not directly encouraged, but were accepted as a sign of God's blessing upon an individual. None of the reactions were particularly new to the Pentecostal tradition, but they occurred with an intensity that had not been witnessed since the beginning of the century. At the time of writing, it is not possible to predict what the outcome of the 'Toronto Blessing' will be. It is evident that many claim to have experienced refreshment from the Lord, but only time will be able to tell the real significance of this interesting spiritual development.

Finally, a much prized tradition that has been on the wane in recent years is the public testimony time. This is an occasion during a service when individuals can testify either to a specific work of God in their lives or express gratitude for the experience of the sustaining power of God. One of the results of the 'Toronto Blessing' has been the reintroduction of the testimony time. Individuals are encouraged to relate their spiritual experiences to the rest of the

---

[26]   The 'Toronto Blessing' was a widely used phrase describing the phenomena experienced during the year 1994–95, the catalyst being the Airport Vineyard Church, based in Toronto, Canada. A plethora of publications have been produced that describe, propogate or criticise the phenomenon. Some of these include, G. Chevreau, *Catch the Fire* (London: HarperCollins, 1994); P. Dixon, *Signs of Revival* (Eastbourne: Kingsway, 1994); M. Fearon, *A Breath of Fresh Air* (Guildford: Eagle, 1994); K. and L. Gott, *The Sunderland Refreshing* (London: Hodder & Stoughton, 1995); D. Pawson, *Is the Blessing Biblical?* (London: Hodder & Stoughton, 1995); D. Roberts, *The Toronto Blessing* (Eastbourne: Kingsway, 1994); T. Smail, A. Walker, N. Wright, *Charismatic Renewal* (London: SPCK, 1995); M. Stibbe, *Times of Refreshing* (London: Marshall Pickering, 1995).

congregation, in the belief that their stories will encourage other members of the congregation to receive these blessings as well.

## Midweek Services

Pentecostal churches have traditionally hosted a mid-week Bible study, with a separate prayer meeting, open to all the congregation and held centrally in the church building. During the decade of 1970–80, these meetings were gradually replaced by mid-week housegroup meetings. These are informal groups, meeting in people's homes. Led by lay people, they typically include a mix of inductive Bible study, prayer and 'sharing', the worship being similar to that found on Sundays. The use of the gifts of the Spirit, particularly the vocal gifts, may be encouraged, the small groups being seen as places where believers can gain experience in using the gifts.

The turnabout in worship within the churches in style, the time allotted for it, and the significance attached to it, has been remarkable. From worship being viewed merely as the 'preliminary' activity to be dispensed with as quickly as possible before the preaching, it has become the raison d'être for many churches and individuals within those churches. At its best, the worship has been elemental in ministering to the believers, for in worship they have felt themselves able to enter into the presence of God and encounter him. For unbelievers who have watched, the worship has communicated to them, on an emotional and spiritual level, truth that they have not been able to receive on a rational level. The change in worship has allowed the Pentecostal churches to still have something relevant to offer to a watching world. There are problems and challenges involved in worship, some of which will be addressed, but at its most appropriate, the worship experience for many in Pentecostal churches is precious, necessary and life-changing.

## Contemporary Issues Faced by Pentecostals in Worship

For all the freshness and transformation introduced into church life by the changes in worship style and content, there are major issues that face Pentecostals in their worship. Over the past fifteen years a homogeneity of style has arisen that needs to be questioned. Theological triumphalism has become the hallmark of many of the choruses, along with a highly specific view of eschatology and spiritual warfare. Some of the classic spiritual disciplines have almost disappeared among the plethora of new songs. Below are two of the major issues that need to be addressed.

### The Unquestioning Use of Musical Styles

The musical style of many of the newer choruses has been accepted on the basis of emotions that are raised, and so the words of songs are sacrificed to the music that accompanies them. The style has been heavily influenced by white, west-coast American, soft-rock ballads. Notwithstanding the fact that there are a number of very gifted British songwriters, this musical style has almost become a symbol of what it means to be Pentecostal or charismatic. The fact that churches in Britain are ministering in a multiplicity of circumstances should lead us to question the use of this homogeneous style of music. Age, ethnicity and differing cultural tastes all suggest that there needs to be a much wider understanding and use of musical composition. It is relevant to note that amongst second-generation charismatics, some of whom have joined the 'youth churches', there has been a desire for a greater diversification of style.

### Theological Concerns

Of greater significance than style has been the unquestioning accep-tance of the language used and concepts expressed. For Pentecostals, their worship has always been the vehicle for their theology, bringing it to life and giving it validity. The framework for an individual believer's commitment to Christ is created and sustained by the language and concepts used in corporate worship.

A contemporary example of this process of 'experience – theology – experience' can be seen in the wake of the 'Toronto Blessing'. Without going into long descriptions, it is enough to say that many Pentecostals have been spiritually encouraged by the ministry shaped and encouraged by the Toronto Airport Vineyard Church. Early observations made it clear that one of the recurring models of ministry was for people to be prayed for individually, and for the one praying to call upon the Spirit to rest in greater power upon the prayer candidate, using the prayer formula 'more, Lord, more'. At times, people would be blown upon, a symbol of the coming of the Spirit as a gentle wind; an alternative, or occasionally complementary, approach would be to pray that 'rivers of living water' would flow out of the believer. The experience of believers who had explained their encounter with the Spirit in terms of breath, wind or rivers was then encapsulated in songs that used the same imagery,[27] these songs becoming the ongoing vehicle for believers to explain their experiences. However, the songs and the images have begun to serve as a framework to explain future experiences, whilst providing a framework of anticipation regarding what believers might expect to experience. Thus, the legitimate use of metaphor becomes fixed in a quasi-biblical explanation that legitimises future experiences.

Ironically, if people have such a narrowly defined set of expectations, there is a possibility that this, albeit unconscious, cycle of understanding and expectation may be a hindrance to the sovereign free work of the Spirit.

*a. The Danger of Triumphalism*
The contents of the songs sung generally refer to instantaneous change that leaves little room either for doubt or a recognition that for many people change is a gradual process. Similarly, there is little understanding that for many Christians, there are periods of 'the dark night of the soul' when it is difficult to sense the presence of God at all. A popular song printed in a song sheet used by all the three major white classical Pentecostal groups in 1994 highlights this feature:

> His Spirit in us releases us from fear
> The way to Him is open, with boldness we draw near;
> And in His presence our problems disappear,
> Our hearts responding to His love.[28]

---

[27]  See 'Down the mountain, the river flows, and it brings refreshing wherever it goes; through the valleys and over the fields, the river is rushing and the river is here', 'Over the mountains and the sea, your river runs with love for me', 'I have felt the wind blow', 'The day of the streams is over, the time of the river is here', 'There's a wind a-blowing', *Spring Harvest Praise 1996* (Uckfield: Spring Harvest, 1996), nos. 24, 113, 60, 125, 132.

[28]  *Power Praise* (Eastbourne: Kingsway, 1994), no. 99.

Pentecostal theology and worship does not easily respond to the times of doubt and the seeming absence of God. As a result, people can end up living in a state of dualism. They can be experiencing the most difficult problems, and yet in church be singing of the potential of the Lord's deliverance and freedom from their problems. For some people, this dichotomy is described as 'speaking out in faith' the desires of one's heart, whilst believing that God will respond to such certainty; for others, it is viewed as living in denial. Our worship needs to be honest, expressing life as it is, not just as we wish it were. Biblically, alongside the psalms of glorious victory and procession, are the psalms of darkness and abandonment. Worship that is 'in spirit and in truth' must reflect both these experiences, without descending into stoical fatalism, or escaping into a fantasy land of over-realised eschatology.

Smail states, 'Worship must have a place not just for the moments when hearts lift high and eyes are shining and joy abounds, but for the dull days when we are empty and unresponsive in ourselves and can only hold out empty hands for the bread and wine, the body and blood, the redeeming gift of his living but crucified self that Jesus gives us from the cross.'[29]

### b. *An Inadequate View of Spiritual Warfare*
Alongside this supposedly immediate transformation of the individual's situation is the declaration of the victory of Jesus in the nations of the world. There has been a discernible shift in emphasis from some of the earlier Renewal songs which focused on the need for loving relationships between believers. Contemporary songs are more aware of the need for the church to be involved in changing society and primarily of the need for a religious revival.

This shift from an unhealthy continuous emphasis on relationships to an outward focus on society is to be welcomed. However, with this change of perspective has come the challenge to develop a biblical model of spiritual warfare. To presume that, because we are singing about spiritual warfare, we are actually engaged in it is fallacious. The danger of becoming removed from the society around us and retreating into a ghetto of our own making, with arcane language and over-realised eschatology, is ever-prevalent. Equally there is, understandably enough, a lack of clarity regarding the nature of revival. The

---

[29] Smail et al., *Charismatic Renewal*, 112.

hope that many will turn to an authentic personal trust in Jesus as their personal Saviour is ever present. However, questions regarding the political nature and structures of society are never really addressed. The need for spiritual warfare to be directed in words and deeds against the powers and principalities of the corporate political system is rarely mentioned.

The church's role, as seen in the songs, is to rise up and 'claim the land', often expressed in military jargon, and to pray for a revival in the nation:

Now is the time to march upon the land
Into our hands He will give the ground we claim.
He rides in majesty, to lead us into victory,
The world will see that Christ is Lord[30]

There is power in the name of Jesus,
Like a sword in our hands.
We declare in the name of Jesus
We shall stand! We shall stand!
At His name God's enemies
Shall be crushed beneath our feet.
For there is no other name that is higher
Than Jesus![31]

Let your word run freely through this nation,
Strong Deliverer, break the grip of Satan's power.
Let the cross of Jesus stand above the idols of this land
Let anointed lives rise up and take their stand . . .[32]

One example of spiritual warfare that has been heavily emphasised, but which has received little critical engagement from within the Pentecostal and charismatic contexts, is the role of 'positive confession'. The idea of 'claiming the land for Jesus' is the ultimate hope of many Christians. However, according to the teachings of the theory of 'positive confession', it is accomplished initially by the believers gathered together in worship and praise; their verbal declaration begins

[30] *Power Praise*, no. 150.
[31] *ibid.*, no. 162.
[32] *ibid.*, no. 107.

a general turning to God by the nation at large. Based on a belief that views heavenly powers and principalities as onlookers on worship, there is a stream of songs that reflect this belief that the words we use have a power to command blessing or the ability to 'bind the evil one':

> We have a vision for this nation;
> We share a dream for this land.
> We join with angels in celebration
> By faith we speak revival to this land.[33]

> I will build my church, and the gates of hell
> Shall not prevail against it.
> So you powers in the heavens above, bow down!
> And you powers on the earth below, bow down!
> And acknowledge that Jesus, Jesus, Jesus is Lord![34]

> Shout to the Lord, shout to the Lord,
> Shout to the Lord of hosts.
> And it breaks the heavy yoke, breaks the heavy yoke
> When you shout, you shout to the Lord.[35]

For the individual involved in corporate praise, it may seem exciting to belong to the only movement that is going to see change in our society, and for that movement to be the prelude to the advent of our Lord, but the triumphalism of our hopes may not be matched by realities around us. The passion of Pentecostal hope and the desire for the glory of God to be evident in the nation–states needs to be allied to a practical involvement in changing the power structures around us.

At the risk of sounding cynical, could it be that if there is not a revival in the next few years, Pentecostals will move away from the theme of revival with a palpable sense of disappointment?

## c. The Place of Pentecostalism in History

Land writes, 'Pentecostalism exists in continuity but differentiating discontinuity with other Christian spiritualities . . . It is more Eastern

---

[33] *ibid.*, no. 111.
[34] *ibid.*, no. 85.
[35] *ibid.*, no. 27.

than Western in its understanding of spirituality as perfection and participation in the divine life. In this regard, it has much to learn from persons like Gregory of Nyssa, Macarius the Egyptian and St. Symeon the New Theologian. It is both ascetic and mystical.'[36]

However, a weakness of Pentecostalism is that, at times, it seems to take the attitude that the only church history of any importance took place after 1906. It therefore sees itself as isolated from the liturgical developments and contributions of other Christian traditions. As a result, for Pentecostals with their emphasis on worship, there is a danger that freshness is found solely in the new – the new song, the new emphasis in preaching, the new style of ministry, rather than in mining the rich seams of church history and rediscovering forms of worship that could be reintroduced in a contemporary setting.

### d. The Place of Intercession

Confession and intercession can often be neglected in Pentecostal worship, or at least relegated to a mid-week meeting. The change in emphasis from what could become times of dreary introspection during communion services to the new-found freedom of the individual believer can easily negate the need for confession, and with it the chance for the believer to experience the reality of forgiveness. Within the range of choruses, from the high-energy praise songs to the tender intimacy of worship, there needs to be the space for people to come under the conviction of the Spirit and then to be able to respond with confession and receive the assurance of sins forgiven. Smail concludes, 'that is how we can be constantly renewed in our relationship to him, so that what he gives us in the Spirit is not soiled, distorted and misused in our sin-stained hands'.[37]

### e. The Danger of Individualism

The focus for many of the worship songs is the individual believer's personal walk with God, and so intercession can become limited to wholly personal matters, often relating to healing and wholeness. These prayers for psychological adjustment can shut out the clamour

---

[36]    S.J. Land, *Pentecostal Spirituality: A Passion for the Kingdom* (Sheffield: Sheffield Academic Press, 1993), 30.

[37]    Smail et al., *Charismatic Renewal*, 112.

of the world with its global needs and tragedies. It is possible to insulate ourselves from the pain that people bear and the situations that seem hopeless, even as we claim to be using the gifts of power and proclaim God's victory. To speak to a situation from a place of power can be easier than to stand with a person, to feel their pain and intercede with them at real cost. Thus, Smail writes, 'Intercession always has about it some of the agony of Gethsemane and the costly identification of Calvary, where, with Christ, we are helpless with the helpless, needy with the needy, and on their behalf we offer ourselves, our time, our energy, our concern, our love, acknowledging our total dependence on God and our humble waiting for him to respond to us in ways and at times of his own choosing. It is when intercession has that Calvary dimension at the heart of it that the resurrecting answers can be given and the Easter triumph can begin.'[38]

## Conclusion

It would be wrong to close with these somewhat negative questions. Firstly, it needs to be pointed out that the leaders of the Pentecostal denominations are aware, and vocal, in outlining some of the present problems in Pentecostal worship.[39] They are among the ones who have lived through the changes of the past three decades, and while appreciating and benefiting from all that God has done, they are also aware of the need for new paths ahead.

Secondly, I believe that Pentecostalism holds within its own traditions the antidotes to some of the issues that have been raised. Inevitably, what follows can only be a very personal and tentative identification of some concerns and proposed antidotes. Nevertheless, I offer it as a contribution to the discussion.

---

[38] Smail et al., *Charismatic Renewal*, 113–114.

[39] 'As I travel around the world I have fun and I have heartache when I look at the exercise of spiritual gifts. I am not prepared to have any of this "yea, yea, yea, hearken unto me, thus saith the Lord, three bags full . . .". I don't want that rubbish. Most of the vocal gifts are nonsense. I am sorry.' Wynne Lewis speaking at Cotswold Christian Centre, Winchcombe, October 1993. Quoted by Nigel Scotland, *Charismatics and the Next Millenium* (London: Hodder & Stoughton, 1995), 149.

## Pragmatism

Pentecostalism has been tainted by pragmatism throughout its history. Since, for Pentecostals, God is a creative Spirit, alive and active, following the Lord means accepting the inevitability of change. At times, this results in Pentecostals laying themselves open to very questionable theology and praxis, since for them theology is not so much a creed as an experience. The unhealthy pragmatism of accepting whatever may be the latest gimmick will only change as Pentecostals find a renewed confidence and conviction in their own history and evangelical theology. This need not mean that they will consign themselves to being part of some monolithic edifice, but it will mean that, from a secure base, they will be able to analyse and make reasonable responses to the changing theologies and practices currently in vogue. The insecurity that assumes that God is always doing something new elsewhere may ignore and negate the work that God may well be doing within their own churches. When the full range of worship – communion, preaching, prayer, singing and ministry – is restored to its rightful form, Pentecostals have much to offer the wider church.

## Communion

The view concerning communion needs to be examined while the significance and necessity of fellowship around the table needs to be explored. It is here that the grace and forgiveness of Jesus is made manifest and tangible to individuals, regardless of whether they feel divine joy or whether they wish to repent. Combined with the tenderness of worship songs, this becomes a greater witness to the love of the Almighty for a rebellious world than many of the biggest evangelistic ventures.

## Theological Maturity

Pentecostals have never desired to preach merely theologically-correct sermons. Early preachers were often unschooled, but vibrant with conviction. There have been problems with the desire for inspiration outweighing theological and biblical accuracy, but in these days when there is a greater openness to preachers from other traditions and a greater interaction with theological issues, there is the real possibility that Pentecostal preaching will reflect the maxim of 'minds on fire'.

In particular, a greater concentration on a theology of the cross in the context of the sovereignty of God is to be sought. While many Pentecostals share the desire for revival, the history of Pentecostalism should point to an awareness that however much we pray and plead with God to send revival, sometimes in his sovereignty he does not act as we think he should. Since we cannot presume on what God will or will not do next, we need to be prepared to minister to the world and worship from within a framework of a 'theologica crucis' as well as looking and hoping for the 'theologica gloriae' of an Easter and Pentecost faith.

The Pentecostal and charismatic denominations have radically affected the church and the expectations of Christian believers in the twentieth century. In worship they have rediscovered a particular form of intimacy with God and stressed the immanence of God. Nevertheless, as they approach the twenty-first century, they face the same dangers that their forefathers encountered at the turn of the present century – the problems of excessive emotionalism, spiritual 'sensualism' and the danger of becoming increasingly irrelevant to the wider world.

Yet at the same time, the expectations of a post-modern generation provide Pentecostals with an entirely new and different arena within which to worship and witness. This generation, which longs for authentic spiritual experiences, may be ready to respond to the Pentecostal message of a God who wishes to communicate with his people, before whom we can live our lives, and whose presence we can experience. With society changing so quickly, and the trends in church life lasting for shorter periods of time, it is difficult to know what Pentecostal worship will look like in even ten years time. Our only hope is that as we are open to the true voice of the Spirit, with our lives firmly rooted in the Word of God, we will be 'led into all truth' by him, 'who is able to keep us from falling and to present us before his glorious presence without fault and with great joy; to the only God our Saviour be glory, majesty, power and authority through Jesus Christ our Lord, before all ages, now and forevermore. Amen'.[40]

---

[40] Jude 24 f.

Chapter Nine

# The Ordinances: The Marginalised Aspects of Pentecostalism

Richard Bicknell

Part and parcel of a maturing process is the need felt by successive generations to evaluate the beliefs of their predecessors. The tradition received is often not as important to those who receive it as it was for those who fought to establish it. Evaluative questions such as 'why do we believe and practise such and such?' are important for every generation. Yet they are especially poignant for the current generation of Pentecostals who are actively seeking to interact with their own tradition and history. This chapter represents the extension of this evaluative process to one particular aspect of Pentecostal understanding, namely that which the majority of Pentecostals have chosen to call the 'ordinances', specifically water baptism and the Lord's supper.

Those with some knowledge of this subject area will no doubt discover 'gaps' in both content and conclusions. That which is presented here simply represents the view of the author who hopes to stimulate the reader into thinking about Pentecostal theology and practice, and those that know better into 'filling in the gaps' through contributing to the discussion themselves.

## Defining the Subject Area: Pentecostal Understanding of the Ordinances

This first section outlines what Pentecostals have said concerning baptism and the Lord's supper. Commentary has been kept to a minimum in order to allow Pentecostals to present in their own words that which they believe.

## The Ordinances .

### Ordinance or Sacrament?
In opposition to claims that baptism and the eucharist[1] are sure channels
of grace conveying that which they signify (sacramentalism), Pentecostals affirm a purely symbolic view of the ordinances. The choice of
the term 'ordinance' itself represents a deliberate attempt to avoid such
sacramental ideas. The use of the term 'sacrament' is generally avoided
in Pentecostal circles for it is assumed that where employed, 'it is done
so with the intention of conveying the thought that grace is somehow
conveyed to the recipient through the rite itself'.[2]

### Baptism: Confessing Salvation

#### a. Regeneration?
In contrast to sacramental interpretations which see baptism as initi-
ating or effecting salvation, Pentecostals view baptism as part of the
ongoing personal response of believers to the commands of Jesus
subsequent to their initial response at salvation. As Gee[3] has stated
clearly, 'baptism in water follows saving faith, arises out of it, but must
never be confused with it'. Thus, baptism is not regenerative, that is,
it does not convey salvation; rather, it is simply a sign that regeneration
has already occurred. Thus, most Pentecostals would follow Gee[4] in
rejecting the baptism of infants (paedobaptism) as 'superstition' for it
disregards the place of personal response. 'Without faith', says Gee
'baptism becomes sheer mockery.'[5]

---

[1] Sacramentalists usually prefer to use the term eucharist, rather than supper,
communion or breaking of bread.
[2] T.G. Hills, 'The Ordinances' (typescript, n.d.), Elim Archives, Cheltenham.
H.D. Hunter notes that although 'ordinance and sacrament can have the same
basic meaning ... Pentecostals have deliberately spurned the word "sacrament",
because it seemed to imply a self-contained efficacy' ('Ordinances', in S.M.
Burgess, G.B. McGee and P.H. Alexander [eds.], *The Dictionary of Pentecostal
and Charismatic Movements* [Grand Rapids: Zondervan, 1988], 653.)
[3] D. Gee, 'Baptism and Salvation', in *Water Baptism and the Trinity* (Missouri:
Gospel Publishing House, n.d.), 9.
[4] *ibid.*, 7; Gee regards paedobaptism as the source of the notion of baptismal
regeneration. He further warns against the 'equally superstitious notion' which
regards baptism as having 'supernatural efficacy as a saving agency'.
[5] *ibid.*, 8.

### b. Confession of Salvation

Baptism is 'the outward sign of the inward cleansing of the conscience wrought by faith in Christ upon repentance from sin'.[6] As a sign, baptism expresses 'pictorially' a believer's 'dying and rising' with Christ, namely their point of salvation which Pentecostals believe is best expressed by the total immersion of the participant. Baptism is therefore seen primarily as a confession of personal salvation: the value of baptism, notes Gee, is that 'it supplies an immediate, simple and definite outward act whereby the inward work of grace in the heart is borne witness to'.[7]

### c. Obedience in Baptism

Gee wrote of the 'duty and privilege of baptism' arguing that it is not a case of baptism to get to heaven, but rather 'baptism is a matter of delight to "fulfil"'.[8] Refusal to be baptised has been regarded with severity, not because of any inherent power in the act, but because it was understood as 'wilful neglect and rebellion', even calling into question the 'possession of grace . . . (which) can alone bring salvation'.[9] Furthermore, Gee[10] argued that any refusal to enter the 'waters of baptism' simply highlights the insincerity of any initial confession.

Understanding baptism in terms of obedience and disobedience derives from its status as a command of Jesus. Thus participation is both expected and encouraged. As Lancaster has noted, 'If any man hesitated over obeying this command, he could be reminded that the Lord who gave it had himself submitted to it . . . declaring that "thus it is fitting for us to fulfil all righteousness".'[11] The baptism of Jesus therefore 'sets us an example in obedience'.[12] Thus Pentecostals insist that 'while baptism is not essential to salvation, it is necessary to full Christian obedience'.[13]

---

[6]  *ibid.*
[7]  *ibid.*, 8. f.
[8]  *ibid.*, 13.
[9]  *ibid.*
[10] *ibid.*
[11] J. Lancaster, 'The Ordinances', in P.S. Brewster (ed.), *Pentecostal Doctrine* (Cheltenham: Elim, 1976), 82.
[12] *ibid.*, 85.
[13] *ibid.*

#### d. A Means of Grace? Baptism as Confirmation

While Pentecostals reject talk of a mechanical transfer of saving grace, baptism can, given certain presuppositions, be regarded as a means of grace; as Lancaster comments, 'in the waters of Baptism, the believer ratifies his commitment to Christ and God confirms through the inner witness of the Spirit His acceptance and approval of that faith. In this, it becomes a means of grace and a source of great joy to those who meet its demands sincerely.'[14]

### The Lord's Supper: In Memory of Christ's Death[15]

#### a. Memorialism

Memorialism is central to the Pentecostal supper. Corporately, Pentecostals partake of bread and wine 'in memory of the Lord's death'[16] whilst individually recalling their initial response to the preaching of the cross: 'his table carries us back to the most vital moment in our lives, the moment when Jesus became real to us'.[17] Thus, as Wilson has noted, 'the partaking of the bread and wine is understood simply as a memorial . . . and complements the extreme emphasis on the death of Jesus as the paramount item of the Christian faith'.[18] Aware that recollection of the cross alone may limit Christ's command to 'remember me', Pentecostals have occasionally stressed the need to remember 'all that he was, and still is'.[19]

#### b. Obeying Jesus

Recalling their initial commitment to Christ prompts believers to further 'recommit' themselves, renewing their 'covenant relationship with God' in a 'pledge of undying affection'.[20] Within this context

---

[14] *ibid.*

[15] This section leans heavily on research regarding Elim's view of the Lord's supper. However, given the common sources of British Pentecostalism, much of the information presented will no doubt be relevant to all camps.

[16] Elim Alliance Statement of Faith.

[17] W.R. Jones, 'His Table', *Elim Evangel*, (24 October 1970), 708.

[18] B. Wilson, *Sects and Society* (London: Heinemann, 1961), 19.

[19] Jones, 'His Table', 708.

[20] H. Burton-Haynes, 'The Breaking of Bread', *Four Essentials of a Virile Pentecostal Church* (Cheltenham: Grenehurst, n.d.), 13.

of Christian commitment, the notion of 'obeying Jesus' through participation in the ordinance is pressed home with force:

> As he instituted the communion service, leading his followers in the first such remembrance feast [!] Jesus pleaded 'remember me', and thus pulled at the heart strings of every true believer. Such an appeal at such a time cannot be ignored. Is there any reason sufficient to warrant a Christian's disobedience? Imagine if our Lord were there, right before you, his nail-pierced hands outstretched, asking you, begging you, pleading with you, commanding you, 'Remember Me'.[21]

Again, as in baptism, participation is seen in terms of obeying Jesus. However, the words, 'Do this . . . as often . . .' suggest not only necessity but also perpetuity. Consequently, the Pentecostal emphasis upon weekly participation has often been supported by this notion of 'obedience'.

### c. Just Bread and Wine?

Pentecostals observe a symbolic view of the bread and wine, describing them as 'emblems' or 'symbols,' rather than 'host' or 'body and blood'. As with the use of the term 'ordinance', symbolic terminology is actively retained in order to exclude sacramentalism, for if they are symbols, they cannot become the reality, that is, the physical body and blood of Christ. Furthermore, since the bread and wine are seen as symbols, it matters little whether real bread and wine are used in the Pentecostal supper. Thus crackers may be used instead of unleavened bread and grape juice instead of fermented wine.[22] Some have claimed biblical warrant for this latter practice; thus 'genématos tés ampelou' (fruit of the vine, Matt. 26:29) is interpreted as unfermented wine.[23]

### d. The Presence of Christ

In view of the fact that the emblems are symbolic, the 'real (bodily) presence'[24] of Christ in them is rejected. Consequently, transubstan-

---

[21] T. Walker, 'Why Communion?', *Elim Evangel* (17 July 1976), 10.
[22] Most Pentecostal churches use non-alcoholic red fruit juice.
[23] W.P.F. Burton, *What Mean Ye by these Stones?* (London: Victory Press, 1947), 11.
[24] The term, 'real presence' refers to the physical and bodily presence of Christ in the emblems, through a supposed supernatural process of transformation.

tiation and consubstantiation are rejected.[25] Since Christ is not in the emblems, he cannot be 'offered' as in the Catholic sacrifice of the mass. For Pentecostals, Christ's body is not 'localised in the bread and the wine . . . but manifested by the power of the Holy Spirit'.[26] It is not the real presence but the 'realised presence of the Lord that makes the feast'.[27] Pentecostal writers exhort their readers to expect Christ himself to be at the communion service, writing 'in his own ordinance he is ever present',[28] 'he will be there, will you?'.[29] Thus, as a 'specific point of encounter',[30] and a 'Divine contact point',[31] the communion has been regarded as the 'focal point of fellowship with Christ'.[32]

### e. The Benefits of His Death
Communion with Christ in the supper is thought to bring a number of benefits for the believer who partakes. Hollenweger comments, 'Pentecostals expect (from the supper) strengthening of their inner being, strength in everyday temptations and healing from sickness'.[33] Dye states that there is in the supper 'opportunity for the revitalisation of our spiritual lives'.[34]

However, it is not through the elements that the believer is strengthened. Rather, it is the presence of Christ in the believer that is the source of this strength: 'Communion is like food in our spiritual lives. Christ communicates his life to us. We are spiritually strength-

---

[25] J. Maybin, 'The Lord's Table', *Elim Evangel* (31 August 1974), 10.
[26] Burton-Haynes, 'The Breaking', 14.
[27] *ibid.*
[28] *ibid.*
[29] Burton, *What Mean Ye, 40.*
[30] J. Lancaster, Interview with author (14 January 1995), tape recording and transcript at Regents Theological College, Nantwich.
[31] C. Dye, 'What Happens When We Take Communion?', *Direction*, 67, (December 1994), 8.
[32] Lancaster, 'The Ordinances', 88.
[33] W. Hollenweger, *The Pentecostals* (London: SCM, 1972), 386.
[34] Dye, 'What Happens?', 8; P. Parker comments, 'Our hungry hearts are richly filled, our sinful lives are marvellously rested and restored and our yearning hopes are completely fed'. Thus, although the material elements are not enough to 'satisfy hunger for one hour', this feast 'satisfies the hunger of the Spirit indefinitely'. ('The Lord's Supper', *Elim Bible College Correspondence School*, 40. 13.)

ened and our experience of Christ is nourished.'[35] Thus, the supper
also signifies reception of Christ for 'he becomes part and parcel of
our very life and nature, strengthening and sustaining us by the
imparted inward nourishment of his presence in our souls'.[36]

### f. Salvific Grace?

One thing that is clearly not available at the supper is salvific grace;
the supper cannot save. As Canty comments, 'we achieve salvation
through the physical act of Christ dying and we acquire it through
the normal channels of communication'.[37]

### g. The Participants

Participation in the supper is 'only for those who have entered the
New Covenant', involving 'conversion: a change of life, of heart
and of mind, a blotting out of our sins and a coming to know the
Lord'.[38] The action of the supper itself is seen to confirm that only
the regenerate should partake, for only those who have experienced
the benefits of Christ's death can enter into a memorial of that death.
Burton, one of the first Pentecostal missionaries, comments further,
'we find that believers in touch with their Lord had their rightful
place at the table: those who had received his word and were
baptised'.[39] Pentecostals have traditionally maintained an 'open' table
allowing non-members to participate provided that they are
believers.[40]

## Elim's Special Ordinances

### Laying on of Hands, Anointing with Oil

Elim's original statement of faith, produced by George Jeffreys,
contained two further ordinances, the laying on of hands and
anointing with oil. As far as can be deduced from Jeffrey's own

---

[35]　Dye, 'What happens', 8.
[36]　*Elim Lay Preacher's Handbook* (London: Elim, 1946), 101.
[37]　G. Canty, *In my Father's House* (London: Marshall, Morgan & Scott, 1969), 54.
[38]　*Elim Lay Preacher's Handbook*, 101.
[39]　Burton, *What Mean Ye*, 12.
[40]　A policy which derives from the very heart and foundations of Brethrenism.

writing, the laying on of hands had to do with the baptism in the Spirit, the empowering of the weak, and personal revival and restoration.[41] The intent of anointing with oil is altogether more obvious – it is for the healing of the sick. In both cases, the act is not seen as a sure channel, guaranteeing healing or restoration, but rather the recipient is raised up as a result of the 'Lord's glorious work'.[42] However, in Jeffreys' theology, healing was regarded as being 'available' for the regenerate believer as a consequence of Christ's atoning death. Participation and reception of these ordinances has not been as strictly defined as with baptism and the Lord's supper. Thus it is fair to say that these ordinances are regarded primarily, though not exclusively, as provisions for the regenerate.[43]

## The Shape of the Pentecostal Discussion

To consider only the content of the Pentecostal discussion would be to give an unrealistic impression of the Pentecostal approach to the ordinances, for it may suggest that all Pentecostals have approached the matter with the same care and attention as the few from whom the above conclusions are drawn. Thus, it seems wise to consider also the general approach to the ordinances in Pentecostalism.

### An Evangelical Agenda

On the whole, the content of the Pentecostal discussion of the ordinances, like much of Pentecostal theology, has followed an evangelical agenda.[44] Over the past 150 years, as a reaction to the

---

[41] G. Jeffreys, *The Miraculous Foursquare Gospel – Doctrinal* (London: Elim, 1929), 8–10.

[42] Thus Jeffreys (*ibid.*, 8) states the act 'can only be efficacious when done in the name of the Lord'.

[43] For some interesting comments on these special ordinances, see Lancaster, *Pentecostal Doctrine*, 90–91.

[44] Although anointing with oil and laying on of hands are hardly the product of an evangelical understanding, we are talking of more than just baptism and the Lord's supper here, for evangelicalism supplies a general anti-sacramentalist outlook by which acts are seen as symbolic and non-effectual.

devaluation of the need for a personal response to the gospel in the over-emphasis on the action of the sacraments, evangelicals have emphasised the need for personal faith.[45] Their particular under-standing of the ordinances arises out of this 'reactionary' environment.

By recapitulating the historical evangelical/sacramentalist debate, the Pentecostal discussion of the ordinances has itself taken on a polemical character. Thus, discussion has been taken up with reaction-ary statements disqualifying sacramentalist claims rather than with positive and constructive statements. The rejection of sacramental categories and ideas (regeneration, vivification through the act, mecha-nistic transfer of power); the use of symbolic terminology to further exclude sacramental interpretations (ordinance, sign or symbol, bread and wine, rather than body or host, etc.); the emphasis of faith as a presupposition for participation; the stress upon the imperative to participate rather than the benefit to the participant; and the individu-alistic interpretation of the ordinances as part of an ongoing personal response to the gospel, all reflect the concerns of evangelicalism.

### A Pentecostal Approach

Although Pentecostals have at various points in their history greatly emphasised the practice of the ordinances, detailed discussion of the nature of the ordinances has been almost entirely lacking.[46] Where statements appear they rarely move beyond basic definitions and assertions,[47] usually comprising short articles or even shorter statements of faith. This discussion has tended to focus upon baptism and the Lord's supper, and one would be hard pressed to find anything of significance regarding the laying on of hands and anointing with oil in their role as ordinances – here, attention has focused not so much on the act itself but rather upon the intended result of healing and restoration.

---

[45]    P. Schroetenboer (ed), *The Text of the Lima Report on Baptism, Eucharist and Ministry with an Evangelical Response* (Carlisle: Paternoster Press, 1992), 1–3.

[46]    The ordinances clearly have not received the same emphasis as other issues such as Spirit baptism and the gifts of the Spirit, especially glossolalia (tongues), all of which have been discussed in numerous articles.

[47]    Regarding the nature of the ordinances, only two sources were found; Lancaster, 'The Ordinances' and Hills, 'The Ordinances'.

Pentecostals have tended not to concentrate upon such issues from a doctrinal perspective, preferring to express the practical benefits resulting from the celebration of the ordinances. Thus the Pentecostal discussion has remained largely descriptive and prescriptive and only rarely has it entered into any evaluation of Pentecostal belief. Consequently, realisation that Pentecostal understanding may have been coloured or influenced by anything other that the biblical text itself (e.g. the influence of Reformed exegesis or an evangelical outlook) has not been commonplace. For Pentecostals, self-examination has largely been a recent phenomenon.[48]

Failure to develop the discussion beyond evangelical categories and ideas is in turn a reflection of the general Pentecostal approach to theology. Up until recent years, 'theology' has not been regarded in a positive light. For Pentecostals, practical experience has been prized above theological intellectualism. Given its association with the 'dry and dead' intellectualism of the Established churches that Pentecostals have been keen to avoid, 'theology' has often being regarded as counter-productive to 'faith'. Pentecostalism has never really felt the need to develop a comprehensive theological scheme commensurate with its Pentecostal perspective, but has remained content with simply rehearsing the conclusions of evangelicalism[49] out of which it sprang.

### Origins of the Pentecostal Understanding

Most Pentecostals are anti-sacramentalist. Yet Pentecostalism arose in a context not unfamiliar with sacramental categories and ideas. In the early days of the Pentecostal movement, it was ecumenical in character and those responsible for its early development were from differing theological traditions: T.B. Barratt, a Methodist minister, no doubt shared the Wesleyan sacramentalist position;[50] A.A. Boddy, an Anglican minister,

---

[48] With notable exceptions such as Donald Gee, whose work *The Pentecostal Movement* (London: Victory Press, 1941) is increasingly being appreciated. He was truly the 'Apostle of balance'.

[49] More properly, nineteenth century Protestant nonconformity.

[50] 'The Methodist communion scarcely deviates at all from the Anglican form, except that there is permission for extempore prayer at the end; and the strong sacramentalism of the Wesleys has by no means been altogether lost.' (Y. Brilioth, *Eucharistic Faith and Practice: Evangelical and Catholic* [London: SPCK, 1930], 194); according to Desmond Cartwright, the official

endorsed infant baptism;[51] and Cecil Polehill was also of an Anglican background. Through their organisation, the Pentecostal Missionary Union (PMU), Polehill and Boddy campaigned for 'nondenomination-alism', encouraging members to stay faithful to their respective traditions. Gee comments regarding the outlook of the infant movement, 'the stress was not upon any system of doctrine . . . some from practically every section of the church participated in the movement'. Had the present Pentecostal understanding of the ordinances arisen from this period, via the same people, there can be little doubt that it would reflect something of the sacramentalist positions of the early 'fathers'.

This 'ecumenical spirit' was not to remain for long. Even at this early stage there were signs of stress; a clash between sacramental spirituality and evangelicalism was inevitable. Gee writes, 'Among those who came into the movement were multitudes from the free churches. The matter of infant sprinkling, for example became a very vexed question . . . some of the earliest members of the Council [of the PMU] later felt themselves compelled to resign.'[52]

The adoption[53] of an evangelical position coincided with a general change in outlook among Pentecostals. It was becoming increasingly difficult to maintain an ecumenical stance as other denominations were largely rejecting the Pentecostal message, and with it those that had come into 'Pentecost'. There was also a growing awareness that this non-denominational phenomenon was itself becoming a movement. Polehill, Boddy and the old 'non-denominational' PMU were reaching the end of their period of influence and the new leadership were more concerned with the survival and organisation of this new movement than maintaining an ecumenical vision. Those that took the helm quickly realised that the survival of Pentecostalism would rest upon their ability to provide a theological basis for the movement. To this end, an evangelical theology[54] was 'adopted' as a working premise for the movement.

---

50  *(continued)* historian for the Elim Church, Barratt later changed his view to that of an 'evangelical Baptist', through pressure from his denomination.

51  E. Blumhofer, 'Alexander Boddy and the Rise of Pentecostalism in Great Britain', *Pneuma*, 8.1. (1986), 32.

52  Gee, *The Pentecostal Movement*, 82.

53  Hollenweger suggests the term 'adoption' as the model for understanding the rise of evangelical theology in Pentecostalism. (*EPTA Bulletin*, 10, 1 and 2 [1992], 45.)

54  More properly, Protestant nonconformity.

Whilst it may be true to say that Pentecostalism does not owe its origin to any outstanding personality, nevertheless with regard to theological presentation, one name clearly stands out: 'the name of Thomas Myerscough stands in many Christian circles as a synonym for sound, sane, scriptural exposition of the word of God', wrote Boulton.[55] Myerscough's influence upon both the theology and organisation of the movement was second to none: George Jeffreys, Elim's founder, who set in place their 'Fundamentals'; Percy Corry, Dean of the Elim Bible College; E.J. Phillips, Elim's Secretary General; and W.F.P. Burton who wrote Elim's only complete work on the Lord's supper all came under the teaching of Myerscough through the PMU Bible School at Preston.[56] Yet his influence was not limited to Elim, for Myerscough also played a large role in the formation of the Fellowship of Assemblies of God in Great Britain and Ireland and was always part of the leadership.

More importantly for our study, Myerscough was of an evangelical (Brethren) persuasion. He was probably not so much a theological innovator as a catalyst in confirming and giving expression to the existing evangelical impulse within the movement. It was probably through him that many evangelical (Brethren) concerns became entwined with the message of Pentecostalism.[57]

## A Pentecostal Theology?

With the exception of the so-called Pentecostal distinctives,[58] Pentecostal discussion has moved along familiar lines with few surprises: a

---

[55]   E.C.W. Boulton, *George Jeffreys: A Ministry of the Miraculous* (London: Elim, 1928), 13; Gee (*ibid.*, 63) was also full of praise for him, writing, 'Mr. Myerscough was an outstanding expositor of the Holy Scriptures, and all who enjoyed the privilege of coming under his influence have been well grounded in the word of faith'.

[56]   *ibid.*, 63.

[57]   Desmond Cartwright, Elim's historian and archivist at the Donald Gee Centre, Mattersey Hall, is emphatic in his belief that it was through Myerscough that Elim began to practice the breaking of bread. (Telephone conversation, 26th April 1995.)

[58]   Namely that which distinguishes Pentecostalism from other denominations, mainly related to the baptism in the Spirit as a secondary experience after salvation leading to increased power for service.

'carbon copy' of evangelical theology with 'Pentecostal' nota bene. It should be of no surprise, therefore, that in their discussion of baptism and the Lord's supper, Pentecostals boast little that can be called 'original' or specifically 'Pentecostal'.

However, when Pentecostalism exploded onto the sedate canvas of British Christianity earlier this century, what was evident was not their theological discussion so much as their practice. Thus, although in their beliefs Pentecostals stood firmly within an evangelical framework, in their practices they so radically reinterpreted that framework as to render it almost unrecognisable. Consequently, the 'Pentecostal' understanding of the ordinances will probably not be found within the pages of some well thought out theological treatise; more likely it will be detected in their practices. That which at first sight appears to be an 'undeveloped theology' might simply signal a different 'pragmatic' approach to theology, one which makes practice its defining statement.

Clearly, the Pentecostal understanding of the ordinances cannot be entirely explained as a rehearsal of evangelical theology. Where the Pentecostal understanding of the ordinances departs from evangelicalism it invariably reflects some aspect of Pentecostal practice. Thus, where evangelicals emphasise the non-effective and symbolic nature of the ordinances, in their practice Pentecostals have tended to focus much more upon the result (i.e. 'tangible' communion with Christ, revitalisation, restoration, physical healing and Spirit baptism are all associated with participation in the ordinances).

Nothing is perhaps quite so expressive of a British Pentecostal understanding of the ordinances in practice than that which can be observed in the 'great Foursquare Gospel demonstrations' of the late twenties and thirties that took place in the Royal Albert Hall, London. These meetings not only dominate the historical skyline of British Pentecostalism but are also significant for its theological understanding. In them almost all the features of the distinctive Pentecostal testimony can be seen at work.

These meetings were divided into three parts: the morning service, during which the sick were anointed with oil and prayed for; the afternoon service, at which recent converts were baptised; and the evening service, which concluded the day's events with the celebration of the Lord's supper. Many of those who attended these meetings were converts from previous revivalist campaigns who were viewed as 'witnesses' to the success of previous Foursquare initiatives.

Setting the ordinances in this context helps to explain certain emphases within the Pentecostal discussion. Thus, the emphasis upon 'witness' in baptism, the importance of the mode of baptism and 'proclaiming' the Lord's death in the supper were no doubt reinforced in these gospel demonstrations. Emphasis upon salvation through the death of Christ permeated the whole meeting; it was preached in the sermons, proclaimed and commemorated in the supper, expressed pictorially in baptism and seen as the basis for healing through anointing with oil. It should be of no surprise therefore that Pentecostal understanding should reflect this and that even after the demise of these meetings, the ordinances should retain an almost exclusively salvific reference.

## Areas of Difficulty in the Pentecostal Discussion

### The Theology of Reaction

*a. Pentecostal versus Catholic: The Problem of Polemics*
In keeping with their evangelical Protestant background, Pentecostals exhibit a fundamental distrust of all things Catholic. To many Pentecostals, Catholicism represents the great evil in the world, Revelation's 'whore of Babylon'.[59] Much of Pentecostal theology has been presented as a reaction to Catholic ideas.[60] Consequently, the Pentecostal discussion of the ordinances has often been expressed negatively in terms of that which they do not believe rather than in positive and constructive terms. Ironically, Catholic theology has, to a certain extent, dictated the agenda for the Pentecostal discussion of the ordinances.

A clear example of this is the use of the term 'ordinance'. Pentecostals recognise the lack of scriptural basis for the exclusive application of this term to baptism and the Lord's supper. Yet it has remained in use precisely because it excludes sacramental interpretations. Aside from this 'polemical' use, there is little, scripturally or semantically, to support an exclusive application of the term 'ordinance' to baptism

---

[59] Wilson, B. *Sects and Society*, 2.
[60] Hills thus poses the question, 'has our theology been developed in a rather negative way through our revulsion of all that we would want to reject in sacramentalism?', ('The Ordinances'), 2.

and the Lord's supper.[61] The application of the term 'ordinance' to the Lord's supper and baptism conveys that they are practices appointed by God, but no more than that. Its use does not explain why other ordinances or commands are not included in this exclusive category. The explanation that they are 'the express commands of Jesus'[62] is not enough, for other commands would surely have priority in Pentecostalism's salvific and pneumatological context, including 'you must be born again' or 'wait for the promise of the Father' (the baptism in the Spirit). Yet these are not regarded as ordinances per se. Without some qualifying remarks, the term 'ordinance' alone does not fully convey the significance of the supper and baptism.

### b. Individual versus Institution: Losing Corporate Identity

By concentrating its efforts upon personal faith over against corporate identity, with all of its association with institutional and sacramental faith, the Pentecostal understanding of the ordinances may have been robbed of corporate significance. Thus, the Lord's supper has been seen purely as an act of personal response to the death of Christ. Pentecostal exegesis bears this out. Paul's reference to the 'body of Christ' (1 Cor. 11:29) has in the past been understood almost exclusively as referring to the physical body of Christ on the cross rather than being a reference to the church as a 'body'. Likewise, baptism refers to incorporation into the church, the body of Christ (1 Cor. 12:13); yet Pentecostal theology has approached baptism almost entirely from the perspective of an individual response to faith.

### c. Obedience versus Benefits: 'Losing the gift'[63]

It is also possible that the emphasis upon obedience as the impetus for participation in the ordinances arose in consequence of a loss of the

---

[61]    In the Authorised Version, the term has a wider application than just the Lord's supper or baptism, referring generally to that which had been appointed. Thus, in interpreting the New Testament, the term 'ordinance' was utilised with this broader understanding in mind, translating a number of words relating to this idea of divine commands. The term is never used with reference to baptism, and can only be applied to the supper after some exegetical acrobatics!

[62]    Lancaster, *Pentecostal Doctrine*, 80.

[63]    This phrase is used in connection with the theology of Zwingli, one of the Reformers. It voices the accusation that Zwingli's theology had lost the aspect of mystery, or more specifically a mysterious transfer of grace. This is

element of 'mystery'. Faced with the difficulty of interpreting the ordinances apart from sacramental categories (baptism did not regenerate; the Lord's supper did not vivify) and an even greater unwillingness to ascribe any significant action to the ordinances for fear of implied sacramentalism, there may have been a tendency to stress only the imperative nature of participation. This approach, of course, guarantees participation, but it is of no use in providing an explanation or interpretation of the actions and experience of the participant. As we shall see, stressing the imperative nature of the ordinances without equal emphasis upon their role and meaning tends towards a minimalistic approach. The participant simply does what is required to fulfil 'obedience'.

### The Marginalisation of the Supper

In his book, written in 1972, Hollenweger comments on the centrality of the supper in Pentecostal worship, noting that although there is no fully developed eucharistic doctrine in the Pentecostal movement as a whole, there is nevertheless a well-developed pattern of eucharistic devotion and practice.[64] Three decades on, however, the practice of breaking bread in the Sunday morning 'communion service' has become marginalised. Thus, ironically, the very practice that gave reason and definition to the 'communion/breaking of bread' service has been reduced to a bare minimum, generally incorporating the reading of 1 Corinthians 11, thanksgiving for the bread and wine and its distribution and consumption. This sentiment is echoed by Allen who, interestingly enough, places the demise of the Pentecostal supper within the same thirty-year time frame, writing 'When, in the early 1960s, I came into a Pentecostal assembly (from Anglicanism) the words of that old service (Anglican communion) came alive as never

---

[63] *(continued)* referred to as the 'gift'. A detailed examination of Zwingli's theology proves this accusation to be false. The Zwinglian supper is often falsely characterised as being 'bare', yet Zwingli's denial of salvific power was *not* a denial of divine action in the eucharist. By faith, Zwingli expected an encounter with Christ; for he taught that though Christ was not literally present in the emblems, to those who eat in faith, Christ is truly, sacramentally, and mysteriously present in the supper, communing with the celebrant. In this encounter, Zwingli expected God to act, 'feeding the soul', strengthening faith and setting free by the power inherent in the sacrament. The Lutheran accusation that the 'gift' (divine action) is lost is unjustifiable.

[64] Hollenweger, *The Pentecostals*, 385.

before, Sunday after Sunday, around the Lord's Table. Tongues, prophecy, heartfelt thanksgiving – all this as together we centred our thoughts on the crucified yet triumphant Christ! Thirty years on things have changed.'[65]

Allen cites various recent trends, writing 'some are saying that a weekly Breaking of Bread is too often for it to be meaningful and now do it less frequently. Others experiment with the form. In some places, the actual breaking of bread occupies a mere five minutes of a two-hour service largely consisting of singing.'[66]

It is precisely because Pentecostals have failed to achieve a distinctive understanding of the supper that it has become a mere shadow of what it should be. It is regarded as a 'divine contact point', yet the presence of Christ is in no way limited to it; Christ's presence is expected to be manifested at other times, not just in the supper.[67] Clearly Christ's presence was expected and felt on other occasions and not just 'especially' in their celebration of the supper. That a special sense of Christ's presence is not contingent upon the supper at all is assumed by Boulton[68] who writes 'Sunday morning arrived and the stewards were busy in the endeavour to find accommodation for the people. And now the service is in full swing. Soon the happy throng is just bathed in Holy Ghost song. A glance at the faces of the singers is sufficient to reveal how deeply they feel the truths that they sing. Their beaming faces and radiant faces provides convincing evidences of the earnestness which holds them.'

There seems to be some confusion. Although one is told that it is during the supper that the Lord draws closest, the experiences recorded above suggest that there is some ambiguity regarding this matter. Similarly, one is told that there are certain benefits available

---

[65]   D. Allen, 'Whatever happened to the Breaking of Bread?', *Redemption*, (March 1993).

[66]   *ibid.*

[67]   Boulton (*George Jeffreys*, 114 f.) quotes Gee who, commenting upon his visit to a number of Pentecostal congregations in Ireland, states 'the closing week-end was spent at Ballymena. On every hand we had been assured of a good time here and we were not disappointed. From the very first, when we had a brief time of prayer before an open-air meeting on Saturday evening, right through the meetings on Sunday there was a rare sense of His presence.'

[68]   *ibid.*, 129.

from participation in the supper, albeit not communicated through the emblems. However, that which is said to be a specific action of the supper, namely 'revitalisation', 'restoration' and the 'strengthening of faith' is again not limited to the supper itself. All these can be found outside of the supper context. Many of the choruses and hymns of Pentecostalism reflect the notion that revitalisation and refreshing, in fact everything that the Christian needs, can be found in Christ, and therefore by definition, at any time.[69]

Thus it is hard to imagine what 'special' role can be accorded to the supper for all of its benefits can be gained outside of its context, through communion with Christ. There appears to be little difference between the predicted effect of the supper and those of any other meeting; both have exactly the same potential to supply the needs of the believer, for in both communion with Christ is assured.

Further ambiguity is introduced by the suggestion that physical healing is somehow available through the Lord's supper. Thus it has not been unusual to hear the one officiating claim that 'there is healing at the table'. In attempting to promote a continuity of approach to the supper, Hills[70] has challenged the above assumption for it contradicts a purely symbolic approach. Thus, he writes, 'it would be easier to accept the proposition that the supper is only a memorial, if pastors dropped the practice of informing worshippers that "there is healing at the table", which is generally understood to be a reference to physical healing'. Furthermore, comments Hills, 'if healing is available at the table, what is its specific source; is it present in the emblems we take? Surely not, for we have been told that they are only bread and wine.'

### The Relationship of Baptism to Salvation

Given that baptism is not essential to salvation, when should one be baptised? There has been a general lack of urgency surrounding the

---

[69] 'Come and dine', the Master calleth, 'come and dine';
you may feast at Jesus' table all the time.
He who fed the multitude, turned the water into wine
to the hungry now He calleth 'come and dine'.
W.G. Hathaway, *Elim Choruses* (Eastbourne: Victory Press, 1968), 5.
[70] Hills, *The Ordinances*, 4

practice of baptism with prospective candidates waiting weeks, sometimes years, following their initial commitment. It is a measure of our
ambiguity and lack of discussion that the practice differs from church
to church. There is no real consensus in this area.

### The Question of Development?

The final question to be addressed relates to whether there is there a
holistic Pentecostal theology. It is precisely because of their roots in
Protestant nonconformity that Pentecostals reject sacramental categories and ideas. Yet Pentecostal reaction to sacramental spirituality has
not relied solely upon the Reformed arguments of nonconformity,
but represents a development of that Reformed position in its emphasis upon the role of the Spirit, and in viewing that role as the antithesis
of sacramental action. For the Pentecostal, the notion that the sacrament conveys salvation 'ex opere operate' is rejected in true Reformed
style as promoting 'religion by works', but also because vivification is
the role of the Spirit and not the sacrament. Thus, whilst sacramental
Christianity is initiated in the sacrament,[71] which also supplies the
'grace to live up to the demands of Christian life', Pentecostal
Christianity is initiated by the Spirit and energised through the
(physically apprehended) 'baptism of the Spirit', but this apart from
the sacrament.

   This marks a clear development of the anti-sacramental polemic
characteristic of the Reformed tradition. Pentecostals also reject
sacramentalism, not solely upon the basis that it promotes salvation by
works, but also because the work of the Spirit in vivifying all of
Christian life displaces the need for occasional sacramental vivification.

---

[71]   'By these sacraments (baptism, eucharist) which symbolise Christ's death
and resurrection and the outpouring of the Spirit at Pentecost . . . converts
are brought into a saving encounter with Christ in his mystery and begin to
enjoy the life of grace'; see F.A. Sullivan, 'Sacraments', in Burgess et al.,
*Dictionary*, 765f.